THE LADY IN THE PINK SUIT

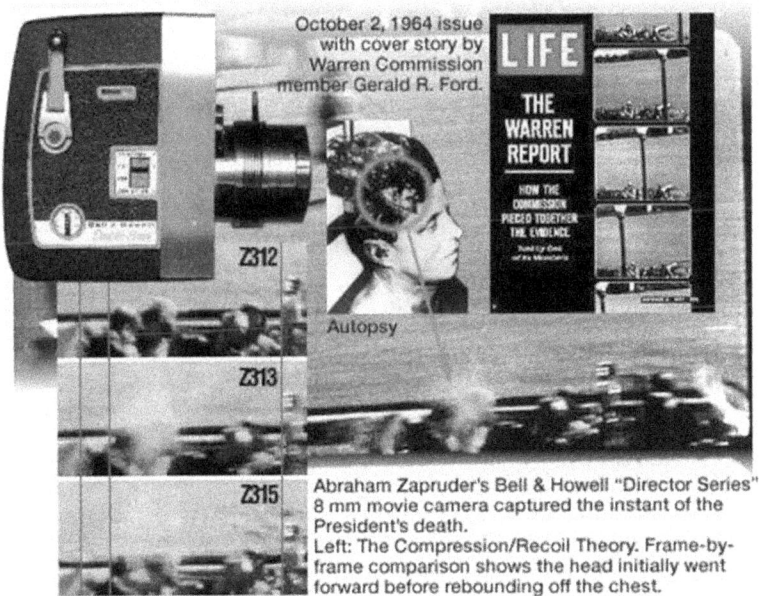

October 2, 1964 issue with cover story by Warren Commission member Gerald R. Ford.

LIFE

THE WARREN REPORT

HOW THE COMMISSION PIECED TOGETHER THE EVIDENCE

Autopsy

Z312

Z313

Z315

Abraham Zapruder's Bell & Howell "Director Series" 8 mm movie camera captured the instant of the President's death.
Left: The Compression/Recoil Theory. Frame-by-frame comparison shows the head initially went forward before rebounding off the chest.

PHAM THUDZUNG

WORKBOOK PRESS LLC
187 E Warm Springs Rd,
Suite B285, Las Vegas, NV 89119, USA

Website: https://workbookpress.com/
Hotline: 1-888-818-4856
Email: admin@workbookpress.com

Ordering Information:
Quantity sales. Special discounts are available on quantity purchases by corporations, associations, and others.
For details, contact the publisher at the address above.

ISBN-13:   978-1-953839-12-1 (Paperback Version)
              978-1-953839-11-4 (Digital Version)

REV. DATE: 11/10/2022

TABLE OF CONTENT

_____

PROLOGUE

"What are you reading, Sir?" I asked the Hierophant.

"The Lady in the Pink Suit" is a metaphor, the Greek priest replied sagely, "The Matrix is real in a sense that most people think they've lived in Freedom. In reality, they've been slaves, both mentally and physically. The Deceptive System has controlled their thoughts, their behaviors, their lives, and their future through the media, the news, the radio, the internet... The Deceptive System has told them how they should feel and what they should think, who their good friends are, and who their deadly enemies are... In order to survive, they've believed in what the Deceptive System has dictated to their brains".

"Is there a way out of this maze?" I stared at him perplexedly

With a gentle smile, he gave me the manuscript, "Find out the Truth for yourself. You're one of them; you've been trapped in the Matrix."

"How could I get out of it, Sir?" I begged

Looking around, I saw nobody. Where did the Hierophant go?

I turned on the pages and pondered about the mystery....

April ...

When the light blue sky fills with some wandering clouds, the meadows are full of beautiful flowers;

the birds are tweeting among the green branches…
Spring is here!

Instead of celebrate a Happy Easter, I feel sad.
Every year, when April arrives, I can't forget the
fateful day April 30, 1975 when the South Vietnam
was collapsed. My family followed people in
Saigon tried by all means to escape to another
unknown land for survival. At that time, I was a
young girl. I had no understanding what happened
to my country; I sensed a tremendous fear grasping
me in a whirlwind of confusion. After that, I was
too busy with a new life in a foreign country, a
different language, strange customs, work… no
time for Vietnam! No time to search for the reason
why I've become a citizen of the United States of
America. President Kennedy did not agree to
continue the presence of the US military in Vietnam
in 1963. Why the American troops still there until
1975?

How many years have gone by since the day I left
home?

It was April 30 again…

My eyes caught the headlines on an old Life
Magazine: Assassination of President John F.
Kennedy. How could the death of an American
President be related to the appearance of a group of
Vietnamese people from the Far East settled in the
USA?

I'd like to consider this unsolved mystery from a
point of view from some Americans then observe

the event from the angle of some Vietnamese immigrants.

Would you join me?

———————

CHAPTER 1
Helen Augier and Robert McCarthy

November …

Only a few more days were Thanksgiving! Helen Augier hasn't finished the shopping list in preparing the ingredients for the traditional American dinner on this special holiday celebration, yet she still had to work! Usually she did not feel so boring to listen to the patients' chief of complaints as today. Helen Augier was in Second Year of the Psychiatric Residency Program at St. Peter's Hospital. Glancing at the watch: 4:37pm, in less than half an hour she would have been free! Right now, she had to take notes in a consultation with Brandon Dorward, a patient with the diagnosis of multi personality-schizophrenic disorder. She greeted him with a smile,

"Good afternoon, how are you today, Mr. Dorward?"

He stared vacantly at the Resident Doctor.

"Did you take the medications?" Helen Augier checked the chart.

"I swallowed whatever the nurse gave to me."

"What are you now?" The Doctor asked.

"Me?" Brandon laughed,

"I'm God! Long, long time ago… In the Wild West Jungle, among the fierce wolves and malicious monkeys, the bucks, deer, and other animals… there were three snakes: a female and two males; there was also a tigress."

"Where are you at this moment, Mr. Brandon Dorward?"

"Let me continue," Brandon said,

"The male snake, Kaa and female snake Nagaina lived in the wilderness with their two offspring. The male snake, Kaa was the Lord of the Jungle. However, the wolves and the monkeys didn't agree. They planned a plot to kill him. The female snake, Nagaina knew about it, because she was slick and clever, however; she kept quiet. The reason, would you inquire? She was jealous with Tigress: Kaa sometimes sneaked out to be with Tigress; she was a beauty. In the meanwhile, Akela, the Leader of the Wolf Pack vowed to raze Kaa to the ground so the Leader of the Wolf would be the Lord of the Jungle. The Bandar-log, a tribe of monkeys also wanted to destroy Kaa; they did not like Akela either. Nagaina had her own plan as well. She crept out to meet another male snake, Carinatus who promised to plan for her future with him..."

The young Resident Doctor's mind abandoned the patient's psychotic world, she thought about the dress she would put on today at dinner with Congressman Robert McCarthy's family. Robert McCarthy was an extraordinary man. Besides the busy schedule at Texas House of Representative, where he was appointed for the 33District, Robert McCarthy also had a Law Firm which he worked as a Prosecutor. Now, Congressman Robert McCarthy aimed for the Democrat Senate seat of the State of Texas. Helen Augier loved and admired Robert

McCarthy since the first time they met in a dinner party at the Governor's Mansion. Robert McCarthy was the Assistant to Helen's uncle, Judge Mitchell Augier. Professor George McCarthy-Robert's father taught Human Behavior and Brain Sciences at University of Texas, Dallas; he married to Marion, a piano teacher at Westwood Junior high school. Helen Augier idolized Mrs. Jacqueline Kennedy Onassis, the First Lady then widow of President John F. Kennedy. Later, she married with the Shipping Magnate Aristotle Onassis. The image of Jackie Kennedy has become an icon of American History; her fashion was still followed by numerous women all around the world. Helen thought that she would wear something like this amazing lady….It was a pink dress with a double pearl necklace?

"Ah, Doctor… Would you want to know the rest of the story?" the patient reminded the young Doctor.

"Uh... Oh! My goodness... It is five already. I have a dinner tonight with Congressman McCarthy's family..."

Brandon Dorward stared at Doctor Helen Augier, "Please remember don't put on a pink suit, Doctor."

"Why?" Helen Augier asked.

"Mrs. Jacqueline Kennedy's pink suit was stained with blood." Dorward said.

Suddenly, the young Resident Doctor felt a cold stream running down her spine. She collected her notes, signed in the chart and said,

"Take your medications; I'll see you next time."

…

Helen stopped by her father's house to give him a gift for Thanksgiving; she entered the two- story- cottage in the suburb of Houston, Texas. Returning to the childhood home, Helen had a mixed feeling of both happy and disquiet. Her mother image has been replaced by the step mother. Helen's father – Doctor Michael Augier, the Cardiologist married Ms. Lynn Brown, a single business woman. Helen's mother- Mrs. Kathy Augier, a CPA accountant- lost her life after a long battle against leukemia. The daughter opposed to this marriage and refused to call the step mother "Mom". The Augier family was devoted Catholic believers; they attended mass very Sunday and Helen graduated from Sacred Heart of Mary School from Kindergarten through twelfth grade. As a young girl, Helen always carried with her the rosary and prayed every day. Oh, how many times this precious gift from God has helped her go through those rough paths of life! Helen always kept the rosary in a little container and put in her purse wherever she went. One thing the young Doctor could not explain to herself was: with her background training in science and modern technology, why should a Medical Doctor needed the cross of Jesus as a lucky charm?

Helen put on a pink dress and pearl necklace; this was the replica of Mrs. Jackie Kennedy's style. Looking at her image in the mirror, she saw the frowning of her step mother, Lynn said,

"I'd put on a light blue dress instead."

"Why so?" Helen asked while combing her hair.

"Because…" the step mother said.

Helen walked toward the door. She didn't want to
hear any further; she thought, "I don't need your
opinion."
She asked the step mother,
"Please tell Dad that I have a gift for him. I put it on
the mantle. Thank you!"

Pulling into the drive way, Helen saw Robert with a
corsage waiting for her. He greeted Helen,
"Come on in. You're so beautiful! I have a surprise
for you."
He kissed her slightly on her cheek as he gave her
the flower.
"What is it, tell me, please!" She said.
"You will know later." He answered.
"OK then." She smiled.
Helen liked Robert's family. There was a warm and
friendly atmosphere in the McCarthy's family
where she visited a few times. The McCarthy lived
in an old, Victorian home in the suburb of Houston.
Leaning on the pillar, Helen thought about Scarlett
O'Hara… One time, Robert showed her around the
big house. There were a huge living room, a library,
five bed rooms, a sun room, and the attic. Helen
followed Robert climbing up the stairs to the top of
the house where it kept the heirloom, the photo
album of the family from Robert's great
grandfather's… Helen was curious about a box that
was locked with a written "Do Not Open".
She asked Robert,
"What is in that box?"

"I don't know. All I was told was: Do not touch that thing." He said.

"Why? What is in there?" She kept on.

"Mom said that it was something Dad kept as a souvenir when he was a surgeon in the Emergency Room at Parkland Hospital. Robert explained.

"Would you like the photographs when I was a baby?" he called Helen as he picked up a stack of pictures.

"You look like a Gerber baby!" Helen laughed.

Robert put a light kiss on Helen's cheek,

"Come for Thanksgiving dinner with my family, yes?"

"OK" she leaned her head on his shoulder...

*

These people were at the Thanksgiving dinner today at the McCarthy family: Robert's father, Doctor George McCarthy, Professor of Human Behavior and Brain Sciences at University of Texas, Dallas. Dr. McCarthy used to work at the Emergency Room at Park Land Hospital in Dallas; he changed the career from a surgeon to a university professor after the death of President Kennedy, November 1963. Robert was ten years old at that time, he didn't know the reason his father left Park Land Hospital; all he could remember was his father became quieter and spent a great deal of time to be alone in his studio contemplating on something. Robert's mother, Mrs. Marion, a piano teacher, Uncle David -a banker-, his wife, Michelle - a pharmacist and their daughter, Cathy, who just had her third birthday last months; Uncle Benjamin McCarthy- a retired policeman-, his wife, Elizabeth - a nurse- and their sons, Jason who was a PhD candidate in Political Sciences at University of Texas, Austin, and Dennis; a Sergeant in the US Army. Jason liked Robert; he often asked the Congressman about some political issues. Aunt Elizabeth came early to give Mrs. McCarthy a helping hand in the kitchen. The dining table was full of a traditional dinner for this special occasion: the Brined Maple Turkey with cream gravy. In addition to sausage stuffing, carrots, and Brussels sprouts, there were delicious desserts: pecan pies and pumpkin cakes with cream cheers glaze.

Mrs. McCarthy proudly added,

"Don't forget my Best ever Green bean Casserole."

"All of us must try velvety mashed potato, it's from my garden."

Uncle Benjamin put a big bowl on the table.

The guests gathered around, Professor McCarthy stood at the head of the table with his wife on his right hand; Robert was next to Helen, then the relatives.

"Let's hold hands and say the Thanksgiving prayer." Professor said

All bowed their heads. Helen felt the warmness of Robert's hand in hers while Professor George McCarthy said the prayers.

"Thank you for inviting me for this dinner." Helen said.

"You're very welcome."

Mrs. McCarthy kindly replied as she passed the dishes.

"Please wait!" Robert asked, "I have an announcement to make."

Everybody directed one's gaze at the Congressman while Robert opened a jewelry box showing Helen a diamond ring, he proposed,

"Will you be my fiancée?"

"Oh! Robert! I'd love to." Helen exclaimed.

"Mom, Dad, Uncle and Aunt, I'd like to introduce my fiancée, Doctor Helen Augier."

Robert said after he put the ring on Helen's finger.

"Congratulations! Congratulations!" the family and the relatives chanted.

"Cheers!"

.....

After dinner, some played cards in the living room; others enjoyed the delicious pumpkin pies while watching the TV. Mrs. McCarthy asked her husband,

"George, will you take pictures of Robert and Helen on their engagement?"

"Of course, come on everybody!" Uncle Benjamin prepared the camera.

"Here, Helen! I want to be next to you and Robert in the picture..."

"Say cheese!"

They sat down for coffee and chatting. Professor McCarthy asked Jason,

"Have you finished your paper yet? Did the picture of the "occipital lobe of the brain" help?"

"Thanks a lot, Uncle George, but I still not quite understand how..." the PhD candidate in Political Sciences said.

"Do you really need to know Human Anatomy in order to be a politician, Jason?" Uncle David laughed.

"In my Prelim paper, I chose *'The Assassination of President Kennedy'*, I still can't figure out if the President had been truly shot from the back or..." Jason explained.

"Goodness sake! People have talked about that over fifty some years." Mrs. Marion McCarthy put a plate of biscuits on the table.

Aunt Elizabeth was warming up the coffee pot, she said

"The Warren Commission concluded that Lee Harvey Oswald acted alone in killing Kennedy and wounding Texas Governor John Connally and that Jack Ruby also acted alone when he killed Oswald two days later."

"However," Robert joined the conversation, "the findings of the Warren Commission have proven controversial and have been challenged by later studies."

"What does the President Kennedy's Assassination National Archives records released on November 18, 2013 tell us? Isn't that what truly happened on November 22, 1963?" Dennis inquired.

"I don't think so," Uncle David said, "On the contrary, the more you try to figure out what the Truth is, the more you get lost in tangles of theories, but none of them can really explain the whole picture."

"Indeed, the "magic bullets - three shots in less than six seconds" by Lee H. Oswald is a cover up for some things more sinister behind the scene." Uncle Benjamin shared his opinion.

"Let's change the subject," Professor McCarthy reminded the relatives, "We talk about something else, OK?" Turning to Robert, he asked,

"Have you and Helen set a wedding date yet?" Everybody chanted,

"When is the wedding date?"

"Will it be at First Baptist Church in Houston?" Once more, Helen noticed Professor McCarthy did not want to discuss about President Kennedy.

.....

Isn't the engagement period the happiest moment in a woman's life? Helen squeezed her busy schedule of a doctor at the hospital to be with Robert, especially at his campaigns for the Democrat seat in the Senate Upper House in Austin, Texas. Today, Robert just finished a press conference to take heat off the base about National Health Care, Helen expressed their thankfulness to the supporters and the audience; a man in his team hurried placed in her hand a note. While people waving the slogans and banners to applause the future Senator Candidate, Helen glanced at the paper:

"Mr. Robert McCarthy, your father has a stroke. He's at Texas Medical Center now."

Helen whispered to her fiancée,

"Dad has a stroke. We have to leave."
Robert tried to compose himself, but Helen could see his hands were trembling. He told the crowd, "Thank you very much, everybody. Helen and I truly appreciate your support and help on my way to the Upper House in Austin. Right now, I must take care of some family matter. We'll meet again in the next campaign. Thank you."
"Thank you" Helen said.
"See you! Mr. Robert McCarthy!"
"We love you both!"

Robert and Helen rushed to the parking lot. Fastening the seat belt, the Senate candidate stared at the sky,
"God, why must it happen?"
They arrived at the hospital and were told to wait outside the UCI. Through the windows, Robert saw his mother crying near his father's bed. The professor body was almost covered by tubes and devices to keep him alive.
Later, Robert met with his mother. Robert hugged Mrs. Marion McCarthy, in tears, she told the story, "I got a call this morning from the university that Dad fainted and collapsed during a lecture. They called the Ambulance...."
"Did he take his medications for high blood pressure?" Robert asked.
"I think he did. You know that he has diabetes, too" the mother answered.
"Please tell me if I can help with anything." Helen said.

Later, the Senate candidate Robert McCarthy met Doctor Brown, the surgeon in charge of the UCI. Doctor Brown explained the MRI image,

"Professor George McCarthy has an ischemic stroke as a result of an occlusion in the cerebral artery on the right side, which causes the loss of movement and sensation on the left side of his body, including aphasia..."

"Will he be able to recognize family members, Doctor?" Mr. Robert McCarthy asked.

"At this moment, I cannot confirm that; however, every patient is different. You'll find that out in the near future. Right now, all I can say is he's blood pressure, pulse, temperature...are stable." and he added,

"We now apply IV rtPA to dissolve the clot and improve blood flow in that part of the brain... We might also use endovascular procedure to remove the clot..."

"When could he go home, Doctor?" Mrs. McCarthy asked.

"Before that we need to transfer him to a rehabilitation center for Physical Therapy to help him get back to some activities prior to the stroke." Doctor Brown replied.

.

After two weeks in the hospital, Professor McCarthy was transferred to a Rehabilitation Center. Mrs. McCarthy stayed with him most of the time there. Robert and Helen came to see him on a Saturday morning; they met Mrs. McCarthy by her husband's bedside. The Anatomy Professor became an invalid: hemiparalized and slurring of speech; however, he recognized his family and maintained a fair long term memory.

Robert asked his father,

"Do you need anything, Dad?"

"Don't worry about me", the Professor tried to keep a sense of humor even he responded in a slurred tone, "Let me know your wedding date, I'll be there, definitely!"

"Of course, we count on you, Dad. We'd love to receive your blessings on that day." Robert and Helen said.

"Thank you, Helen. I'm glad to have you in the family."

He turned to the future daughter in law,

"May I have a few words with you ?"

"Yes, Dad; please speak - we are listening." They bent down by his bed.

Professor divulged the message,

"I'm sorry that I have a stroke; I'm now a burden to everybody."

"Dad, please don't say that..." Robert interrupted his father.

"Let me talk, for I don't know how much longer..."

"...Marion and Robert, you know I have a box in the attic..." Professor kept on,

"...the box I kept as a souvenir of Parkland Hospital with the words "Do Not Open?"

"Yes, we know that box... and nobody has ever touched it. Why do you need to mention it today?"

Professor firmly ordered,

"That's exactly I want you all promise with me Do Not Open it."

Mrs. McCarthy directed her eyes at her Robert and Helen as they fixed their eyes on Professor McCarthy,

"We promise." They said in unison.

Professor tried to gasped some air as he finished the talk,

"I'm glad. Don't ever forget that. Robert, I truly don't want you involve in politics... Don't get any further than being a Senate... Remember to tell your children the same thing..."

The Senate candidate wondered about the reason behind these words, but he dared not to disturbed his father at this moment.

Robert looked into the Professor's eye and said,

" I will keep your words, Dad" he helped his father lying down while Mrs. McCarthy put a pillow under her husband's head. Helen covered him with a blanket. She didn't think that she understood the Professor's message. However, they held his hands tightly in theirs. Robert saw tears on his mother's eyes; he felt his heart sobbing.

.

After that visit, Robert involved with more campaigns and speeches toward the running for the Senate House while Helen had an overtime schedule; they skipped seeing Professor McCarthy. Then suddenly Robert got a message from his mother,

"Dad is in the hospital again, he has a septic pneumonia."

"How did it happen, Mom?"

Robert phoned as he was running to the garage. The mother sobbed weakly,

"He has had a fever, sore throat, cough and nasal congestion for a few days, the nurse at the Rehabilitation Center gave him some Tylenol but the temperature has not been reduced; instead it rose up to 105F... I requested a Doctor; the Doctor came and examined Dad. He said that he was afraid it was more serious than he anticipated. He said it was more likely Dad got a sepsis. He transferred Dad to the ER..."

Once more, Robert saw his father's body with tubes and IV lines... This time Professor McCarthy was unconscious. Helen also rushed to be at the scene. The Senate candidate Robert looked fixedly at the breathing machine that kept his father alive. At this moment, his father was diagnosed: Bacteremia-Strep pneumoniaea. They gave the Professor antibiotics by IV but it did not lower the temperature...

Robert paced back and forth in the room; his mother folded and unfolded a napkin while tears rolling down her cheeks. Helen fixed her eyes on the breathing machine. Everything was deadly quiet, so quiet that Robert could hear the clicking of the clock on the wall. It reminded him that time was running out...

A few days later, Doctor Patrick Rosh told Mrs. McCarthy and Robert that Professor McCarthy was brained death. The family had to make the most difficult decision: turning off the breathing machine.

After the funeral, Robert had to put the memory of his father behind and to focus on his goal: to be a Senator of District 8 - Houston, Texas.

Robert and Helen got married. After the wedding, they planned; they resided in an affluent suburb of Texas. The Senate candidate did not want to stop his ambition at this level; he aimed to be one of the two United States Senators from Texas.

The wedding of Senator of District 8, Houston-Texas Robert McCarthy and Doctor Helen in the summer at First Baptist Church aroused a widespread interest and excitement. As the newlyweds stepped out of the church, the crowd chanted,

"God bless you!"

Helen was so beautiful in the Amelia white wedding gown; next to her, Robert had his best look in the Joseph & Fleiss Tuxedo suit.

Senator McCarthy and his wife waved to their supporters,

"Thank you! Please come to our reception!"

At the wedding reception, Helen had a floral pink dress; the lilies of the material matched with the pearl necklace. Helen admired Mrs. Jacqueline Kennedy Onassis; she had a wardrobe of a few suits and dresses resembled the former First Lady's fashion: pearl necklaces. The wedding cake was so beautiful and delicious; the music was sweet; the two families and guests gave the newlyweds a lot of gifts Helen and Robert couldn't ask for any blessings better than this special occasion.

The day after the wedding, Robert and his wife went to their honeymoon in Hawaii. This was a gift from Helen's parents. Then, they planned to visit Uncle Benjamin McCarthy in Dallas before returning to work. Scott- a clerk at Robert's office offered to be the chauffeur since he planned to buy some antiques in that area. He told the newlyweds, "You're just relaxed and take the back seats; I'll take care of the road."
"Thank you very much." Robert said.
While Robert texting a message to his mother, Helen opened her purse to look for the lipstick. Next to her makeup, there was the rosary. Helen took it out and prayed to the Blessed Mary.

Was it because of the rain that Scott ran into an accident that night? Scott drove a SUV with Robert and Helen were the passengers; he just exited from I 45, TX6 on the way toward College Station/Bryan; a pickup truck made a left turn and hit the SUV by the side; where Robert was sitting. Helen cried out as she saw the blood,
"Oh, Robert, are you OK?"
Pressing her fingers on the cut of Robert's left arm, Helen saw that the impact of the collision threw her purse to the window by Robert's side; as the result, the purse became the cushion which prevented a serious injury to his left arm. Someone could justify

to Helen that was only a coincidence; but Helen knew in her heart: she was praying to the rosary when the accident happened. Did the Virgin Mary protect Robert?

The driver from the pickup truck stopped the engine and walked toward the SUV. He exchanged the information with Scott then the police came.

Robert told his wife,

"Luckily, I'm not in a serious condition."

Helen looked at her dress; there were some drops of blood stained from Robert wound. Suddenly, she remembered the words from the step mother,

"I wouldn't wear that dress if I was you..."

She felt a cold stream running down her spine. Mrs. Jacqueline Kennedy's pink suit had some stained blood of her husband, President John F. Kennedy.

CHAPTER 2
The First Visit to Dallas

A few days later, Robert and Helen arrived at Uncle Benjamin McCarthy's house in Dallas, Texas. Robert introduced Helen to his Uncle's family: his wife, Elizabeth and their sons, Jason and Dennis. Everybody was happy to meet the bride who truly enjoyed Tex-Mex cuisine! After dinner, the Senator found his Uncle, Jason and Dennis in the den; the old Police officer was self –absorbed with running rolls of films on different screens.
Robert asked,
"What are you doing, Uncle Ben?"
The retired policeman looked at his nephew,

"I have studied the JFK Assassination for over twenty years; yet I'm still in a maze..."
Jason put his hand on his father's shoulder, he said,
"I was impressed by your work, so I chose my PhD thesis The Assassination of President John F. Kennedy; however, I've got stuck as well!"
Dennis joined in the conversation,
"What do you think, Robert? Who killed John F Kennedy?"
"There're quite a few theories about the death of President Kennedy." Robert replied.
Helen pulled a chair to add her opinion,
"The Warren Committee stated that Harvey Lee Oswald committed the crime."
"Let's start from the beginning, shall we?"Uncle Ben said.
Elizabeth brought in a big bowl of popcorn with a smile, she asked
"I want to share with you, too!"
"Thank you, honey,"
Mr. McCarthy said then read the documents, "*The Wikipedia* summarized nicely the events of the assassination..."

John Fitzgerald Kennedy, the 35th President of the United States, was assassinated at 12:30 p.m. Central Standard Time (18:30 UTC) on Friday, November 22, 1963, in Dealey Plaza, Dallas, Texas. Kennedy was fatally shot by a sniper while traveling with his wife Jacqueline, Texas Governor John Connally, and Connally's wife Nellie, in a presidential motorcade. A ten-month investigation from November 1963 to September 1964 by the Warren Commission concluded that Kennedy was assassinated by Lee Harvey Oswald, acting alone, and that Jack Ruby also acted alone when he killed Oswald before he could stand trial.

Lee Harvey Oswald (October 18, 1939 – November 24, 1963) was, according to five U.S. government investigations, the sniper who assassinated John F. Kennedy, the 35th President of the United States, in Dallas, Texas, on November 22, 1963.

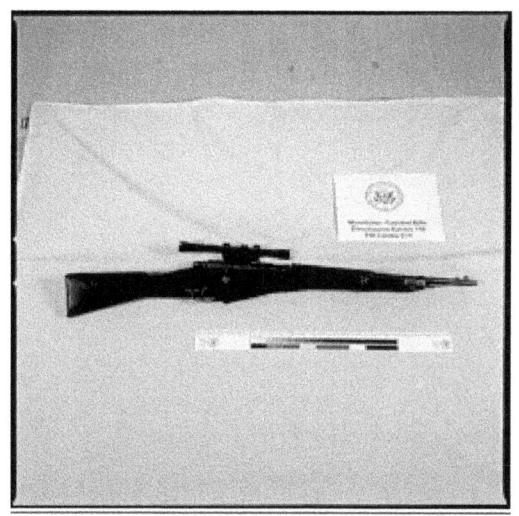

The 6.5 mm Carcano carbine owned by Lee Harvey Oswald

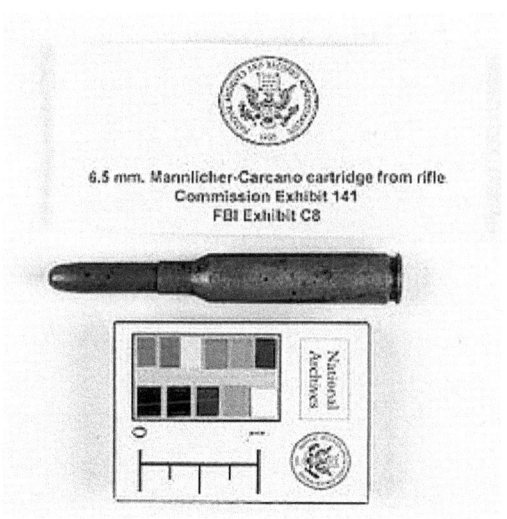

CE-141, or Warren Commission Exhibit 141, the unfired 6.5x52 mm round of ammunition left in the assassination rifle above.

In March 1963, Lee Harvey Oswald, using the alias "A. Hidell," purchased by mail order a 6.5 mm Carcano Model 91/38 carbine, also improperly called Mannlicher-Carcano, with a 4x scope He also purchased a revolver from a different company, by the same method. Both weapons were signed for in the name of Lee Harvey Oswald. It is officially accepted that the rifle was fired from the Texas School Book Depository in Dallas, Texas to assassinate United States President John F. Kennedy as his motorcade drove by on November 22, 1963. The Warren Commission exhibited photographs of Oswald holding the rifle, a palm print found upon examination of the rifle, and detective work tracing its sale, all eventually led to Oswald.

This excerpt is from November 22, 1963 by Jeremy Bojczuk.

The morning after the assassination, officials in Washington made two important discoveries: About seven weeks before the assassination, a man calling himself Lee Oswald had visited the Soviet Consulate in Mexico City, where he met an official who was suspected by the CIA of being a member of the KGB's assassination department. The obvious implication was that the Soviet regime had been involved in President Kennedy's assassination. The man in Mexico City who had claimed to be Oswald was probably an impostor. The implication now was that the Soviets had been falsely implicated, presumably by individuals or groups within the US security apparatus. The events in Mexico City generated two competing conspiracy theories: either the Soviets were behind the assassination, in which case US intelligence and security institutions had failed to do their job, or evidence within the US Political System behind the assassination.

"These findings fit very well with the solution to the assassination: Lee Harvey Oswald had killed President Kennedy alone concluded by the Warren Commission, and he had done so for no political or ideological motive. Two days after the JFK assassination, Oswald himself was shot dead, in the basement of the Dallas police headquarters by Jack Ruby. This man also acted as a loner. Less than an hour later, J. Edgar Hoover, (CIA Director) reported in a conversation with Nicholas Katzenbach, the Deputy Attorney General:

"… I am concerned about, is having something so that we can convince the public that Oswald is the real assassin."The CIA Director continued, "Mr. Katzenbach, I think that President Johnson might appoint a Presidential Commission..." I agreed that the priority was not to investigate the assassination but to "convince the public that Oswald is the real assassin". On Sunday, November 24, Oswald was being led through the basement of Dallas Police Headquarters toward an armored car that was to take him to the nearby county jail. At 11:21 a.m. CST, Dallas nightclub operator Jack Ruby stepped from the crowd and shot Oswald in the chest. Oswald was taken unconscious by ambulance to Parkland Memorial Hospital–– the same hospital where doctors tried to save President Kennedy's life two days earlier. Oswald died at 1:07 p.m.

Which one is the "real Oswald"?

At noon on November 22, 1963, on a street in Dallas, the president of the United States is assassinated. <u>He is hardly dead when the official version is broadcast</u>. In that version, which will be the definitive one, <u>Lee Harvey Oswald alone has killed John Kennedy</u>.

The weapon does not coincide with the bullet, nor the bullet with the holes. The accused does not coincide with the accusation: Oswald is an exceptionally bad shot of mediocre physique, but according to the official version, his acts were those of a champion marksman and Olympic sprinter. He has fired an old rifle with impossible speed and his magic bullet, turning and twisting acrobatically to penetrate Kennedy and John Connally, the governor of Texas, remains miraculously intact.

Oswald strenuously denies it. But no one knows, no one will ever know what he has to say. Two days later he collapses before the television cameras, the whole world witness to the spectacle, his mouth shut by Jack Ruby, a two-bit gangster and minor trafficker in women and drugs. Ruby says he has avenged Kennedy out of patriotism and pity for the poor widow, Jacqueline Kennedy.

Jack Ruby

(Jack Ruby was born as Jacob Leon Rubenstein; March 25, 1911 – January 3, 1967) was a nightclub operator in Dallas, Texas. On November 24, 1963, Ruby fatally shot Lee Harvey Oswald, who was in police custody after being charged with the murder of John F. Kennedy two days earlier. A Dallas jury found Ruby guilty of murdering Oswald, and Ruby was sentenced to death. Later, Ruby appealed his conviction and was granted a new trial. As the date for his new trial was being set, Ruby became ill and died of a pulmonary embolism due to lung cancer. Ruby said he had been distraught over Kennedy's death and that his motive for killing Oswald was "...saving Mrs. Kennedy the discomfiture of coming back to trial." Others have hypothesized that Ruby was part of a conspiracy. G. Robert Blakey, chief counsel for the House Select Committee on

Assassinations from 1977 to 1979, said: "The most plausible explanation for the murder of Oswald by Jack Ruby was that Ruby had stalked him on behalf of organized crime, trying to reach him on at least three occasions in the forty-eight hours before he silenced Oswald.

Ruby was about to shoot Oswald who is being moved by Dallas police. Det. Jim Leavelle is wearing the tan suit. Det. L.C. Graves is wearing the dark suit.

The House Select Committee on Assassinations in its 1979 Final Report opined: Ruby's shooting of Oswald was not a spontaneous act, in that it involved at least some premeditation. Similarly, the committee believed it was less likely that Ruby entered the police basement without assistance, even though the assistance may have been provided with no knowledge of Ruby's intentions… The committee was troubled by the apparently unlocked doors along the stairway route and the removal of security guards from the area of the garage nearest the stairway shortly before the shooting... There is also evidence that the Dallas Police Department withheld relevant information from the Warren Commission concerning Ruby's entry to the scene of the Oswald transfer. When Ruby was arrested immediately after the shooting, he told several witnesses that he helped the city of Dallas "redeem" in the eyes of the public, and that Oswald's death would spare "... Mrs. Kennedy the discomfiture of coming back to trial." At the time of the shooting, Ruby said he was taking phenmetrazine, a central nervous system stimulant.

Ruby's explanation for killing Oswald would be "exposed ... as a fabricated legal ploy", according to the House Select Committee on Assassinations. In a private note to one of his attorneys, Joseph Tonahill, Ruby wrote: "Joe, you should know this. My first lawyer Tom Howard told me to say that I shot Oswald so that Caroline and Mrs. Kennedy wouldn't have to come to Dallas to testify."

Another motive was put forth by Frank Sheeran, allegedly a hit man for the Mafia, in a conversation he had with the then-former Teamsters boss Jimmy Hoffa. During the conversation, Hoffa claimed that Ruby was assigned the task of coordinating police officers who were loyal to Ruby to murder Oswald while he was in their custody. As Ruby evidently mismanaged the operation, he was given a choice to either finish the job himself or forfeit his life.

Dr. Jerry Kroth wrote in his theses:" Ruby died of lung cancer although he never smoked. Ruby believed he had been injected with cancer cells. The CIA was experimenting with injecting mice with cancer cells in the early 1960's. Ruby indicated that JFK had been killed by a conspiracy. Cause of death: Lung cancer."

Robert held up his hand above his head to cut in the reading,

"The death of Oswald and Ruby are definitely conspiratorial as the reason of killing President Kennedy. Let's focus on the Single Bullet Trajectory."

THE SINGLE-BULLET THEORY (or magic-bullet theory, as it is commonly called by its critics) was introduced by the Warren Commission in its investigation of the assassination of President John F. Kennedy to explain what happened to the bullet that struck Kennedy in the back and exited through his throat. Given the lack of damage to the presidential limousine consistent with it having been struck by a high-velocity bullet and the fact that Texas Governor John Connally was wounded and was seated directly in front of the President, the Commission concluded they were likely struck by the same bullet.

The theory, generally credited to Warren Commission staffer Arlen Specter (later a United States Senator from Pennsylvania), posits that a single bullet, known as "Warren Commission Exhibit 399" (also known as "CE 399"), caused all the wounds to the Governor and the non-fatal wounds to the president (seven entry/exit wounds in total).

According to the single-bullet theory, a three-centimeter (1.2″) -long copper-jacketed lead-core 6.5×52mm Mannlicher-Carcano rifle bullet fired from the sixth floor of the Texas School Book Depository passed through President Kennedy's neck and Governor Connally's chest and wrist and embedded itself in the Governor's thigh. If so, this bullet traversed 15 layers of clothing, 7 layers of skin, and approximately 15 inches of tissue, struck a necktie knot, removed 4 inches of rib, and shattered a radius bone. The bullet was found on a gurney in the corridor at the Parkland Memorial Hospital, in Dallas, after the assassination. The Warren Commission found that this gurney was the one that had borne Governor Connally. This bullet became a key Commission exhibit, identified as CE 399. Its copper jacket was completely intact. While the bullet's nose appeared normal, the tail was compressed laterally on one side.

In its conclusion, the Warren Commission found "persuasive evidence from the experts" that a single bullet caused the President's neck wound and all the wounds in Governor Connally. It acknowledged that there was a "difference of opinion" among members of the Commission "as to this probability", but stated that the theory was not essential to its conclusions and that all members had no doubt that all shots were fired from the sixth floor window of the Depository building."

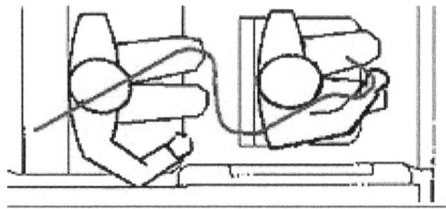

PHOTO: Trajectory of CE399 projected according to some critics. Trajectories such as this one gave rise to the term "magic bullet."

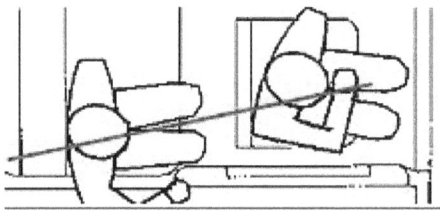

Trajectory of CE399 projected according to modern analysis. Note relative positions of seats.

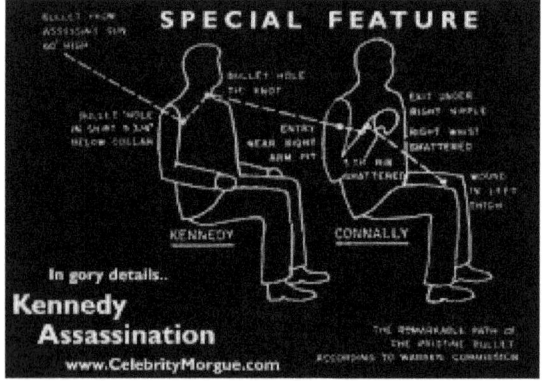

CBS news did a reenactment in 1967 involving several expert riflemen firing from a 60 foot tower at a moving sled using a similar Mannlicher-Carcano rifle.

None of these expert riflemen hit the target twice on their first try and 7 of them failed to do so on any try. They also were able to fire several practice rounds before the test.

Warren Commission Tests The Warren Commission's tests were equally bad. The WC paid 3 expert riflemen to duplicate Oswald's alleged feat. These shooters fired 18 rounds using Oswald's gun and scope.

They fired 3 rounds with just the iron sites. These shooters missed the head and neck area of the target 18 out of 18 times using the telescopic sight and 2 out of 3 times when they used the iron sites.

Some of the shots missed the target completely. They were able to take as long as they wanted for the first shot. They were firing from a height of only 30 feet. Oswald fired from a height of 60 feet. They were also shooting at stationary targets instead of a moving limousine.

"We reject the Single Bullet, so actually how many bullets were there?" Helen asked,

Dennis responded with a smile, "It's really more confusing; the FBI stated that three bullets were fired during the Kennedy assassination; the Warren Commission agreed with the FBI investigation that three shots were fired but disagreed with the FBI report on which shots hit Kennedy and which hit Governor Connally."

II. THE NUMBER, TIMING, AND SOURCE OF THE SHOTS FIRED AT THE PRESIDENTIAL LIMOUSINE

A. Warren Commission Findings

The Warren Commission concluded that three bullets had been fired at the Presidential limousine from the sixth floor, southeast corner window, of the Texas School Book Depository. Finding that the first pierced the President's neck, the Commission also indicated that "[although * * * not necessary to any essential findings * * *, there is very persuasive evidence from the experts to indicate that [this] * * * same bullet * * * also caused Governor Connally's wounds.

The Single–Bullet Theory and the Holes in JFK's Shirt and Jacket

Because of the unreliable documentary evidence from the autopsy, the precise location of the bullet wound in President Kennedy's back is not known. However, the bullet holes in his shirt and jacket, the precise locations are known.

These locations allow us to test the plausibility of the single–bullet theory. The question is whether both garments could have ridden up sufficiently for their holes to be consistent with a shot that: originated from the sixth floor, and exited through the throat at the same angle, in order to cause Governor Connally's injuries.

The Downward Angle

The FBI calculated the angle from the easternmost sixth–floor window to Kennedy's upper back. After making allowances for the slight downward slope of the road, it was determined that any bullet fired between frame 210, the first instant at which a sixth–floor gunman could have seen Kennedy, and frame 225, when Kennedy can first be seen to be injured, would have travelled downward at an average angle of 17° 43′ 30″ to the horizontal can represent the implications of a downward angle of about 17–18° by using a model. President Kennedy's exact position in the car is not known, but an examination of still photographs and the Zapruder film allows certain assumptions to be safely made:

Kennedy was sitting with his back against the seat.
His head was tilted slightly forward.
His right elbow was on or just above the side of the car, a little below the level of his shoulder.
His left arm was not raised.
The bullet hole in the back of the jacket is: 53/8″ below the top of its collar. The hole in the back of the shirt is 5¾″ below the top of its collar. With the garments in their normal positions, the hole in the jacket was either level with, or a small fraction of an inch below, the hole in the shirt:

The following photograph, taken by Phil Willis at the same time as frame 202 of the Zapruder film, shows that the jacket was in its normal position less than half a second before Kennedy came into view from the sixth–floor window:

With the shirt and jacket aligned normally, the holes are far too low for the hypothetical bullet to have come out of the throat at the required angle. The bullet holes would have had to be about four inches higher, close to the level of the collars:

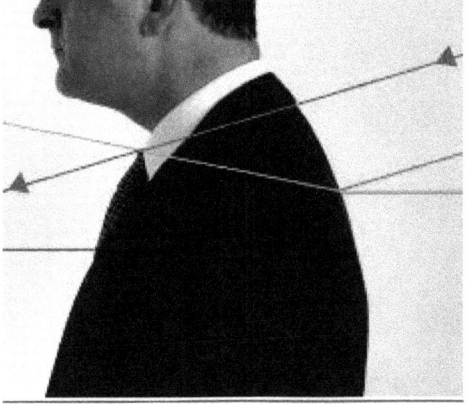

Some photographs, taken further from the time of the shooting than the Willis photograph, show the right shoulder of the jacket slightly raised as the president waved to the crowd. Even with the arm in this position, the bullet hole is much too low:

For the bullet hole to approach the level of the shirt collar, the back of the jacket would have had to ride up far beyond the level shown in any photographs of Kennedy during the motorcade:

When the collars of the shirt and jacket were in their normal positions, the two bullet holes were at almost exactly the same level. This suggests that if both garments had ridden up when the bullet passed through them, they had ridden up by almost exactly the same amount. Buttoned–up shirts are generally much more restricted in their movements than are jackets. Even if the jacket hidden up sufficiently to allow a bullet to enter the president's back near the level of the collar, the shirt could not have done so:

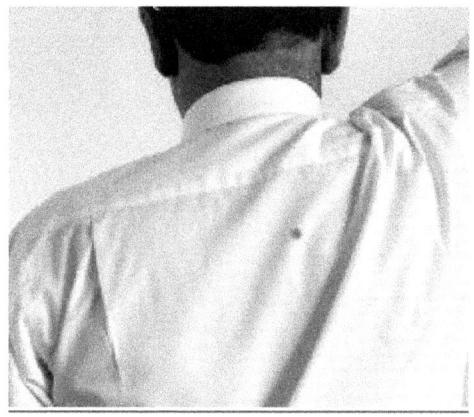

The known location of the hole in the shirt is not consistent with a hypothetical shot from the easternmost sixth–floor window that came out of Kennedy's throat.

The Truth, the Hole and the Single–Bullet Theory

No doubt the physical dimensions of our model, and the physical properties of his clothing, differ from those of President Kennedy. But any such differences are surely insignificant. It is clear that the hole in Kennedy's jacket, and especially the hole in his shirt, could not have been caused by a bullet entering his back at an angle of 17° or 18°, continuing in a straight line, and coming out of the throat just below the Adam's apple.

The location of the bullet holes disproves the single–bullet theory.

The original photographs on this page are issued under a Creative Commons Attribution Share Alike license, which means that you may use these images for any purpose, whether personal or commercial, provided you:

Mr. McCarthy smiled,

"Do you know that President Kennedy did not die because of either the Single Bullet or three bullets which the Warren Commission stated they were from Oswald's rifle?"

Helen looked at the retired policeman in perplex, she inquired,

"Would you please explain, Sir?"

Jason interrupted,

"Dad, save the fatal shot for me!" then he told Helen,

"I promise you a very unbelievable act in the JFK assassination from... Ah, but now I'd like to talk about the JFK autopsy, which is also very intricate. This is the excerpt from Wikipedia."

The autopsy of President John F. Kennedy was performed, beginning at about 8 p.m. EST November 22, 1963, on the day of his assassination and ending at about 12:00 AM EST November 23, 1963, at the Bethesda Naval Hospital in Bethesda, Maryland. The choice of autopsy hospital in the Washington, D.C. area was made by the President's wife, First Lady Jacqueline Kennedy. She chose the Bethesda Naval Hospital because President Kennedy had been a naval officer.

Death certificates: Kennedy's personal physician, Rear Admiral George Gregory Burkley, signed a death certificate on November 23 and noted the cause of death as "Gunshot wound, skull". Buckley described the head wound as "shattering in type causing a fragmentation of the skull and evulsions of three particles of the skull at the time of the impact, with resulting maceration of the right hemisphere of the brain.

Dr. Charles Crenshaw, surgeon at Parkland Hospital: The head wound was difficult to see when he was laying on the back of his head. However, afterwards when they moved his face towards the left, one could see the large, right rear parietal, occipital, blasted out hole, the size of my fist, which is 2 and a half inches in diameter. The brain, cerebral portion had been furred out and also there was the cerebellum hanging out from that wound. It was clearly an exit wound from the right rear, behind the ear. A right occipital area hole has the size of my fist.

Doris Nelson, emergency room nurse at Parkland Hospital: We wrapped him up.... And I saw his whole head ... There was no hair back there ... It was blown away. Some of his head was blown away and his brains were fallen down on the stretcher.

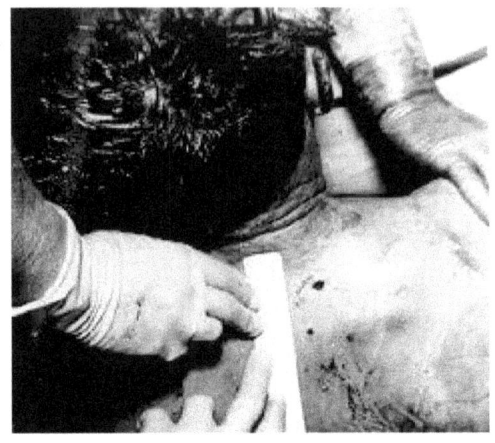

"How would the descriptions of Dr. Crenshaw fit this photograph?" Dennis asked.

Robert kept on reading," He also noted "a second wound occurred in the posterior back at about the level of the third thoracic vertebra". A second certificate of death, signed on December 6 by Theran Ward, a Justice of the Peace in Dallas County, stated that Kennedy "came to his death as a result of two gunshot wounds (1) near the center of the body and just above the right shoulder, and (2) 1 inch to the right center of the back of the head."

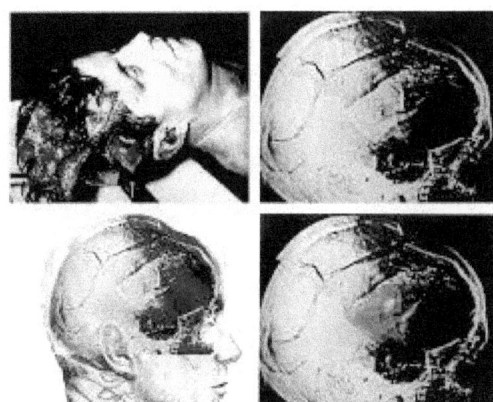

Figa1 Fig 1a

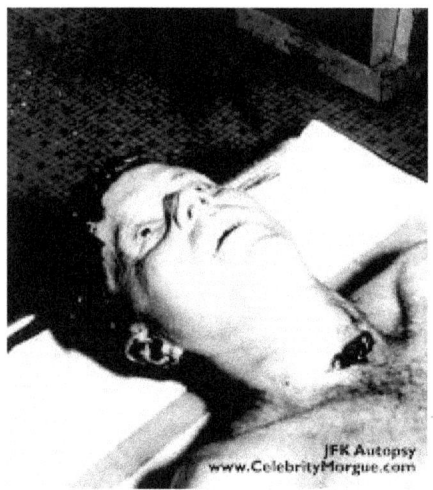

Fig 1bi

Elizabeth pointed to the images on the screen; she
requested an answer, "Tell me, please, how could
the photographs of Figa1, Fig 1a, and Fig1b be from
the same person?"
"Good observation!" Mr. McCarthy laughed, "I also
think there are some suspicious in the JFK autopsy
reports."
"How do you explain it, Sir?" Helen wanted to
know
"The answer is not simple," Mc McCarthy said,
"Now, we will search for the death of the Police
Officer Tippit.".
"Uncle Ben, should we focus on the autopsy instead
of go to another murder?" Robert asked
"That's exactly right!" Mr. McCarthy opened a file
and turned on the projector, "These are the models

that caused a great deal of disagreement among the
reporters."

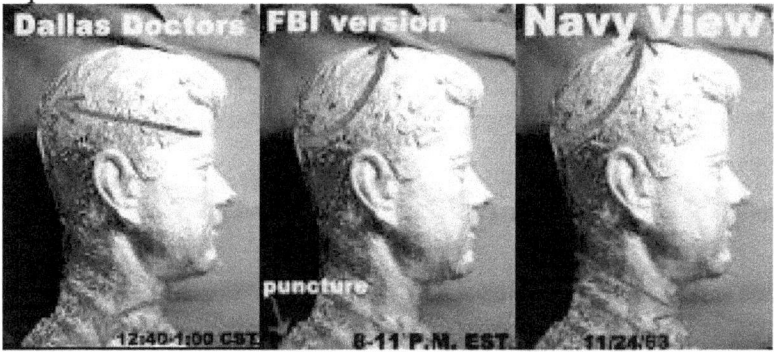

"I can't understand those Doctors and Professionals
were not able to come up with one accurate report
for the American people and the world?" Elizabeth
sighed.
"There were two murders, approximately at the
same time on November 22, 1963 at Dealey Plaza.
There were two corps, one from President Kennedy,
the other from Police Officer Tippit, and they
switched between the two dead bodies." Jason
explained.
"What! What did you've just said?"
Everybody stared at Jason, who showed his PhD
thesis to the audience and proudly announced,
"Yes. I spent four years to do some research on this
matter. "
"Tell us, please. Why and who killed Tippit?"
Helen inquired.
"The Warren Report claimed that Lee Harvey
Oswald was responsible not only for the

assassination of President Kennedy, but also for that of a Dallas policeman, J.D. Tippit, who was shot dead on a suburban street around 40 minutes after Kennedy had been shot in Dealey Plaza" Robert said.

"There are other theories about the death of this policeman." Mr. McCarthy made a comment.

Dedication Ceremony
Officer J.D. Tippit
Historical Marker

Where Was Oswald During the Tippit Shooting?

The only confirmed sighting of Oswald at around this time was by his housekeeper, Earlene Roberts, who saw him standing at a bus stop outside his rented room, waiting for a bus which would eventually pass the Texas Theater, the site of Oswald's arrest about 45 minutes later. The bus was heading north. The site of Tippit's murder was nine–tenths of a mile away to the south. Roberts saw Oswald no earlier than 1:03pm (Warren Commission Hearings, vol.6, p.448 and Warren Commission Hearings, vol.7, p.439), a maximum of

seven minutes before Tippit was killed. The FBI
(Warren Commission Hearings, vol.24, p.18) and
the Secret Service (Warren Commission Document
87, p.340) independently measured the time they
took to walk briskly from the rented room to the site
of the murder. Both took 12 minutes. Without
assistance, Oswald could not have reached Tippit in
time to shoot him.

I found an interesting article by Robert D.
Morningstar- Who is really buried in Arlington?
Dennis said, and then he read to the group. "In June
26, 1992, in Chicago, I was invited by Mr. Douglas
Carlson to address a closed session of President
Kennedy assassination researchers at the Third
Decade JFK symposium on my discovery within the
Zapruder film several alterations which employed
what I have dubbed "Gestalt Editing Techniques",
also I reported the discovery visible condensation
trails in frame Z-295. The discovery of this
condensation trail by this writer in New York City
and independently by researcher Roy Schaeffer in
Dayton, Ohio in 1992 proves conclusively the
presence of a shooter high on the Criminal Court
Building.

J.D. Tippit's killing has always been pictured as a
chance encounter in the Oak Dale District between
an alert, cruising hero policeman and a "suspect" in
the shooting og JFK based on the APB (All Points
Bulletin) put out the minutes before by the Dallas
Police Department. Tippit's death has always been
pictured as a random killing forced by
circumstances on the Fleeing of Oswald. I recalled

that he had been buried the following day (November 23, 1963) in a seal casket because his wound had purportedly disfigured his face. Tippit's body was disappeared from 10th and Patton that afternoon (1:15pm, November 22nd, 1963), was processed through two hospitals within two hours, and was never seen again by kith or kin. I remember his funeral shown on CBS; a light brown coffin was left to rest surrounded by Mrs. Tippit, their three children and waves of weeping policemen.

Amazing Coincidence

In Jim Bishop's account, much to our amazement, besides being shot in the torso several times, Tippit was described having been shot at the right temple, especially the right temporal area, the very same region of the head where the fatal shot passed through President's Kennedy head.

I was stunned. My mind boggled at the thought that this might be more than a mere coincidence- that the man accused of killing both Tippit and JFK could shoot two people within 45 minutes of each other, within four miles apart, one with a rifle from a high building and the other with a handgun at a short range (on the run), and inflicted exactly the same types of wounds.

Medical Discrepancies: I had already read some of the unusual medical discrepancies between the photos and X rays of President Kennedy's autopsy in several books. On the Third Decade Conference, at a panel of the foremost experts of America in the JFK assassination, I inquired whether anyone had ever consider the possibility that we might be seeing rear view photos and X rays of Tippit substituted for those of JFK. Some cynics laughed in the audience, but from the podium, the moderator, Mr. George Michael Evica, author of "… And We Are All Mortal", responded with a most unusual answer: "It's interesting that you asked this question, I've studied about JD Tippit, and when I went down to Dallas I found out that Tippit bore a remarkable resemblance to President Kennedy, so much so that his friends in Dallas Police Department used to rib him and called him Jack and JFK". I also inquired whether anyone had ever seen Tippit's autopsy report. Later, Dr. Dan DuPont, a researcher from N. Hollywood, CA, approached to me to discuss my inquiry. He promised to send me a copy of Tippit's autopsy report to assist in my research. In late July, 1992, I received from Dan DuPont a 1964 manuscript by Gary Murr entitled "The Death of Officer J.D. Tippit". It contained the report of the FBI Special Agent Arthur Carter on the autopsy of Officer J.D. Tippit, conducted by the Texas Coroner, Dr. Earl Rose. While study the entry wound diagrams by Dr. Rose, I saw the remarkable similarity between Dr. Rose's Tippit diagrams and the wound I perceived in the purported JFK's lateral X ray. I realized that the lateral X ray purported to be that of the late president might be in fact that of Officer J.D. Tippit. Dr. Rose description of the path taken by the bullet through Tippit's brain approximates the trajectory described by the Warren Commission and House Select Committee on assassination reports of the bullets path through President Kennedy's brain.

"Here is a note that was ignored by the Warren Commission." Jason read to the group.

Tippit was shot by two men, one of whom was Billy Seymour...six witnesses, ignored by the Warren Commission, saw two men shoot Tippit. One of them resembled Oswald...Seymour ran toward the Texas Theater. Richard Sprague-The Taking of America 1, 2, 3, 1976.

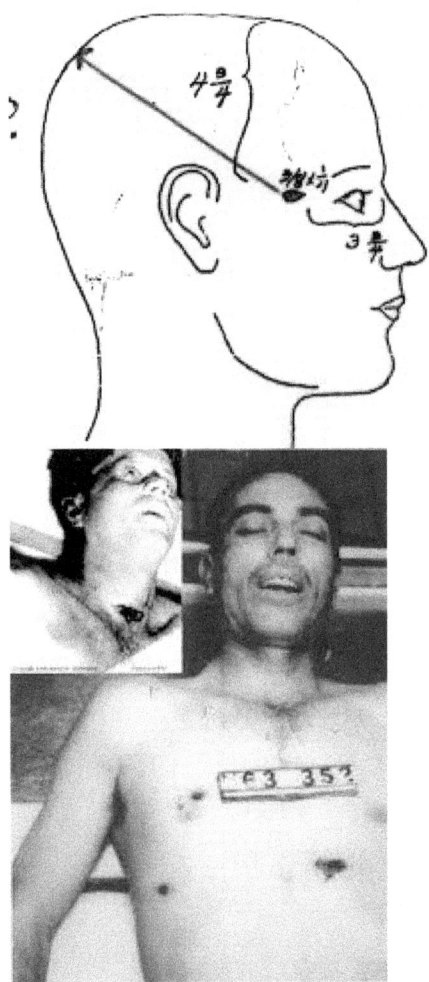

"If we searched for images of Tippit's autopsy, they are mixed up with JFK's autopsy. I'd like you pay attention to the shirt with the stripes, for I'll come back on that matter later." Mr. McCarthy said

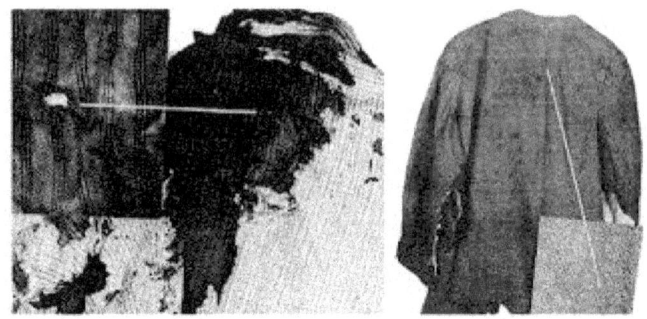

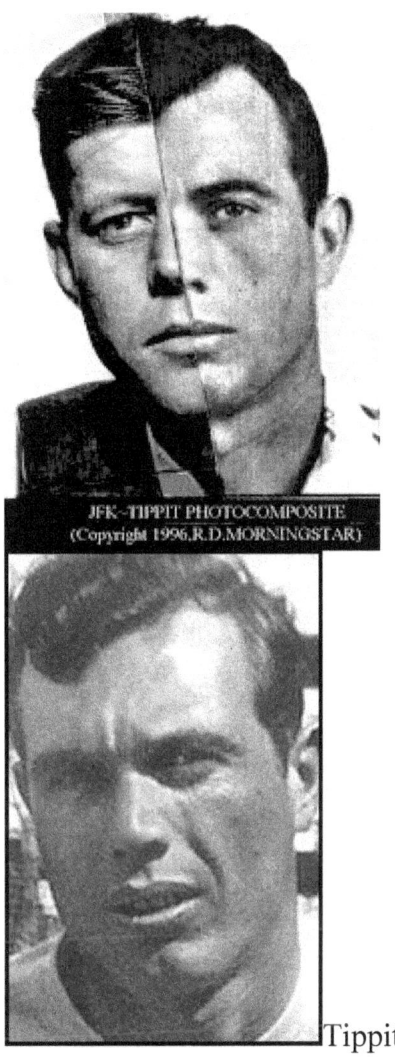

JFK ~TIPPIT PHOTOCOMPOSITE
(Copyright 1996.R.D.MORNINGSTAR)

Tippit

JFK

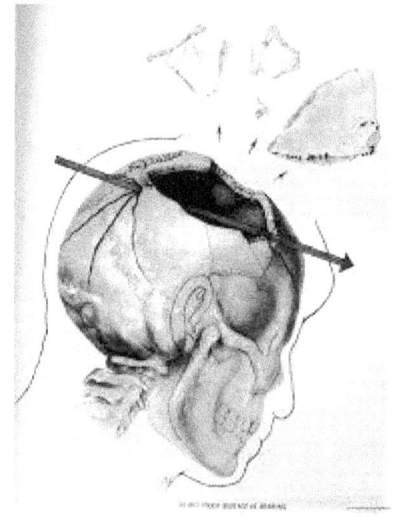

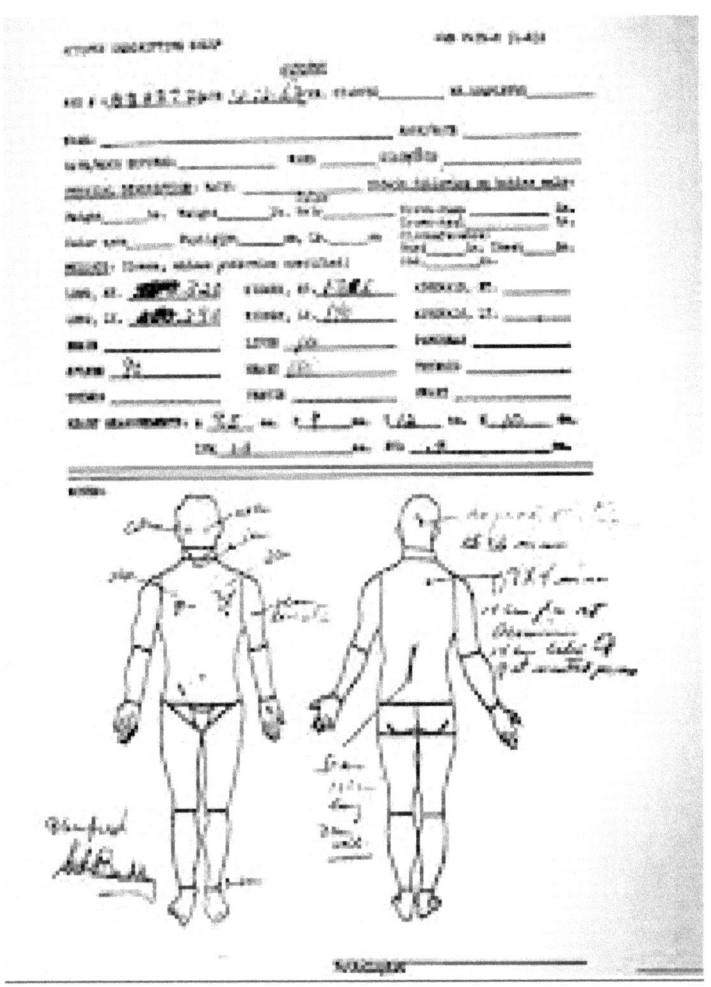

MF d 2 people within short range (on the run), and inflict exactly the same resolved to inquire f each other, within 4 miles of each other, one with IA Robert said, "Here's a discussion of the possibility that the man who murdered Tippit was Curtis LaVerne Crafard, also known as Larry Crafard instead of Lee Harvey Oswald as stated by the Warren Commission. At the time of the assassination,

1.   Curtis LaVerne

Crafard

Lee Harvey Oswald. Photo taken in Minsk.
COMMISSION EXHIBIT No. 2892

Crafard was purportedly employed at Jack Ruby's Carousel Club as a multi-purpose employee. His job allegedly consisted of being a handyman, clean-up man, part-time bartender, and also answering the telephone (WCE 2250). Crafard was also ostensibly living at the Carousel Club at the time of the assassination. According to the official version of events, on the day following the assassination, Crafard made a sudden departure from Dallas and allegedly hitchhiked to his cousin's home in Clare, Michigan (ibid). As this writer explains below, Crafard was not only demonstrably mistaken for Oswald by several witnesses, but there is a chance that he was the man who murdered Tippit. (Crafard was mistaken for Oswald, this was the reason that Oswald was charged with Tippit's murder).I had already read of some unusual medical discrepancies between photos and x-rays of the President in autopsy; I then inquired whether anyone had ever seen any pictures of Tippit's autopsy. The answer is confusing into the JFK's cases.

"What is the purpose of killing Officer JD Tippit?" Helen asked.
"Ah! You must read this paper to understand the death of JD Tippit." Jason answered.

THE AF1 TAPES & SUBSEQUENCES EVENTS AT ANDREWS AFB ON NOVEMBER 22, 1963: "What Was Supposed to Happen vs. What Did Happen" By Doug Horne, Author of "Inside the Assassination Records Review Board"

At my request, a friend of mine, psychologist Steven Kossor of Pennsylvania, recently used the sophisticated audio equipment he employs in his hobby as an audiophile to create an enhanced excerpt for me of the key passages in the Clifton version of the "Air Force One Tapes" (the GPO/NARA version released to the public in 2012, based on the Clifton version of the AF1 conversations, which is about 27 minutes longer than the version previously released by the LBJ Library), pertaining to the selection of JFK's autopsy site (Walter Reed Hospital vs. Bethesda Naval Hospital); and the mode of transportation to be used to move JFK's body from Andrews Air Force Base to the autopsy site (a mortuary style ambulance vs. helicopter).

Those portions of the AF1 tapes have always haunted me, since a tug-of-war was clearly going on between major actors onboard Air Force One, and major actors at the White House Situation Room ("Crown"), regarding where JFK's autopsy would be performed, and how the body would be transported there. Many people who have studied these conversations have undoubtedly wondered the same things: "What was being planned- – and why – and how did those plans change after AF1 landed at Andrews AFB. – and why?- This rather lengthy and detailed essay will share with its readers my considered opinions after ruminating about this subject off and on for 32 years, since 1981– when I first became aware of the LBJ Library version of the AF1 tapes by reading David Lifton's forensic thriller about the JFK assassination, Best Evidence.

CONTEXT IS EVERYTHING

Everything in this essay is grounded around one basic, undeniable fact: that the heavy, bronze, reddish-brown ceremonial casket from Dallas, in which JFK's body was taken aboard AF1 at Love Field in Dallas, was empty when the public saw it unloaded from Air Force One on live television shortly after 6:04 PM on November 22, 1963, and placed into a light gray Navy ambulance. We know this is so because President Kennedy's body arrived at the Bethesda morgue twenty minutes BEFORE the motorcade from Andrews AFB, transporting the Dallas casket in a light gray Navy Pontiac ambulance, arrived at the front of the Navy hospital. If the timeline that supports the above conclusion can be trusted, then the only conclusion possible is that JFK's body had been removed from the Dallas casket onboard the airplane, prior to the arrival of Air Force One at Andrews, and somehow spirited to Bethesda Naval Hospital before the Andrews motorcade arrived. It is essential that the reader review the basic facts proving that the body's chain-of-custody was broken enroute the autopsy, before we move on to the principal topic of this essay, which is:

"What do the AF1 tapes reveal about what was intended that night; what actually transpired; and how did those events deviate from what had been planned, and why?"

The timeline can indeed be trusted, and I shall demonstrate why. Two Navy enlisted men, Dennis David and Donald Rebentisch, were part of the working party that unloaded JFK's body at 6:35 PM at the Bethesda Naval Hospital loading dock that evening.

Mr. David was a First Class Navy Corpsman serving as "Chief of the Day" at Bethesda, and was instructed by the Secret Service detail (which had literally taken over Bethesda that afternoon) to assemble a working party of sailors, so that the President's casket could be unloaded, and taken into the morgue, when it arrived in a vehicle at the Bethesda morgue's loading dock. HM1 Dennis David was the supervisor of the working party, and Donald Rebentisch was a member of this working party. As reported in Best Evidence, both men, in the early 1980s, had independent and identical recollections of offloading a cheap aluminum shipping casket from a Hearse (a black Cadillac mortuary-style ambulance built specifically for the funeral trade) at the morgue's loading dock, and of taking the casket into the morgue, and setting it down, before being dismissed.

Dennis David's best recollection when interviewed by the ARRB staff in 1997 was that this event occurred at about 6:45 PM; the precise time of the event was fixed with precision in 1997 when the ARRB staff acquired the November 26th, 1963 typed after-action report of USMC Sergeant Roger

Boyajian, whose Marine Barracks security detail had provided physical security during the autopsy. (Mr. Boyajian still had an onionskin carbon copy of the report in 1997. He sent the ARRB a high-quality photocopy; which he authenticated by letter.) In his after-action report, which pertained only to the physical security provided for President Kennedy's autopsy, Boyajian wrote: "At approximately 1835 the casket was received at the morgue entrance and taken inside." This pins down much more accurately Dennis David's estimate to the ARRB staff that the shipping casket event had taken place at about 6:45 PM. The military time of 1835 hours (6:35 PM civilian time) in Boyajian's report, which was a contemporaneous document typed four days after the autopsy, trumps Dennis David's estimate in 1997 (very accurate, as it turns out) of 6:45 PM, and can be authoritatively considered the true arrival time of the shipping casket. Later on, during the night of the autopsy, after the autopsy had been concluded, in response to a question from HM1 Dennis David, Dr. J Thornton Boswell, one of the three pathologists who had conducted JFK's autopsy, confirmed to David that JFK had indeed been in the shipping casket his working party had unloaded from the Hearse at the morgue loading dock hours earlier. [David told Lifton in 1979 that both Dr. Humes and Dr. Boswell (the two Navy pathologists who participated in the autopsy) had been present on the loading dock, along with their commanding officer, Captain Stover, and what he believed to be the Surgeons General of the Army and Air Force.]

In contrast, both the local newspapers, and a Secret Service report, reported that the light gray Navy ambulance containing the Dallas casket, Jackie Kennedy, and Robert Kennedy, had arrived at 6:55 PM in front of Bethesda Naval Hospital, and newspapers the next day reported it had sat there for twelve minutes, before being driven away to the back of the building (its destination at that time – about 7:07 PM– per the two FBI agents who led the way in their own vehicle, was the morgue loading dock). We have a high degree of certainty, therefore, in both key aspects of this timeline – that is, in the arrival time of both caskets at Bethesda. The shipping casket (which Boswell confirmed to Dennis David had contained JFK's body) arrived twenty minutes prior to the Andrews motorcade and the light gray Navy ambulance, and furthermore, the Navy ambulance had then (according to newspaper reports the next day) sat out in front of the hospital for an additional 12 minutes before even moving. Dennis David also recalled clearly – in 1979, long before he ever knew about the Boyajian report – that after his working party unloaded the shipping casket from the Hearse, he went to the forward part of the hospital and subsequently watched the Andrews motorcade arrive, about 20 or 30 minutes later, from a second floor office window. As it turns out, his sense of time was quite accurate even many years later in 1979, for the Andrews motorcade arrived exactly 20 minutes after the casket arrival mentioned in the Boyajian report. This speaks highly to Dennis David's reliability as a witness.

It gets even worse, as far as the body's chain-of-custody goes. The staff of the House Select Committee on Assassinations (HSCA) learned in the late 1970s that the two FBI agents sent to Bethesda to obtain any bullets removed from the body, James Sibert and Francis O'Neill, helped two Secret Service agents (Roy Kellerman and William Greer) offload the Dallas casket (which had to be empty) from the light gray Navy am arrived at the morgue loading dock, using a wheeled conveyance (almost certainly what was known as a "church truck"). This was reconfirmed by the ARRB in 1997 when these two men were deposed; and former FBI agent James Sibert clarified for the ARRB that they set it down in the morgue anteroom. So this second casket entry was quite distinctive from the first one, in that:

(1) it was a different casket than Dennis David's working party offloaded [a heavy bronze ceremonial coffin, as opposed to a cheap, unadorned, lightweight gray aluminum shipping casket];

(2) It was delivered by a different vehicle [by a light gray Navy Pontiac ambulance, as opposed to a Hearse, which was a black Cadillac mortuary-style ambulance]; and

(3) Different people, or "actors," unloaded the casket from the vehicle which delivered it [namely, the second casket delivery was offloaded by four

Federal agents wearing suits, whereas the first casket delivery was offloaded by Navy sailors in working uniforms]. Based on inferences in an internal FBI interview report, this second casket entry by the four Federal agents occurred at approximately 7:17 PM. Unknown by the two FBI agents at the time, the Dallas casket was empty when they moved it into the morgue anteroom. (The two Secret Service agents had to know otherwise, for they had been onboard Air Force One during the flight back to Washington from Dallas.)

The "French Farce" continued that evening, for there was a second entry of the Dallas casket at 8:00 PM. The Honor Guard, or Joint Service Casket Team, after chasing a "decoy ambulance" into the darkness and getting lost, finally found the Dallas casket sitting out front in a light gray Navy ambulance (which one of the two present that night is unclear), and performed their intended ceremonial function by following it to the back of the hospital, manhandling the heavy bronze casket up the narrow steps leading to the morgue loading dock platform, and by then taking it into the morgue proper. The time of this third casket entry (and the second entry for the Dallas casket that night) was recorded in the after-action report of the Military District of Washington (MDW). So the time of this final casket entry – 8:00 PM– is also unassailable. And its actors are startlingly different from the other two casket entries that preceded it: the Joint Service Casket Team, hastily assembled at Andrews AFB, consisted of members of the Army, Navy, Air

Force, Marine Corps, and Coast Guard – all wearing the dress uniform of their respective services, and white gloves. [Unlike the Marine Barracks security detail supervised by USMC Sergeant Boyajian, they carried no weapons.] Furthermore, after setting the heavy bronze casket down next to one of the morgue examining tables, they witnessed the casket being opened, and saw JFK's body removed from the heavy, reddish-brown ceremonial coffin. Those who were playing a "shell game" with President Kennedy's body that night understood that the mortified and embarrassed Casket Team had to be allowed to perform its ceremonial function – that is, to "find" the casket that they had lost in the darkness; to take it into the morgue; and to see it opened and to be reassured that all was well, and that the slain Commander-in-Chief's body was inside. The illusion of an intact chain-of-custody had to be created for this most important audience, and for those supervising its performance, General Phillip Wehle (Commandant, MDW), and his aide, Lt. Richard Lipsey. The first two casket entries that night – the shipping casket at 6:35 PM and the first Dallas casket entry at about 7:17 PM – remained unknown to the Joint Service Casket Team, and to Wehle and Lipsey. [Lipsey later freely admitted knowledge of a "decoy ambulance" to the HSCA staff in an interview in the late 1970s, but seemed completely unaware of its implications; presumably, he and General Wehle were given a benign explanation for the "wild goose chase" conducted in the dark by both of them, and by their honor guard that night. Many of the enlisted Navy personnel on duty the night of the autopsy at Bethesda were aware of a "decoy" Navy ambulance, and its existence was even admitted to them by some of the Secret Service agents at the Naval Hospital.]

So – now that the reader understands the context within which we will be evaluating the Air Force One tapes and other critical data – we can proceed to our examination of the initial tug-of-war over the autopsy site, and the mode of transportation for JFK's body enroute the autopsy. Something was very much amiss that day. It behooves us to try to understand just what was going on:

(1) Why would anyone want to remove JFK's body from the Dallas casket onboard Air Force One?

(2) How did JFK's body arrive at Bethesda Naval Hospital prior to the Andrews AFB motorcade?

(3) What plan for the autopsy and the body's movement was hatched while AF1 was in flight, and how was that plan altered in its execution? and

(4) What happened to JFK's body at Bethesda in-between its early arrival at 6:35 PM, and the official commencement of the autopsy at 8:00 PM before a large audience of at least 35 people at the Bethesda morgue?

WHY WAS JFK'S BODY REMOVED FROM THE DALLAS CASKET ONBOARD AIR FORCE ONE, AND WHEN?

Author William Manchester makes quite clear in his 1967 book, The Death of a President, that there was a prolonged, serious, intense, and acrimonious struggle for custody of President Kennedy's body at Parkland hospital on November 22, 1963 after he was pronounced dead. The Dallas County Medical Examiner, forensic pathologist Dr. Earl Rose, was adamant that he perform a Texas autopsy in accordance with Texas law; and the Secret Service was equally adamant that they would not permit a Texas autopsy, and insisted on taking President Kennedy's body back to Washington without an autopsy being performed in Texas. His vivid description of this battle can be found on pages 297-305. Another account can be found in the DVD video of the documentary "The Men Who Killed Kennedy," in which O'Neal funeral home ambulance driver Aubrey Rike and Dr. Paul Peters of Parkland Hospital describe, in front of the motion picture camera, the intense (and at times, profane) altercation as they witnessed it.

Never mind that William Manchester sides with the Secret Service and the desires of the emotionally overwrought Kennedy entourage, and viciously criticizes Earl Rose for bad judgment. For what it's worth, Dr. Rose had the law behind him, and the Secret Service did not. There was no Federal jurisdiction over an assassinated President at the time, and Texas law prevailed. We know now, in hindsight that the autopsy performed at Bethesda Naval Hospital that night was badly flawed at the very least (that is the most charitable thing we can say about it today). In view of the improper and substandard procedures followed at the Bethesda autopsy; in view of the fact that many autopsy photos known to have been taken are now missing; in view of the fact that the three surviving skull x-rays (at least two are missing) are not originals, but are altered copy films; in view of the fact that some autopsy notes were burned and other notes are missing, that the first draft of the autopsy report was burned, that one signed copy is now missing, and the extant copy in the National Archives is the third written version of the autopsy protocol; in view of the fact that the brain photos in the JFK autopsy collection at the National Archives cannot be photos of JFK's brain; and in view of the all Americans who want to know what really happened to President Kennedy in 1963 surely wish that an honest and honorable professional like Dr. Rose had been allowed to do his job and perform an honest and competent autopsy on John F. Kennedy's body. If Dr. Rose had been allowed to do his job, I do not think we would now be faced with the massive cover-up that surrounds the medical evidence in JFK's assassination.

The point here is to emphasize that for about 30 minutes, the Dallas County Medical Examiner courageously stood his ground and attempted to prevent the theft of President Kennedy's body from Parkland Hospital by the Secret Service. Ultimately, the Secret Service agents with the Dallas casket (which was on a wheeled conveyance called a "church truck") pulled aside their coats and showed their weapons, and literally threatened to run Dr. Rose over with the casket (per Dr. Peters, who witnessed the altercation) if he did not get out of the way. Dr. Rose was pushed aside by Secret Agents and other members of the Kennedy entourage, and the Dallas casket, with JFK's body inside, was spirited away to Love Field in O'Neal Funeral Home ambulance.

The casket was taken onboard Air Force One via the port aft passenger door (the Presidential door) at 2:14 PM local time (CST). It was placed on the port side (left-hand side) of the aircraft in the aft compartment, after several seats had been removed to make room for the coffin, prior to its arrival. Jacqueline Kennedy boarded the aircraft at 2:18 PM. The swearing-in of the new President, Lyndon Baines Johnson, took place at 2:38 PM. Air Force One (SAM 26000) took off at 2:47 local time, and its wheels touched down at Andrews AFB two hours and thirteen minutes later, at 6:00 PM EST. At time 6:04 PM, the wheels were "on the blocks" (i.e., the chocks were in place).

As previously discussed above, we know that President Kennedy's body arrived at the Bethesda Naval Hospital morgue loading dock, in an aluminum shipping casket, at 6:35 PM; and we know that the bronze Dallas ceremonial casket (in which JFK's body left Dallas) was not driven up in front of the Bethesda complex until 20 minutes later, that it remained stationary for twelve minutes in its Navy ambulance, and was not set down in the morgue anteroom by the four Federal agents who offloaded it until about 7:17 PM, over 40 minutes later. Therefore, we know that the bronze Dallas casket must have been empty when it was offloaded from AF1 on national television shortly after 6:05 PM on November 22, 1963.

So when was JFK's body removed from the Dallas casket, and why?

The "why" seems obvious to me. The Secret Service was intent upon preventing a Texas autopsy – anyone who has read my book, Inside the Assassination Records Review Board, will understand that the Secret Service could not under any circumstances allow an honest autopsy of President Kennedy's remains. An honest autopsy would have revealed that he was shot from both the front and from behind, and was a victim of crossfire, and therefore of a conspiracy. The goal of the "dirty" Secret Service agents in the immediate aftermath of the assassination – those involved in the coup – was to spirit the body to a designated site where the "crime scene" (i.e., the body) could be "sanitized" – that is, where all evidence of frontal shots [both frontal entrance wounds and bullet fragments] could be removed from the body – hence, the extended altercation at Parkland Hospital with Dr. Rose and law enforcement officers over the custody of the body. [It was necessary to remove all evidence of frontal shots prior to autopsy so that the autopsy results would conform with the official cover story or "legend," namely, that JFK had been shot by a lone gunman, firing from above and behind him, in the Texas School Book Depository.] Given the intense and prolonged nature of the altercation between Dr. Earl Rose and

Roy Kellerman and his men at Parkland, I conclude that JFK's body was removed from the Dallas casket immediately after it was taken onboard Air Force One as a "security precaution" by the coup plotters, in case Dr. Rose and local law enforcement arrived, unannounced, to take custody of President Kennedy's remains.

This possibility must have seemed very real to Roy Kellerman and his Secret Service compatriots' – the altercation at Parkland Hospital had been intense and had nearly required physical violence for its resolution. There is no other logical or rational reason I can think of for removing JFK's body from the Dallas casket after it was taken onboard Air Force One. This is the only reasonable explanation. This was the beginning of the medical cover-up in the JFK assassination.

The "when" is also fairly obvious? After the swearing-in of LBJ, at 2:38 PM, the Kennedy entourage maintained a vigil, an "Irish wake," beside the casket in the aft compartment of the aircraft, throughout the entire flight. So the body could not have been removed from the Dallas casket at any time after the swearing-in. In fact, Manchester writes that even during the swearing-in, JFK's loyal and distraught Air Force Aide, General Godfrey McHugh (who had refused at attend the swearing-in of LBJ), was standing at attention beside the casket of the fallen Commander-in-Chief. So the only opportunity for Secret Service agents to remove JFK's body from the Dallas casket would have been immediately after it was taken onboard at

2:14 PM, and prior to the swearing-in at 2:38 PM. Jacqueline Kennedy boarded at 2:18 PM, and Manchester tells us in The Death of a President that she immediately went to the bedroom on the airplane to compose herself. Manchester also writes about a state of pandemonium shortly after the casket came onboard during which Godfrey McHugh went forward to the cockpit more than once to demand that the aircraft take off immediately. It is apparent, therefore, that the best and only opportunity for the Secret Service to remove JFK's body from the Dallas casket was between 2:18 PM (when Jackie Kennedy boarded) and 2:38 PM (the time of LBJ's swearing-in). This might have rather handily been accomplished under cover of some excuse like: "Please clear the compartment, while we secure the casket to the deck." The body would presumably have been spirited out of the aft starboard galley door, which was in the same aft compartment of the airplane where the casket was located. (See the diagram titled "Plan of Air Force One" at the end of Manchester's book.) JFK researcher and Air Force One expert James Sawa agrees with me that the body was almost certainly taken out of the starboard aft galley door. As documented by Manchester, there was an ongoing luggage transfer at Love Field of LBJ's luggage from Air Force Two (SAM 86970) to Air Force One (SAM 26000), which would have provided the opportunity to place JFK's body (which had been wrapped in two sheets at Parkland Hospital, one around his head and one around his body) in either the forward or aft luggage compartment of Air Force One. The aft luggage compartment seems more likely to me than the forward luggage compartment, based upon the photographs of the two luggage compartments taken by Sawa and displayed during his 2003 presentation at the Cyril Wecht Conference at DuQuesne University. The forward luggage compartment, per Sawa's photographs, was very crowded and contained large electronics cabinets, filled with radio equipment, that left minimal space for cargo; the aft luggage compartment, per Sawa's photos, was an unobstructed space with a very long longitudinal bench, devoted solely to cargo stowage. There was plenty of space for a human body lying in a horizontal position in the aft luggage compartment, based on Sawa's photograph, taken at the Air Force Museum in Dayton, Ohio. In summary, David Lifton's conclusion in his 1981 book Best Evidence, that JFK's body must have been spirited away in an Air Force One luggage compartment prior to takeoff, still stands up today, since we know unequivocally that it was taken onboard in the bronze Dallas casket (per ambulance driver Aubrey Rike, who saw the lid closed at Parkland and who stated that the casket was never opened before going onboard the aircraft at Love Field) – and since it could no longer have been inside the Dallas casket when it was offloaded at Andrews (per Dennis David and Sergeant Roger Boyajian).

And guess what? There is a reference in the new Clifton version of the Air Force One tapes to something going on with the body prior to takeoff. I will quote below from the verbatim transcript I made in 2012, from a radio conversation between Roy Kellerman (code name "Digest") and his boss at the White House Situation Room, the Head of the White House Secret Service Detail, Gerald Behn (code name "Duplex"), at time 32:21 on the GPO/NARA MP3 sound file:

Digest: we're at the airport, 26000, everybody aboard.

Duplex: OK, go ahead.

Digest: We're waiting for the swearing-in at the plane before takeoff.

Duplex: Of the – that's of Volunteer [LBJ's code name]?

Digest: Roger.

Duplex: Say again, Roy, say again.

Digest: We are waiting for judge to appear for swearing-in.

Duplex: That is for Volunteer, is that right?

Digest: Yes, we are having one, ah [garbled] to have it done here before we take off, Jerry.

Duplex: That's affirmative. Do you have any idea yet what, ah, Lace (Jackie Kennedy) wants to do and what Volunteer wants to do on their arrival here?

Digest: No. I will call you back. Suggest – we have a 2 hour 15 flight into Andrews. We have a full plane of at least 40.

Duplex: OK, go ahead.

Digest: I'll have to call you again after – after the, ah, body. Ah, however, I'm sure the, ah, Volunteer boys will go over his car and so forth. We will need [garbled] and several others.

.

Shortly after this exchange Kellerman terminated the conversation. The quote speaks for itself, I think: "I'll have to call you again after the, ah, body." Something that was happening with "the body" – after it had been taken onboard – caused Kellerman to have to sign off. This is consistent with my conclusion that JFK's body must have been removed from the Dallas casket shortly after it was taken onboard, and before the swearing-in of LBJ. Remember, the Dallas casket was taken onboard at 2:14 PM, four minutes before Jackie Kennedy boarded at 2:18 PM. Kellerman told Behn that everyone was onboard (which means it was past 2:18 PM when he commenced this conversation), and said twice that everyone was waiting for the swearing-in, which means the swearing-in had not yet happened. And during this period, between 2:18 and 2:38 PM, something was taking place with "the, ah, body." Something that caused Kellerman to say he would have to call Behn back.

HOW DID JFK's BODY ARRIVE AT BETHESDA NAVAL HOSPITAL BEFORE THE MOTORCADE FROM ANDREWS AFB?

The short answer is, "by helicopter." Specifically, by a helicopter that landed at the Bethesda Naval

Hospital complex's Officer's Club parking lot. JFK's body was transferred from that helicopter to a Hearse (a black Cadillac mortuary ambulance), placed inside a shipping casket, and delivered to the morgue loading dock less than five minutes later, at 6:35 PM, when USMC Sergeant Boyajian dutifully recorded the time of arrival of the casket in his notes. He committed his notes to a typed report three and one half days later, a copy of which he provided to the ARRB staff in 1997 after I established contact with him. How I reached these conclusions, and the crucial role of the AF1 tapes (and other evidence) played in reaching these conclusions, is detailed below.

The Clifton version of the AF1 tapes (between time 40:51 on side 1, and about 1 hour and ten minutes – that is, through the end of side 1 of the GPO/NARA release; and continuing from time 3:52 to time 6:05 of side 2 of the GPO/NARA release) reveals an interesting tug-of-war between one group of actors on AF1 – namely, Secret Service agent Roy Kellerman, George Burkley [Military Physician to the President], and U.S. Army General Ted Clifton [Military Aide to the President] – and other actors at "Crown" [the White House Situation Room], whose spokesman on the tapes is Head of the White House Secret Service Detail, Gerald Behn. [President Kennedy's National Security Advisor, McGeorge Bundy, was also at Crown that day.]

All three actors onboard Air Force One – Kellerman, Burkley, and Clifton – made repeated attempts to establish ground transportation from

Andrews AFB to the U.S. Army's Walter Reed Hospital, in Washington D.C., where they wanted the autopsy conducted. As the conversations continued, General Clifton specified on two occasions that he wanted a "mortuary-type ambulance" (in other words, a Hearse) at Andrews AFB to pick up President Kennedy's casket. At one point a "ground return" or limousine was also requested to accompany the mortuary-type ambulance.

The recipients of these radioed requests from AF1 were both General Heaton (the U.S. Army Surgeon General, apparently speaking on the phone from Walter Reed), and Gerald Behn at "Crown." Heaton seemed compliant and willing to do whatever was requested of him. But Behn, from the very beginning, insisted that the autopsy would be conducted at Bethesda Naval Hospital, and that the mode of transportation would be by helicopter. Eventually, General Ted Clifton onboard Air Force One finally comes to accept what Gerald Behn at "Crown" insisted on, which was a Bethesda autopsy, and asks Behn if it is correct that a mortuary-type ambulance will take the body to Bethesda. Behn quickly corrected him, telling Clifton that helicopter transportation would take the body to Bethesda Naval Hospital. Clifton expressed his concern that the bronze Dallas casket may have been too heavy for a helicopter, and so continued to insist on a "mortuary-type ambulance" as a backup.

A Gawler's Funeral Home Hearse Was Initially Assigned to Proceed to Andrews:

In 1996 the ARRB interviewed Mr. Joseph Hagan (President of Gawler's in 1996, and the same man who was in charge of the embalming team at Bethesda on 11/22/63). He told us that Colonel Miller of the MDW initially ordered Gawler's to send a Hearse to Andrews AFB, but that this order was rescinded at the last minute. This begs another question, though:

if the Gawler's Hearse to Andrews was rescinded, was it assigned to go somewhere else instead? Somewhere like the Bethesda Naval Hospital complex?

A Stolen Conversation from the White House Situation Room:

There is a snippet of "hot mike" back chatter coming from "Crown" on the Clifton version of the Air Force One tapes, which begins at time 1:02:20 and terminates at 1:03:13 of side 1; it occurs during a period when no one on AF1 is speaking, and it is clear from context that we are listening to a Situation Room background conversation picked up by an open microphone. Only certain words or short phrases can be heard – not any complete sentences – and the words and phrases quoted below are interspersed between static, garbled conversation, and some voids and silence in between, as well:

Crown: *"... black car... black Cadillac is the... black Cadillac... I'd get him out there anyway, regardless! ... Get him out there anyway, regardless... then maybe... then maybe...* [long pause, including communications chatter, followed by one more, quite distinct] *black Cadillac.*"

My audiophile friend in Pennsylvania who created an enhanced AF1 excerpt for me, Steven Kossor, has not only detected a loud audio "pop" indicative of crude splicing in this segment, but has also detected (using wave form analysis) strange "voids" between segments of the conversation which also reveal alteration of this segment of the Clifton voice recording. He also insists that the first two "black Cadillac" phrases above, and the repeated phrases "get him out there anyway, regardless" and "then maybe" are identical duplications that prove the Clifton tape has been edited. As Steven Kossor has written me:

"... These are duplicate audio signals, not separate transmissions, created mechanically as a result of audio tape storage (print through) and/or editing. Each unique vocal "set" represents an original transmission that is duplicated one or more times. The wave forms are virtually identical (there is no change in emphasis from one to the other), and they occur at approximately equal distances in time after the first occurrence of the sound that they duplicate. The wave form and presentation of the last "Black Cadillac" utterance is different from the earlier ones and probably represents a separate utterance of that phrase in a recording that has apparently been edited multiple times between the first "Black Cadillac" utterance and the last one."

[Aside from this forensic evidence of editing during the "black Cadillac sequence," we also know, based upon the well-documented, missing conversations about the capture and identity of the accused assassin in Dallas – recalled by others in their memoirs, oral history interviews, and books – and from studying other segments of conversation on the tape which appear out of order or incomplete, that the Clifton version of the AF1 tapes, while some 27 minutes longer than the older LBJ Library version, is not complete, and has been edited. There may still be as much as three hours of conversation missing, based on the fact that there were three frequencies in full use for the entire 2 hour and 13 minute flight, according to the report filed by the radio operator on the aircraft.]

The speakers here (apparently two persons) are unknown, but in the portions of the Clifton recording that have not been excised, they are clearly talking about a "black Cadillac." That is very interesting, given that the shipping casket containing the President's body arrived in a Hearse – a black Cadillac mortuary-type ambulance – at 6:35 PM. The additional phrases "I'd get him out there anyway regardless" and "then maybe" are consistent with someone deeply concerned about moving JFK's body and with the time pressure to do so, and some hopeful, or expected outcome. [They are NOT phrases that would seem to apply to the only other black Cadillac I know of that day, the "Queen Mary" follow-up car on Elm Street. It had its own Secret Service numerical designation, 679-

X, and was not ever referred to as a "black Cadillac" in any writings I have ever come across.] And this conversation was picked up from the White House Situation Room, where the radio spokesman that day was the Head of the Secret Service White House Detail, Gerald Behn. [Gerald Behn would have referred to the "Queen Mary" as 679-X, or by its code name designation, "Halfback."] It was Gerald Behn who insisted, from the git-go, on helicopter transportation to move the body of JFK to an autopsy at Bethesda.

The reader should also be aware that when Dennis David met the Hearse at the morgue loading dock, that several "men in suits" (civilians) whom he presumed to be Federal agents got out of the car when it arrived. Were they Secret Service agents? Under the circumstances, there is no reason to believe they were anything else. The Secret Service sent about 40 agents to Bethesda Naval Hospital that afternoon to take over preparations for the autopsy; and it was a Secret Service agent who informed Dennis David that his visitor was about to arrive, and urged him to get his working party to the loading dock. Moving that body from Andrews AFB to the Bethesda morgue, via a helicopter and Hearse, would have been a Secret Service operation, all the way, so it is telling that we hear the phrases "black Cadillac" and "get him out there anyway, regardless" from "Crown," where Jerry Behn (Head of the White House detail) appears to have been running the show.

A Helicopter Was Definitely Sent to Andrews AFB to Pick Up President Kennedy's Body:
In November of 1996, David Lifton gave a remarkable presentation at the JFK Lancer conference in Dallas, in which he played a video interview he had just conducted with the former Marine Corps pilot of a military helicopter sent to Andrews AFB to pick up President Kennedy's body and transport it to Bethesda Naval Hospital. Anyone interested can watch and listen to the video of this interview by obtaining the DVD disc from the 1996 Lancer conference titled: *"Medical Evidence."* Summarizing, the former Marine pilot was a member of the "HMX" helicopter squadron based in Quantico, VA and Anacostia, Maryland. This squadron provided 24-hour, seven days per week "hot team" standby service for the President and high level, VIP Federal officials. Normally they were on duty for 48 hours at a time, and then off duty for the next 48 hours. Lifton's witness (whose identity he protected) stated in the videotaped interview that he was about to go home and enjoy a rare day off on November 22, 1963 when he was called into a special, surreptitious briefing at the Anacostia base where he was working that day. He was ordered to take a helicopter to Andrews AFB, and to be as unobtrusive as possible (including not using the lights on his hello), to await the arrival of Air Force One, and to take President Kennedy's body to Bethesda Naval Hospital. He was ordered to use a VIP helicopter, and was told that others would load the body onto his helicopter. His call

sign for this mission was to be "Nighthawk One." He was told to stay out of public view; to taxi up to the tail of Air Force One after it had landed; and to stay out of the lights as much as possible.

The pilot of "Nighthawk One" landed on the west taxiway at Andrews just prior to sunset (he remembered the orange sky) and parked his helicopter behind some trees near the passenger terminal. He kept the engines running, but turned the rotors off. As soon as he saw Air Force One land, he spun his rotors up again.

He then taxied out to Air Force One in the darkness, and stopped about 100 feet from AF1 on the right rear side of SAM 26000 – on the starboard aft quarter of the airplane. He could see "Army 1" (the helicopter LBJ used that night to go to the White House) parked in the lighted area of the tarmac "where the action was," and noted that the entire port side of Air Force One was illuminated by the television lights. He saw a large casket coming down on the scissors lift from the port aft door, then saw the casket loaded into the Navy ambulance and saw Jackie Kennedy get into the ambulance. At this point he realized that either the plans had changed since he was given his mission, or he had merely been a backup, and no one had told him about the ambulance. As soon as he saw the Dallas casket put into the Navy ambulance, he taxied away into the darkness, requested clearance, and flew his helicopter to Quantico, Virginia.

Undoubtedly, "Nighthawk One's" mission had been requested by Gerald Behn at "Crown," the one official who had insisted throughout the Air Force One conversations on the Clifton tapes that JFK's autopsy be conducted at Bethesda, and that his body be moved by helicopter.

The obvious questions, in view of "Nighthawk One's" departure without President Kennedy's body onboard, are:

(1) Who changed the plan? How did this happen? And

(2) How did JFK's body get to Bethesda Naval Hospital, if "Nighthawk One" did not take it there?

Orders Were Given by "Crown" to Separate Jacqueline Kennedy from the Dallas Casket, and to Send the Casket to Bethesda by Helicopter:

The AF1 tapes reveal unambiguously that Gerald Behn in the White House situation room wanted to separate Mrs. Kennedy (hereafter referred to by her initials, JBK), and all other VIP passengers who were not Secret Service agents, from the Dallas casket. Although JFK's Military Aide, General Ted Clifton (code name "Watchman"), initially insisted on an autopsy at Walter Reed Hospital and the use of a mortuary-type ambulance for transportation, he eventually fell into line with "Crown's" demands and then actively supported Behn's orders. Here are some telling quotes from the Clifton tapes:

Digest: Walter Reed ambulance for body that will go to Walter Reed, over?

Duplex: Say again, say again.

Digest (Kellerman): … [We need] an ambulance from Walter Reed to transport body, over?

Duplex (Behn): Arrangements have been made for a helicopter for the Bethesda Naval Medical Center, over.

Digest: Standby, Jerry – ah, I'll have to get Burkley here.

A short time later Behn clarified his intentions:

Duplex: The, everybody aboard Air Force One, everybody aboard Air Force One, with the exception of the body, will be choppered [transported by a helicopter] into the South Grounds [of the White House. The body will be choppered to the Navy Medical Center at Bethesda, over.

Burkley: The body will be choppered or will go by ambulance to the Navy Medical Center?

Duplex: Will be choppered, will be choppered.

Somewhat later, General Clifton on AF1 (apparently unaware that the Secret Service is running the show in Washington) "reads the riot act" to General Heaton, the Surgeon General of the Army:

Clifton: [material appears to be missing here from both the LBJ Library and Clifton version of the AF1 tapes – there is no "point one" on the tape "… two: we do not want a helicopter for Bethesda Naval Medical Center. We do want a [sic] ambulance and a ground return from Andrews to Walter Reed, and we want the regular, ah, post mortem that has to be done by law, under guard, performed at Walter Reed. Is that clear, over?

Heaton: That is clear; General Clifton. You want an ambulance, and another, ah, limousine, at Andrews, and you want the, ah, regular post mortem by law done at Walter Reed.

Clifton: That is correct.

These instructions, given to the Army Surgeon General (who was at Walter Reed, and not at "Crown"), were undoubtedly why the Gawler's Hearse was originally ordered to go to Andrews AFB by Colonel Miller of the Army's Military District of Washington. This conversation, apparently, also stimulated Dr. Dick Davis, the acting Head of Neurosurgery at the Armed Forces Institute of Pathology (the AFIP was co-located with Walter Reed in Washington D.C.), to assemble a team and set up to perform a craniotomy (the surgical skull cap removal performed at autopsies) at Walter Reed. He told me, when I interviewed him in 1997 while on the ARRB staff, that his team was set up and ready to go, but President Kennedy's body never arrived at Walter Reed.

Then, after the "black Cadillac" conversations overheard at Crown on the Clifton tapes, General Clifton (who now began using his code name, "Watchman") begins to defer to Behn's plans for a Bethesda autopsy:

Watchman: Ah, Duplex, this is Watchman. I understand that [you] have arranged [fadeout] ... mortuary-type of ambulance [garbled] take President Kennedy to Bethesda. Is this correct, over?

Duplex: Watchman, ah, there's been [sic] arranged to helicopter, helicopter, the body to Bethesda, over. After some discussion about whether it is safe to use a helicopter, this ensued:

Watchman: This is Watchman. Ah, don't take a chance on that. Also, have a mortuary-type ambulance stand by in case the helicopter doesn't work.

Duplex: That's affirmative [garbled] That's affirmative, I received.

Watchman: Now, some other instructions. Listen carefully. Ah, we need a ramp, a normal ramp put at, put at the front of the aircraft, on the right-hand side, just behind the pilot's cabin, in the galley. We are going to take the First Lady off by that route, over. Do you understand?

Duplex: I receive, affirmative.

Clifton then asked for a large forklift for the casket at the port side rear door, and a normal ramp for passengers at the port forward door. He then summarized:

Watchman: Duplex, this is Watchman, I say again: at the right front, a ramp for Mrs. Kennedy; at the left rear, if possible, a forklift for the casket; and on the left front, near the pilot, [a] normal ramp, [a] normal press arrangement [garbled], over?

Clearly, at this point General Clifton was implementing Jerry Behn's stated intention to separate JBK from the Dallas casket. Behn had earlier said all passengers were to be choppered to the South Grounds of the White House; and now

Ted Clifton was attempting to ensure that this would happen by arranging for her to exit the aircraft secretly, in the darkness, using the forward starboard galley door – a different door than was going to be used for the Dallas casket.

The question is, WHY? I have inferred that among the many conversations that must have been deleted from the AF1 tapes, were undoubtedly conversations between Kellerman and Behn about the body switch – about the removal of JFK's body from the bronze Dallas casket prior to takeoff, as a "security measure" to keep it out of the hands of the Dallas County Medical Examiner, Earl Rose. This is the context in which the "black Cadillac" discussions overheard at "Crown," and the blatant attempts by Behn and Clifton to separate JBK from the Dallas casket, best make sense.

Now, just because "Nighthawk One" took off from Andrews AFB without JFK's body onboard, that does not mean that there weren't other helicopters available. Please read below this crucial exchange between Kellerman (Digest) and Behn (Duplex), which occurred between time 3:52 and time 6:05 on side 2 of the Clifton tapes (after the Clifton plan to remove JBK from the aircraft in secret was discussed):

Duplex: [after many communications problems]… Go ahead Digest, this is Duplex.

Digest: Again, I repeat, three helicopters [to] transport people to the White House lawn, OK?

Duplex: That is affirmative.

Digest: Roger, OK, White House 102 and 405-X for transportation to, ah, Navy Hospital, OK?
Duplex: That is affirmative.
This is significant. Kellerman is confirming that three helicopters at Andrews were assigned to take AF1's passengers (largely, the Kennedy entourage, including JBK) to the White House, and that two additional helicopters were assigned to transport JFK's body to Bethesda. These are designated by Kellerman as White House assets, and are therefore not HMX "hot team" assets.

Getting the body of JFK to Bethesda was so important that redundancy was laid in: both "Nighthawk One" had been arranged to perform that function, as well as two other assets controlled by the Secret Service (White House 102 and 405-X). Presumably, one of these two White House assets would be used to take the heavy, ceremonial bronze Dallas casket to Bethesda – an event which was highly likely (indeed, almost certain) to be televised on live TV. The second helicopter mentioned by Kellerman would have been needed to surreptitiously transport the actual body of JFK from the luggage compartment on AF1 where it had been hidden during the flight, to Bethesda, where it could have been reunited with the bronze Dallas casket. If this had taken place as planned – a two helicopter rendezvous on the grounds of Bethesda in the darkness – JFK's body could have been placed back into the Dallas casket and no one at the morgue would have known otherwise. Once the very public loading of the Dallas casket onto hello # 1 had taken place, the klieg lights would have been turned off, and the Andrews TV coverage would have ceased. (This is exactly what happened once LBJ's hello, "Army 1," departed. The TV coverage abruptly ended.) Then, in the ensuing darkness, it would have been easy to offload JFK's body from its hiding place in an AF1 luggage compartment and place it on hello # 2.

The most significant quote on the Clifton tapes then takes place almost immediately after Kellerman tells Behn about the two helicopters to be used for the Navy Hospital.

Duplex: Digest, this is Duplex. You accompany the body aboard the helicopter.

Digest: Roger…

After all that had gone before in the AF1 conversations, the reader will understand that this is the proof that the light gray Navy Pontiac ambulance was never intended to take JFK's Dallas casket to Bethesda. In fact, William Manchester makes clear, in two places in his book The Death of a President, that this was a cardiac ambulance (not a hearse), and that it was sent to Andrews by Captain Canada, the commanding officer of the treatment hospital at Bethesda, in case LBJ had experienced any heart trouble. [Rear Admiral Galloway commanded the entire complex; Captain Stover was the C.O. of the medical school at Bethesda; and Captain Canada was the C.O. of the treatment hospital.]

On page 381, Manchester writes:

"Captain R.O. Canada, Jr., Bethesda's commanding officer, wasn't informed of the role his hospital would play. And Godfrey McHugh's tart order for an ambulance had been ignored. Captain Canada did send one to Andrews, but that was sheer chance. Because Lyndon Johnson had served in the Navy, he had been Canada's patient after his massive heart attack on July 2, 1955; the ambulance was dispatched against the possibility that the new President might be stricken again during the flight."

Jacqueline Bouvier Kennedy, On Impulse, Changes the Secret Service /Military Plan to Separate Her from the Dallas Casket:

We know from Manchester's book that Robert F. Kennedy, the slain President's brother and the U.S. Attorney General, was the first person to board AF1 after touchdown. In fact, he appears to have done so in the darkness, just when the bright television klieg lights were briefly switched off as the aircraft approached its designated parking spot. Air Force One had touched down at 6:00 PM local time, and had been taxiing toward its normal waiting area for about three minutes.

Manchester writes on page 387:

"The crowd waiting by the chain fence had realized that arrival was imminent because they heard the whining jets. They couldn't see its silhouette, however; the klieg lights blinded them. At 6:03 PM these were abruptly cut off. The reason was

commonplace. The pilot had to see his way…
Closer and closer the huge ghost crawled until
Swindal [the pilot], looking down, could identify
two of the waiting men. Robert McNamara was
facing him, looking peculiarly tall. Robert Kennedy
had just left the sanctuary of his [pickup] truck
[where he had secreted himself] and was posed in a
tense half-crouch, ready to spring aboard. Swindal
paused momentarily for the crouched." [Did AF1
actually pause momentarily in the darkness to let
RFK onboard before any others? The meaning of
Manchester's writing here is unclear.] The eyes of
the crowd were on the rear hatch, the President's. A
ramp had been readied for the front entrance, and
the Attorney General vaulted on it, unseen; he was
pumping up the steps while it was still being rolled
into place… the aircraft glided forward once again
and parked." The time "on the blocks" was reported
by AF1 as 6:04 PM.
RFK raced to the rear of the aircraft to be with JBK.
Jacqueline Bouvier Kennedy had already displayed
a gritty, stubborn frame of mind during the flight
back.

On page 348, Manchester writes that when Rear
Admiral Burkley, JFK's Military Physician, asked
her if she wanted to change her blood-spattered pink
Chanel suit:
"No," she whispered fiercely. "Let them see what
they've done."
A similar exchange took place with Malcolm
Kilduff, the acting Press Secretary for JFK's trip to

Texas. Manchester, who did not have access to the AF1 tapes, and therefore did not understand the true intent of taking JBK out the forward starboard door...,

Continued on page 348:
The last man to realize that she really meant it was Kilduff. He thought long about how they could offload the coffin at Andrews without pictures being taken. His solution was to open the galley door on the starboard side, opposite the usual exit. That way the great mass of the fuselage would mask both the coffin and the widow; photographers and television cameramen would see nothing. He proposed the plan. She vetoed it. *"We'll go out the regular way* [using the Presidential exit on the port aft side of the aircraft]*," she said. "I want them to see what they have done."*
Ask yourself what was more likely: was General Clifton taking orders from an assistant Press Secretary, or was the assistant Press Secretary taking order from the Commander-in-Chief's Military Aide? It seems obvious to me that Clifton tried to use Kilduff to get Jackie to leave the aircraft in the darkness, via the secret exit ramp previously arranged by Clifton, on the radio circuit to "Crown." And it was naive for Manchester to fall for this specious after-the-fact explanation for a purported plan to remove both the casket and Jackie Kennedy from the forward starboard galley door, since there was no forklift at the forward starboard galley door to take the casket off. The forklift was

at the Presidential door, on the aft port side. Air Force One itself (Clifton) had initiated that arrangement.

On page 390, Manchester writes:

Bob Kennedy explained the transportation choices to his sister-in-law. "There's a helicopter here to take you to the White House. Don't you want to do that?"

"No, no, I just want to go to Bethesda." She saw the gray ambulance, assumed it was the one she had requested, and said, "We'll go in that."

And thus, were all the devious plans of the coup plotters to separate the widow (and all other witnesses) from the Dallas casket torn asunder, and rendered moot. In this instant, while looking out the Presidential exit door at the left rear of the aircraft, the determination of President Kennedy's widow to remain with her husband – she had no idea the Dallas casket was empty, and therefore equated staying with the casket to staying with JFK's body – threw a giant monkey-wrench into the plans of the Secret Service to surreptitiously reunite his body with the Dallas casket. The failure of this plan led directly to the absurd "French Farce" of the three casket entries discussed earlier, and through this discovery of the body's broken chain-of-custody – by investigating what it meant – we have uncovered the clandestine post-mortem surgery that was performed on JFK's body, at Bethesda Naval Hospital, to remove all evidence of frontal shots from his cadaver before the autopsy officially began. No coup plotter in his right mind would have planned the three Bethesda casket entries that actually occurred that night, for the different entries left undeniable evidence of a serious break in the body's chain-of-custody, and of "missing time" prior to the beginning of the autopsy at 8:00 PM. The investigation of what transpired during that "missing time" (between 6:35 PM and 8:00 PM), and of what the three casket entries implied, has led to a true understanding of why the Parkland Hospital wound observations and the Bethesda Naval Hospital wound observations are so markedly different. (Chapter 13 of Inside the ARRB, pages 998-1013.)

Manchester's confirmation that RFK and JBK, with an ad hoc decision, commandeered a cardiac ambulance sent to provide aid to LBJ (and that that vehicle was not the intended mode of transportation for the body) is found on page 391 of The Death of a President, where he writes: *"Beside the driver, gaping, were the heart specialist and nurse who had been sent to attend Lyndon Johnson. At Roy Kellerman's request all three slid out wordlessly and Greer, Kellerman, Landis, and Burkley scrambled in, Burkley on Landis' lap. The Attorney General entered the back, sitting opposite his sister-in-law; Godfrey perched beside her."*

This is the precise moment when the pilot of "Nighthawk One" took off, without the Dallas Casket, and flew to Quantico to put his bird to bed. Kellerman and Greer had no choice but to modify their plan immediately, and to stay with the Dallas casket, which Kellerman surely knew was empty. (He was in charge of all security for the Dallas trip, and as the reader will recall, blurted out a revealing oral utterance on the radio to Gerald Behn prior to takeoff from Love Field, about something happening with "the, ah, body.") As soon as the AF1 personnel failed to separate Jackie Kennedy from the Dallas casket, Kellerman's main task changed from "going with the body on the helicopter" to preventing anyone from opening it while it was still empty. It was for this reason that he stayed with JBK, RFK, and the empty Dallas casket.

Was There Enough Time to Fly JFK's Body to Bethesda to Support a 6:35 PM Arrival at the Morgue Loading Dock? Do the Facts Fit the Hypothesis?
The answer is YES. I closely studied the events on the ground at Andrews by watching my DVD of the A&E network's rebroadcast of the NBC live TV coverage on November 22, 1963, called *"As it happened."*
Using that broadcast and a stopwatch; and the AF1 tapes; and the Chuck Holmes logbook of Andrews-AFB activity on 11/22/63; and Manchester's book, I was able to construct the following timeline:
6:00 PM: AF1 Touchdown. [From the AF1 tapes and the Chuck Holmes Andrews AFB logbook]
6:04 PM: AF1 "on the blocks." [From the AF1 tapes]

6:14 PM: LBJ makes brief televised remarks before microphones. [From the DVD of TV coverage, and Manchester's book] The Navy ambulance has already departed with the Dallas casket, with RFK and JBK onboard.

6:20 PM: LBJ's hello, "Army 1," takes off and the television lights are turned off and the coverage abruptly ends. [From the DVD of TV coverage]

6:26 PM: LBJ and "Army 1" arrives at the South Lawn of the White House [from Manchester's book] 6:26 PM: LBJ and "Army 1" arrives at the South Lawn of the White House [from Manchester's book]

6:30 PM: Air Force Two (more correctly, SAM 86970, since there was no Vice President onboard) lands at Andrews. It would have taxied for three to four minutes before parking, based on the time required for AF1 to taxi to its resting spot. [From the Chuck Holmes special Andrews logbook for 11/22/63]

The time required for a helicopter flight from Andrews to the White House (6:20 to 6:26 PM) was just 6 minutes, and you can be sure that the pilot of "Army 1" was being very careful that night, and was not trying to set any speed records.

In order for JFK's body to show up at the Bethesda morgue loading dock at 6:35 PM (per the seminal Boyajian report) I stipulate that it would have had to arrive by helicopter on the grounds of Bethesda five minutes prior to that, by 6:30 PM.

Was there enough time to fly JFK's body from Air Force One's parking spot at Andrews to the grounds of Bethesda, and arrive by 6:30 PM? YES.

If JFK's body (wrapped in the two sheets in which it left Parkland) had been loaded onto a helicopter by 6:23 PM – three minutes after LBJ's hello departed and the TV broadcast was discontinued – it would have had seven minutes to get to Bethesda Naval Hospital. If JFK's body had been put on a helicopter at 6:21 instead of 6:23, then nine minutes would have been available for the flight to Bethesda. Washington D.C. is a small town, not very large in land area, and Bethesda is immediately northwest of the city limits, not that far from the White House.

My estimated "necessary" arrival time for the helicopter surreptitiously transporting JFK's body to the Bethesda Naval Hospital complex Officer's Club parking lot – 6:30 PM – is indirectly corroborated by an entry in an Army log from MDW's funeral operations center. In a footnote on page 689 of Best Evidence (cloth edition), Lifton wrote that the log indicates that at 5:30 PM word was passed that Kennedy's body was going to Bethesda. A log entry then notes that one Army official notified Admiral Galloway "advising them to provide a security cordon around the heliport at the Bethesda Naval Center, expecting arrival of the remains at approximately 1830 hours [6:30 PM]." This confirms my own estimate of the possible arrival time of the surreptitious flight with the body from Andrews calculated above, and proves my own calculations of the feasibility of getting there on time (to support a 6:35 PM offload at the morgue loading dock) were "spot on."

Is there evidence of a helicopter landing on the Bethesda grounds near the morgue?

The answer is YES.

On page 35 of William Law's 2005 book In the Eye of History, from his interview of Paul K. O'Connor (a Navy corpsman who assisted the Navy pathologists with the autopsy on JFK), he quotes O'Connor as follows:

"Right after we heard the helicopters come over, I distinctly heard one land in the back of the hospital, which was the Officer's Club parking lot. There was a big parking lot. I heard one helicopter land there. I heard another helicopter land at the north side of the hospital where there was a normal helicopter-landing pad. Several minutes later, I can't give you a definite time – maybe five minutes – the back of the morgue opened up and a crew of hospital corpsmen and a higher ranking corpsman brought in a plain, pinkish-gray, what I call a shipping casket. It was not ornate. It was not damaged... They brought it up front where we were. At that time we opened up the coffin. Inside was the body bag."

Dennis David had first told his story about delivering a plain gray metal casket (from a black Cadillac) to a small town Midwestern newspaper in May of 1975. Paul O'Connor corroborated this story about a "pinkish gray" casket to the HSCA staff in 1977, and also told the HSCA staff that the

President's body had been removed nude, from inside a zippered body bag, with a sheet wrapped only around the head. (JFK did not leave Parkland Hospital in a body bag; and his body, when it departed Parkland, was not nude – it was wrapped in a sheet. His head was wrapped in a separate sheet, also.) A third witness to the shipping casket was Navy corpsman Floyd Riebe, who assisted the official photographer at the autopsy that night; he has recalled that the crude shipping casket had ugly turnbuckles on it to seal the lid, and had no prominent side rails for the pallbearers, like the bronze Dallas casket.

Paul O'Connor was interviewed extensively by David Lifton on film in 1980 for his short documentary *Best Evidence*, and subsequently again by Lifton, a few years later, on video for a TV journalism news show. He was also interviewed extensively by Nigel Turner for his multi-part documentary, *The Men Who Killed Kennedy*. Although he is now deceased, the reader has ample opportunities to assess Paul O'Connor's credibility. I find him very credible. His story about the shipping casket never wavered, and his account of a group of Navy corpsmen bringing in the shipping casket dovetails perfectly with Dennis David's account. His memory of one helicopter landing on the north side of the Bethesda Hospital, at the helipad, concurs with Manchester, who records in his book that the H-21 helicopter carrying the Joint Service Casket Team from Andrews landed at that site, out in front of the main building. His account of a second hello landing at the Officer's Club parking lot, behind the morgue, is indirectly corroborated by Dennis David. David told Lifton in 1979 that he believed the black Cadillac ambulance (the Hearse) that delivered the shipping casket to the morgue loading dock had come in through "the back gate." When Lifton asked David to explain why he said that, he explained that the road which brought the black Cadillac to the morgue loading dock wound its way from the back gate, past the Officer's Club, to the morgue entrance. (See page 573 of Best Evidence, cloth edition.) So the route used by the black Cadillac ambulance met by Dennis David passed directly by the Officer's Club parking lot, where O'Connor was certain a helicopter had landed, only about five minutes before the shipping casket was delivered to the morgue where O'Connor worked that night, by a working party of Navy corpsmen.

Everything fits, including the Hearse. Dennis David has consistently recalled that the two people in the front of the black Cadillac were wearing white operating room smocks, and that it was definitely not a military vehicle. It had to have been the Gawler's funeral home Hearse that was originally assigned to go to Andrews AFB, but which was recalled by Colonel Miller "at the last minute." Apparently it was sent to Bethesda instead. Tom Robinson, who in 1963 was a twenty-year-old Gawler's embalming assistant (whose specialty was applying restorative art to cadavers to prepare them for open-casket funerals), said he was present all night long inside the morgue and had a "50-yardline seat" in the gallery. He witnessed things that were NOT WITNESSED by the large audience to the official autopsy that began at 8:00 PM. [Two examples were: (1) him witnessing JFK's skull sawed open to remove the brain – something Humes did not have to do before his large audience at 8:00 PM; and (2) he saw about ten metal fragments removed from JFK's cranium and placed in a vial – this contradicts the official account that there were only two small metal fragments removed from the cranium.] In order to see these events, Robinson must have arrived early, with the body. Therefore, I conclude that he was one of the occupants of the black Cadillac's front seat (wearing a white smock as one would expect an embalmer to wear), and that the black Cadillac met by Dennis David and his working party at 6:35 PM was the Gawler's Hearse.

ONE BIG LOOSE END
On page 690 of Best Evidence (cloth edition), David Lifton writes that in her handwritten notes, recorded two minutes prior to Air Force One's touchdown at 6:00 PM, LBJ's secretary, Marie Fehmer, recorded the following entry: "5:58 Air Andrews – Body w/Mrs. K to Walter Reed." What is of extreme interest to me is that she made this entry just prior to landing, not one hour or more earlier, when the selection of the autopsy site was apparently undecided, and in fact was a subject of controversy between AF1 and "Crown."

Furthermore, author Craig Roberts, in his book Kill Zone, quoted an official Andrews AFB history that stated JFK's autopsy had been performed at Walter Reed Hospital after the body's arrival at Andrews AFB.

Of course we certainly know today that JFK's autopsy was performed at Bethesda Naval Hospital, and that his body first arrived there at the morgue loading dock at 6:35 PM (per Dennis David and the Boyajian report). We also know that while there was sufficient time to get JFK's body to Bethesda by 6:30 PM, using a helicopter, there was no time to spare, either – no time for a diversion.

But in view of all the early talk on AF1 about an autopsy at Walter Reed (begun by Roy Kellerman, and continued for a time by both Dr. Burkley and General Clifton), and in view of the fact that Dr. Dick Davis (the acting head of Neuropathology at AFIP) was set up at Walter Reed and ready to perform a craniotomy on JFK's skull, I have to wonder whether at some point that day, there might have been a plan to alter and sanitize JFK's head wounds surreptitiously at Walter Reed, and then take the altered body to Bethesda, where the damage seen at Bethesda would then be [falsely] represented as "damage done by the assassin's bullet?"

We might never know the answer to this question. All we know today is that the timeline shows that as events actually unfolded, there was no diversion enroute Bethesda from Andrews- – in fact, there was "just enough time" to land at the Officer's Club parking lot at about 6:30 PM and to get the body to the morgue in the black Cadillac (the Gawler's Hearse) by 6:35 PM.

ANOTHER POSSIBILITY IS PROVED IMPOSSIBLE

Various researchers, at one time or another, have speculated that JFK's body might really have come back to Washington on Air Force Two. This can now be definitively ruled out, because of the firm time of arrival of JFK's body provided by the Boyajian report, dated November 26, 1963. Sergeant Boyajian wrote that the casket arrived at the Bethesda morgue at 1835 hours, which equates to 6:35 PM, civilian time. (He was surely talking about the President's body; no other reasonable interpretation is possible. And of course Dr. Boswell, who was present on the loading dock when the shipping casket arrived, confirmed to Dennis David later that night, that it had indeed been President Kennedy in the shipping casket.) We know from a transmission on the new Clifton tapes that SAM 86970 (otherwise known as AF2) took off from Dallas at 3:15 PM CST (thus confirming the takeoff time listed in the reports of two Secret Service agents), and we know from the Chuck Holmes logbook provided to the ARRB (the special operations log for 11/22/63 made by the 1254th ATW [Air Transport Wing] Command Post), that SAM 86970 landed at precisely 1830 hours, or 6:30 PM civilian time.

Presumably, the taxi time for AF2 to get to its designated spot on the Andrews tarmac would be similar or identical to that for AF1 – namely, three or four minutes. This would have AF2 rolling to a complete stop and "on the blocks" at about 6:33 PM at the earliest. Secret Service agent Emory Roberts wrote in his after action report that the landing time for AF2 was 6:35 PM – this was probably the actual time "on the blocks." This allows insufficient time for a helicopter trip from Andrews AFB to Bethesda Naval Hospital. And that's an understatement; in fact, the landing time recorded by Emory Roberts allows no time at all for a trip from Andrews AFB to Bethesda Naval Hospital. The numbers don't lie. So, not only did the pilot and flight engineer on AF2 deny to David Lifton that they ever had JFK's body (or any other body) onboard their aircraft (as reported in the cloth edition of Best Evidence on page 679), but more importantly, the facts on the ground (the landing time of 86970 – 6:30 PM), combined with the known time for a helicopter flight from Andrews to Bethesda (7 to 9 minutes), make it impossible for Air Force Two (86970) to have delivered JFK's body to Andrews in time for it to arrive at the Bethesda morgue loading dock at 6:35 PM.

Consider these additional facts. The actual flight time for AF1 from Love Field to Andrews was 2 hours and 13 minutes. The actual flight time for AF2 from Love Field to Andrews was 2 hours and 15 minutes. The "Great Circle Mapper" software which I consulted when writing my book revealed that, at the cruising speed of 535 mph for the military version of the Boeing 707 aircraft reported by William Manchester (who after all, did interview the pilot of AF1), the trip from Love Field to Andrews should have taken 2 hours and 14 minutes. This is only one minute off of the actual flight times for AF1 and AF2! Everything fits, and is consistent with the arrival time for SAM 86970 in the Chuck Holmes logbook – 6:30 PM – being accurate. (See pages 1790-1792 of Inside the ARRB for a thorough discussion of the capabilities of the two aircraft.) Therefore, there is every reason to have full confidence in the Chuck Holmes logbook.

In the world of great uncertainty that characterizes much of the JFK assassination evidence, it is comforting and satisfying to be able to rule out one distracting possibility, for this allows us to focus with confidence on what really happened, instead of wasting our time on idle and unfounded speculation.

SUMMATION

This essay, I believe, provides a good lesson in historiography. When one studies a problem, one needs to use as many sources of evidence as are available, and take a holistic approach to the problem; that is, to study it with an open mind, and without making any assumptions or preconceptions, while keeping the "big picture" in mind at all times. In this case the problem was defined by this series of questions:

"What can the Air Force One tapes tell us about the autopsy planning while AF1 was enroute

Washington, D.C. from Dallas? Was there anything amiss? Did the plans evolve? Was the final plan executed as planned? If not, why not?"

We now know that there was a vehement disagreement within the Federal bureaucracy over whether the autopsy would be at the U.S. Army's Walter Reed Hospital, or the Navy's Bethesda National Naval Medical Center. The Secret Service won the argument. We know that the AF1 personnel (especially General Clifton) wanted initially to use a mortuary-type ambulance to move the body, whereas the Secret Service at the White House Situation Room wanted to use a helicopter. The Secret Service won the argument: while the empty Dallas casket was moved in a light gray Navy cardiac ambulance, the actual body of JFK was transported to the grounds of Bethesda Naval Hospital in a White House VIP helicopter. We now know that this helicopter from Andrews (with unnamed escorts onboard – presumably Secret Service agents) arrived at about 6:30 PM in the Officer's Club parking lot, and that the body of the assassinated Commander-in-Chief was then encased inside a body bag, and that the body bag was then placed inside a plain, unadorned, lightweight aluminum shipping casket, and taken to the morgue loading dock, where it arrived at 6:35 PM and was offloaded by HM1 Dennis David's working party. The Hearse (the black Cadillac mortuary ambulance) and the shipping casket were undoubtedly provided by the Gawler's Funeral Home. [Something not mentioned above was how "radioactive" any and all questions about the President's casket, or the time of his arrival at Bethesda, seemed to Joseph Hagan of Gawler's when he was interviewed by the ARRB in 1996. He would not speak to us voluntarily without a subpoena, and so he received one. He was evasive and non-credible about all questions related to the Gawler's hearse, his arrival time that night at Bethesda, and the types of caskets he saw at the morgue. However, he did verify that it was his handwriting on the Gawler's business document called the "First Call Sheet," in which he wrote the following words: "Body removed from metal shipping casket at USNH at Bethesda."]

We now know, from the new evidence revealed in Inside the ARRB, that two witnesses, Tom Robinson of Gawler's funeral home, and Navy enlisted x-ray technologist Ed Reed, both witnessed the illicit, clandestine, post-mortem surgery to President Kennedy's cranium – surgery whose goal was to "sanitize the crime scene" by removing all evidence of frontal shots from the body – well before the official autopsy began at 8:00 PM. We now know that the series of skull x-rays and photographs taken of President Kennedy's cranium prior to 8:00 PM (when the autopsy began) represent damage caused by this post-mortem surgery, not by any assassin's bullet. Based on what we know about the autopsy report today, it would not be admitted in evidence at a trial (since the first two written versions, as well as original autopsy notes, have been destroyed), and each individual autopsy photograph and skull x-ray would be subjected to significant challenges before they could be admitted into evidence. The three surviving skull x-rays would not be admitted into evidence at any trial today, for we now know (thanks to the pioneering work of Dr. David Mantik, MD, PhD) that the three skull x-rays in the Archives are not originals, but are altered copy films. We know today that the brain photographs in the National Archives that reside with the JFK autopsy photographs cannot be photographs of President Kennedy's brain: they have been disowned by the official photographer, John Stringer (because they are recorded on the wrong types of film), and by one of the FBI agents present at the autopsy, Francis O'Neill (because there is too much mass present, and in the wrong locations). Furthermore, the large amount of mass present in these brain photos is grossly inconsistent not only with the skull x-rays (which show much brain tissue missing in the forebrain, and in the right cerebral hemisphere), but also with the amount of missing mass noted at Parkland Hospital (at least one third of the brain was observed to be missing by Dr. McClelland), where President Kennedy received emergency treatment in an attempt to save his life.

For all these reasons, it is important to study the Air Force One tapes, and how (and when) President Kennedy's body really arrived at Bethesda Naval Hospital – for this is when the medical cover-up began: on the trip back to Washington onboard Air Force One, and on the ground at Andrews AFB.

As libertarian scholar and activist Jacob Hornberger has recently pointed out, there are two general types of people that one observes when studying how Americans react to the JFK assassination evidence. One category is those who have open and inquiring and even critical minds – people who demand logical and rational answers when they encounter things in the evidence, and in the "official explanation," that do not make sense. Another category of people one encounters are what he calls differentials, those who tend to blindly defer to authority when they encounter things that don't make sense. These are the people who want simplistic explanations to mysteries and conflicting evidence, so that they can sleep well at night. These are the people who don't want to believe that a coup happened in America in 1963, or that there was a massive cover-up by the U.S. government of the medical and forensic evidence in JFK's assassination. These differentials include the minority of the U.S. population who still profess to believe in the Warren Report. It is to the first category of people – at least 80 per cent of all Americans today – those who are "empiricists," who follow evidence wherever it leads them, and who have open and inquiring minds, that this essay is dedicated.

.

"Do you all now understand the meaning of JD Tippit's death?" Mr. McCarthy looked straightly into the group.
"Yes", Elizabeth said,

"They switched the body of President Kennedy and the one of JD Tippit."

"So the autopsy of JFK at Bethesda Hospital in Mary land does not match with the description of the wounds of JFK by the Doctors in Park land, Texas." Dennis added.

"Remember the true rationale of this twist", Robert took a deep breath and said, "is to make the autopsy fit the wounds caused by the Single Bullet by Oswald as the conclusion of the Warren Commission."

"Wait, I have the last question for you all. What is the true identity of the corpse?"

But there is one witness who saw exactly what happened when a bullet struck the President's head. Jackie Kennedy was looking at her husband when he was mortally wounded. And while she did not permit her 313-minute interview with William Manchester to be unsealed during her lifetime, the tapes will ultimately be available - in 2067 - one hundred years after they were made.

They stared at one another, but nobody uttered a single word. Helen looked at the clock, she exclaimed, "Oh, my goodness, it's almost 9 already! I have a conference tomorrow."

"Yes, we must go home. Thanks a lot Uncle Ben for the dinner." Robert said,

"It's very interesting to talk about JFK assassination. Thanks to Jason and Dennis as well."

"Thank you, everybody" Helen said.

"Drive carefully!" Mr. McCarthy said.

On the way home, Robert told Helen, "This evening we learned a lot about the assassination of President Kennedy."

"Yes, it is for sure." Helen replied,
"I'd like to know more about Mrs. Jacqueline
Kennedy Onassis. We haven't discussed about that
at the meeting."
"And I need to explore further on the JFK autopsy."
Robert added, "I plan to see my mother this
weekend, will you go along?"
"I'd like to have a talk with Lynn-my step mother
on Saturday. I'm curious about Lynn as she warned
me not to put on my pink dress- the imitation of the
Pink Chanel of Jackie Kennedy. I want to know
why it bothered her."
"Very well, then we see one another on Sunday to
exchange what we might have found out more about
this puzzle."
"OK"

CHAPTER 3
Dr. McCarthy's Secret & Lynn's Story

This weekend, Senator Robert McCarthy went to see his mother, Mrs. Marion McCarthy.

Robert's mind was preoccupied with thoughts about the murder of Police Officer JD Tippit in coincidence with the assassination of President Kennedy, and the Air Force One Tape from Mr. Doug Horn with the confusion of the transportation of the President's coffin from Parkland in Dallas, TX to Bethesda in Maryland. Whose body was in that coffin? Whose body was buried in Arlington Cemetery? Suddenly, it crossed his mind that his father, Dr. George McCarthy who worked in the ER at Parkland Hospital by the time of the assassination of President Kennedy... then for some unknown reason, he left Parkland and worked at the University of Texas, Dallas as a Professor of Human Behavior and Brain Sciences. Ah! Robert couldn't forget that his father mysterious box with the note "Do Not Open". At the last moment of his life, his father made the whole family promised never open that box. What is inside? Why can't it be exposed?

Pulling the car into the drive way, Senator Robert McCarthy saw his mother opened the door with a smile,

"What's special occasion that you come today? My birthday is not until next month?"

"I just want to see you, Mom?" Robert kissed his mother, and he asked,

"Have you baked a carrot cake for me?"
Mrs. George McCarthy put her hands over the shoulders of her son, she confirmed,
"Of course, I made one especially just for you, Mr. Senator!"
"Thank you, Mom"
After having a cup of coffee with a piece of his favorite cake, Robert asked,
"Mom, I'd like to look at something in the attic."
"I don't know if you can find anything up there… A lot of stuff, but they are not put in any category. I haven't had time to sort them out; after your Dad passed away." Mrs. McCarthy said.
"Do you remember Dad's box with the note Do Not Open? Would you know what the content inside?" Robert asked.
"I have no idea. Once time I pressed him, but I couldn't get anything out from him except, Do Not Open it forever. Is that what you want? I don't know where he put it."
"Don't worry, Mom. I know what I'm looking for." Robert answered as he went up to the attic. Among the boxes, desks, chairs, racks of clothing, Robert found his father – Dr. George McCarthy's box , a small green metal container, on the lid, three words "Do Not Open" painted in red. Robert wiped off the dust and unlatched the secret.
"No! Robert, Stop!"
Mrs. McCarthy called out loud.
Robert turned his back, his mother was behind him. She grabbed the box from his hand; in an angry voice she scolded Robert,

"What on earth did you do that? Didn't you promise with your Dad at his death bed?"

"I'm sorry, Mom", the Senator lowered his head in a begging manner he implored,

"Mom, I need to know a very important truth."

"I don't understand what you're talking about, what truth?"

Mrs. McCarthy requested, she held tightly the box in her hands.

The Senator explained,

"In November 1963, Dad was an ER surgeon at Parkland Hospital, right, Mom?"

"What is the reason to bring up that matter?"

"I think that Dad worked on the case of the assassination of President Kennedy."

"Robert, I really do not want to hear any further." Mrs. McCarthy walked downstairs.

"Wait, Mom," the Senator went after his mother, "Uncle Ben showed me something extremely important. I don't know if the Warren Commission reported the autopsy work on the corpse of President Kennedy or the body of Police Officer ..."

Mrs. McCarthy cut in,

"Again, Robert; I don't understand what you're talking about; and I don't want to hear anything about it, OK? One thing definitely I know for sure: from now on I will keep this box in my room and locked it up."

"Mom, I must know the content inside of the box." Robert begged.

"No. End of discussion." Mrs. McCarthy replied.

…

Helen rang the bell, she glanced at the bouquet of roses for Lynn – the mother in law – The relationship between Helen and Lynn has been rough since the day Dr. Augier; her father announced that he decided to tie the knot with Lynn, a business woman. Dr. Augier explained to Helen that he liked Lynn and wanted to have her for companionship after the death of Helen's mother; nevertheless, Helen ignored her father's reason.

Helen gave the bouquet to Lynn as Lynn appeared at the door.
"How have you been?"
"Tell me, please. What brought you here? I was surprised when you said, "Have a cup of tea together."
The step mother smiled,
"What is your favorite tea?"
"Do you have green tea? Actually, I'd like to ask you a question..."
"I prefer youth berry to others" Lynn said as she poured tea into a cup for Helen,
"What do you have in mind?"
Holding the tea cup in her hand, Helen looked into Lynn's eyes,
"What was the intention that you warned me about the Pink Chanel Dress? You must have read a lot about Mrs. Jacqueline Kennedy, haven't you?"
"I also have a question for you before getting into that subject; usually you don't like me. Please tell me what the meaning of this meeting is?"

Helen was straightly to the point,

"It's about the Pink Chanel Dress, the imitation of Jackie's outfit which I put on the other day. You told me not to wear it, but I did anyway. Then, a very strange thing happened..."

"Yes." Lynn took a deep breath,

"Indeed, Jacqueline Kennedy Onassis is an extraordinary woman. That dress was stained with blood of President Kennedy… You know that I was divorced before I married your Dad?"

"How is it related to Mrs. Jacqueline Kennedy?" Helen was asked.

"Probably you'd have thought that Jacqueline Kennedy had a perfect marriage?" Lynn questioned. "Of course, the President and the First Lady had a wonderful family with two beautiful children, the whole wide world know that." Helen stated, "It's a matter of fact, no doubt about that."

"I want to tell you a little bit about my life. I was married to Fred Alaounis, my high school sweet heart right after the Blackhawk High School Graduation. We went to college together; he graduated and worked at Wells Fargo Bank when I started my Clothing Design business." Suddenly, Lynn change the subject,

"By the way, how is the relationship between you and Robert? Or I'm not supposed to ask?"

""We have a few differences, but no big deal." Helen laughed, "How was your first marriage?"

"You're lucky" Lynn said,

"My first husband is a womanizer, even up to this moment; Fred is sixty two now, yet he's still chasing the skirts! That was the reason we filed a divorce. Avoiding a court hearing, we agreed a settlement on the ground of incompatibility."

"Lynn", Helen became impatient, "How is it related to Mrs. Jacqueline Kennedy, please."

"President Kennedy had a queue of women," Lynn laughed,

"That's the basis I wanted to know how the First Lady handled her problems."

Sipping some tea, Lynn continued,

"To tell the truth; from the high school sweet heart love, my feeling for Fred turned out bitterly a deep hatred when I figured out that he had several affairs behind my back. At one time, I even thought about killing both Fred and Mary (Fred's girl friend). Of course I didn't do anything, but the scheme of hurting both of them crossed my mind several times."

"Wow!" Helen exclaimed, she felt more opening her heart to the step mother. She confessed,

"I've been mad at Robert sometimes - and I'm afraid there's something between Robert and Beth, his secretary. One time, he yelled at me when I brought up that woman's name."

"I had numerous arguments with Fred, we ended up by nowhere. He screamed at me as well, but he kept on going to one night club after another... The woman who worried me the most was Mary. I think-and also I believe that one of Mary's children is Fred's child... I was so anxious and not able to perform my tasks at work; Brandon —my supervisor– recommended Fred and me to see a marriage therapist. Fred attended only one session; he said that he didn't need any "therapy" and kept on his way of chasing the skirts after work... Here's something about the clash between Jacqueline Kennedy and Marilyn Monroe"

Lynn gave Helen a paper,

"Read this so you'd understand a woman's jealousy better."

MARILYN MONROE VERSUS JACQUELINE KENNEDY

(Excerpt from *Are You a Jackie or a Marilyn?* By Pamela Keogh)

"Growing up and throughout her life, Jackie had every imaginable advantage – gracious homes with staff and her own horse, the best education possible, a father who doted on her and husbands who protected her. But perhaps the most important thing Jackie had was a center, a clear identity: She knew who she was and her place in the world.

Marilyn, on the other hand, had none of these advantages. For starters, not even the name "Marilyn Monroe" was originally her own. Instead, it was a studio invention.

Three years older than Jackie, Marilyn was born Norma Jeane Mortensen on June 1, 1926, in Los Angeles, California, to Gladys Baker, an unmarried woman with deep psychological problems who worked as a film cutter at RKO studios. The identity of Marilyn's father was never made known to her (in later life, she claimed to remember a photograph of a handsome man with a mustache), and she was later baptized Norma Jeane Baker.

Unlike Jackie's, Norma Jeane's childhood was uncertain and, at times, harrowing. She had a clear memory of her mother having a fit and being taken out of the house in a straightjacket, and for the rest of her life, she feared that she might end up the same way.

On June 19, 1942, she wed her twenty-one-year-old neighbor, Jimmy Dougherty, whom she barely knew. It is said that Norma Jeane was weeping when her husband left, having been drafted during World War II. A few months later she was discovered while working in a wartime factory and found an even greater love: the camera.

Marilyn's will was formidable; her desire, immense. She wanted, she wanted, she wanted.

She wanted respect. She wanted love. She would marry and divorce twice more. She wanted a home and a loving husband, children even. She wanted to be a world-famous movie star; she fought for decent scripts. In retrospect, when she was recognized all over the world – our blonde bombshell goddess, Marilyn – it all seemed inevitable.

While Jackie had every societal advantage and Marilyn so many strikes against her in her birth, nevertheless; they were more than equal in the fame game. Although Jackie lived a longer life, Marilyn is perhaps more beloved today because people all over the world connect with her on an emotional level. Her desire to be known, to be loved, is as much a part of her appeal as her innocent sexuality."

"I can relate to you better now. At first, I thought you were after my Dad's money" Helen said.
"Here are some pages from Christopher Anderson's book," Lynn added.

Marilyn Monroe called Jackie Kennedy at the White House and confessed she was having an affair with her husband, to which the First Lady responded 'that's great... I'll move out and you'll have all the problems.
In *"These Few Precious Days: The Final Year of Jack with Jackie",* author Christopher Andersen claims Jackie *'knew everything' about Jack's cheating and turned a blind eye, but his relationship with Marilyn 'seemed to bother her the most.'*
And she was right to fear the bombshell actress, because Marilyn's sights were firmly set on becoming the President's second wife. However, she didn't take his cheating lightly.
Jack's close friend, George Smathers, said Jackie was 'damn mad' about his fooling around, but she was willing to look the other way as long as he was careful and didn't humiliate her.
   Marilyn Monroe & Jackie Kennedy

"We ended up with a divorce."
Lynn took a deep breath after pouring out all her problems to her step daughter.
"Did you feel better after the divorce?" Helen asked.

"No, it's not at all!"

Lynn laughed but Helen could see tears rolling down on her cheeks. Helen hugged the step mother. "The thing I was afraid of the most was losing Fred. This fear controlled me completely; I had to follow all its mandates. The therapist, Dr. Brown – told me, "You either give up which you fear to lose so it no longer holds any power over you." I asked him, "How could I ever done that, Doctor? In that case, I'd consider as if I were dead!"

"You did give it up, didn't you?" Helen inquired.

"Indeed. I gave up my marriage with Fred." Lynn burst into a loud cry,

"But, I have not been the same anymore after that. I know that you'd not understand my feeling; anyhow…please focus on my emotion and Mrs. Kennedy's sentiment since the two husbands were womanizers in these cases. Mrs. Kennedy had a difficult time in her first marriage, she also thought about the divorce with the President…"

"The death of Marilyn Monroe is a mystery. Still it's difficult to say that it was an accident or a murder." Helen changed the subject.

"That is true," Lynn agreed; and suddenly her voice became mysterious,

"I rather pay more attention to the Fatal Shot that killed President Kennedy."

"What do you mean?" Helen inquired, "Who is this person? Why did he do it?"

"I don't know what the truth is anymore. One thing I'm certain of is the Warren Commission reports are just a whole bunch of bologna." Lynn made a

126

sarcastic remark, "Why did you say *'he'*? Did you have absolute evidence about the man or men who killed the President? How about if I said that the Fatal Shot was not fired by a man?"

Swiftly, the words of Mr. Benjamin McCarthy (Robert's Uncle) flashed back in Helen's mind, "The Fatal Shot was fired by an unbelievable person, in an unthinkable circumstance."

"Lynn, I'm lost." Helen sighed. She felt a little bit shaking over her body.

"Could you explain this to me, Dr. Helen Augier-McCarthy?" Lynn looked up to Helen

"What's do you have in mind? Just call me 'Helen', please?" the step daughter in law smiled.

Lynn cut a slide of cake; she offered to Helen then continued,

"In the beginning, my purpose was to figure out how the First Lady Jacqueline Kennedy resolved her marriage problem. I hated those women who break others' marriages. I despised the women had affairs with Fred; I think that they were aware that he was a married man, but jumped in bed with Fred anyhow....Strangely, in the case of Marilyn Monroe had affair with President Kennedy, I do not hate Marilyn Monroe....Honestly, I felt sorry for her and for the President. I love them both. On the contrary, I'm scared of the First Lady. Now, Psychiatrist Dr. Augier-McCarthy, please tell me why I feel this way? I'm in the same situation as the First Lady; I should have compassion to the First Lady and despised Marilyn Monroe and hated the President instead?"

The Psychiatrist replied,
"It's called **Reverse psychology** is a technique involving
the advocacy of a belief or behavior that is opposite to
the one desired, with the expectation that this
approach will encourage the subject of the persuasion
to do what actually *is* desired: the opposite of what is
suggested."

"Yes, Doctor, "Lynn said, "What would have happened if the First Lady had had compassion for Marilynn Monroe?"

"What are you saying?" Helen stared into Lynn's eyes, "Were you talking about your situation with your ex-husband?"

"The First Lady and I were in a similar situation: we married to womanized men. Ah, Doctor, do you know the cause of Marilynn Monroe's death and also the reasons of the JFK and RFK assassinations?"

"Why don't the patients just follow the text books? In Psychology/Psychiatry patients are so confused." The psychiatrist thought; and she said, "Focus on your problems only, please."

"Of course, Doctor. Would you want some tea?" Passing the tea to the Doctor- Lynn laughed, "Actually, I love the Tigress-I meant Marilyn Monroe- better than the First Lady. Look at this picture, Helen. Who could be angry at this beautiful Tigress?"

The Tigress... Did someone mention about the love triangle of the two snakes and a tigress in a jungle to Helen? And now Lynn wandered in her thoughts with the same characters. The Doctor told the patient,

"See you next time. I should leave now."

"Would you like to stay a bit longer, your Dad will be home in a few minutes?" Lynn asked

The door opened, Dr. Augier came in.

"Hello, honey! What a surprise, Helen, how are you?"

Dr. Augier kissed his wife and hugged Helen, "How is everything with you and Robert?"

"We're fine. Thanks, Dad; and how have you been?"

Helen kissed her father.

"Lynn believes in proper nutrition, so I'm in great shape!" Dr. Augier laughed.

"It's very nice to see you, Dad; I have to leave now. I have some errands to do."
Helen told her father; turned to Lynn, she said, "I'll come again. Thank you very much for the tea."
"Take care and say Hello to Robert for me, will you?" Dr. Augier added, "The best gift you give me is being nice to Lynn, OK, Helen?"
"I will remember that, Dad." Helen smiled.
"See you!" Lynn hugged her step daughter.
.

Diving home, Helen's mind was occupied with the marriage of President Kennedy and Mrs. Jacqueline Kennedy. She decided to do some searching on this story. The book *Jacqueline Kennedy Onassis: A life Beyond Her Wildest Dreams* by Darwin Porter and Danforth Prince from Blue Moon Productions publisher revealed these facts. Helen read the following pages,

Jackie had had enough. Fed up with his constant womanizing, and having her own dalliances that fueled the fire of her desire for liberation, Jackie told her confidantes that she wanted out. Her anger amped up after Marilyn Monroe's humiliating 'Happy Birthday Mr. President' performance
And it wasn't the first time Jackie threatened to divorce Jack.
By the late 1950s, Jackie was too demoralized by Jack's sexual philandering to continue the public charade. Her father-in-law, Joe Kennedy knew all too well the profound problems and stepped in to warn her. 'There is danger facing you as a divorced

130

Catholic woman', he told her. 'I suggest you put divorce out of your mind', according to the revelatory new book.
Ambition Jackie became the Inquiry Camera Girl of the Washington Herald newspaper in 1952. By that time, she had already decided that her real goal was to become a rich man's wife.

"This is very interesting." Helen made a book mark, "No doubt that later, she became Mrs. Onassis, wife of the richest man of the world!"

Kennedy scion Joe Kennedy offered his daughter-in-law a check for one million dollars to stay in the union. Jackie allegedly told him that the cost of her staying with JFK would rise to twenty million dollars 'if he brings home any venereal disease from any of his sluts', according to the authors. If Jackie had divorced Jack while he was a U.S. Senator, the old man's dreams of having a son in the White House would have gone unfulfilled. And he was more concerned about those political ambitions then he was about Jackie being ostracized by the Catholic Church.
Jackie didn't know what she was getting into when she first met the dashing senator from Massachusetts.
Single Jackie returned to Washington, DC in the early 1950s, leaving a string of lovers behind after a whirlwind trip to Europe, and she was hired as an 'Inquiring Photographer' for the now-defunct Washington Times-Herald.

Before hooking up with Kennedy, Jackie also dated John White, employed by the State Department and once madly in love with Kick Kennedy, Jack's younger sister who tragically lost her life in a 1948 airplane disaster.

'When I first dated her [Jackie], she decided she was the reincarnation of Madame Recamier', a famous French socialite and hostess of salons for the great and near-great in politics and the arts. That dream quickly faded and Jackie confessed she now just wanted to marry a rich and powerful man, and be the power behind the throne. 'I prefer him to be American, but I would settle for a British man, perhaps even a Frenchman. If a Brit, I would want him to look like Prince Philip', Jackie is quoted as telling White. Bartlett knew that Jack was a skirt chaser and he also knew that Jack had to settle down if he wanted to become president. Jackie just might be the one to do it.

'They did seem to like each other, but it was so very casual. At least, Jack was intrigued enough to walk her out to her car which was parked outside my house', Bartlett said.

Jackie was secretly dating John Husted, Jr., a stockbroker from a banking family. But Husted knew he wasn't rich enough to fulfill her desires, despite being locked in each other's arms for months. He did propose and she accepted – until she started dating Kennedy. She surreptitiously slipped the ring in his coat pocket and said good night and goodbye.

*At the time, Jack had been seeing Inga Arvad,
nicknamed 'Inga-Binga,' a reporter for the
Washington Times Herald who wrote the gossip
column on movers and shakers in D.C. She was
rumored to have had a lusty affair with Hitler's
Reichmarschall, Hermann Goring.*

Helen wanted to know more about Mrs. Kennedy's
life,
"How did she deal with the lost of her husband, as a
faithful Catholic?" Helen kept on reading....

*In a letter written in 1953, when Jacqueline Bouvier
was still only 23, she confided to Father Leonard,
an Irish Priest: "Maybe I'm just dazzled and
picture myself in a glittering world of crowned
heads and Men of Destiny– and not just a sad little
Housewife... That world can be very glamorous
from the outside – but if you're in it – and you're
lonely – it could be a Hell"*

*After the funeral of President Kennedy, Mrs.
Jacqueline Kennedy was questioning her faith. She
was no longer certain there was a God and, if there
was, why he would steal away her young husband.
"I am so bitter against God," she wrote a few
months after the assassination of President John F.
Kennedy. "I always would have rather lost my life
than lost Jack." She wrote on a black edged
mourning paper.
"I think God must have taken Jack to show the
world how lost we would be without him," she*

*wrote "But that is a strange way of thinking to me –
and God will have a bit of explaining to do to me if
I ever see him."*

*The letter, one of several shared with the Globe in
the last several weeks, is one in a trove of secret
correspondence that the former first lady had over
nearly 15 years with Father Joseph Leonard, an
Irish priest. Kennedy, who was elegantly mysterious
for so long,*

*Journalist Thomas Maier's The Kennedys:
America's Emerald Kings, which chronicles the
Kennedys through the lens of their Irish-Catholic
roots, received significant press when it was
released late last year because of its revealing
portrait of Jackie Kennedy's deteriorating mental
health in the spring of 1964, after her husband's
assassination. Interviews conducted by Maier with
a counselor to Jackie reveal her despair at her
family's loss. Her husband and her young son
Patrick had both died within a few months of each
other, and in her depression, she was contemplating
suicide. In the crowded field of Kennedy
biographies, Maier's book clearly had the magic
touch-a nugget of insight from a previously
untapped source. Most new Kennedy books have to
settle for the travails of a previously family member,
such as last spring's Sweet Caroline, a biography of
Caroline Kennedy that offered such delectable
gossip as "a spellbinding account of the surreal
years she spent as the stepdaughter of Aristotle
Onassis" and "the times she, too, cheated death."*

Maier's book holds the trump card: Jackie, whose fame as a style icon nearly eclipsed her husband's political career.

"I asked, 'Father, did the Kennedy children ever ask you if there is a loving god, why did these awful things happen in their lives?' He paused, and he said the children never asked, but Jackie did. And that took me by complete surprise. I asked him, 'How so?' He proceeded to tell me the story of how at Bobby and Ethel Kennedy's suggestion, he had tennis lessons in the backyard. Under the guise of giving tennis lessons, essentially, he would counsel Jackie."

Those lessons began in April of 1964, five months after the assassination, at the hard court at Bobby's Hickory Hill estate in McLean, Va. Clearly, the best-known part of their recently revealed discussions was Jackie's consideration of suicide in the wake of her husband's death. But their conversations as recounted by McSorley are also interesting for revealing how unfamiliar (or disinterested) Jackie was with her own faith. McSorley answered some very basic questions about Catholic doctrine for Jackie. When she asked, "Do you think I will ever see him again?" McSorley responded by noting the resurrection of the body. "Oh, that's just one of those myths," replied Jackie. "It never really happened. Nobody ever really came back from the dead

It seems as if their conversations gradually moved away from such topics, towards her regrets about the past-McSorley felt she blamed herself for their marriage's shortcomings-and even towards the future. By the summer, she had decided that for her and her children's health, she needed to leave the memories of Washington and move to New York City. Her correspondence with McSorley continued. He made several visits that fall and winter to their Fifth Avenue apartment, taking John Jr. to the world's fair and answering some of his questions about death.

During Maier's first interview with McSorley, the priest related that he was very concerned at the time for Jackie Kennedy's health.

Helen ran across an article about JFK assassination, "JFK was murdered by his own wife- Jacqueline, the Jesuits Assassin. *Jacqueline Kennedy* was *trained by the Jesuits her whole life and WAS trained*

in...While riding in an open motorcade, President Kennedy was shot in Dealey Plaza on Friday, Nov. 22, 1963 at 12:30 p.m.... This case has baffled people for the last four decades, and is one of the ten most unsolved mysteries of the last one hundred years." (From Hughes, 2002)

Helen quickly closed it up. Feeling tired, she walked to the kitchen to drink some water; she heard the door open. Robert came in. He said, "Sorry, I'm late. I stopped by mother's house." Helen kissed her husband,

"Did you find out anything interesting?"

"I found the box, but Mom didn't let me open it. How was your day?"

Robert hugged his wife.

"I went to see Lynn; we had a good talk… Have you had supper?" Helen asked.

"Yes. Did you?"

"I had a glass of milk. I'd like to retire now." Helen yawned.

"The same is here. I'll take a shower and hit the shack! " Robert laughed.

While they were in bed Robert turned and tossed; and Helen kept on staring at the ceiling.

"I'd like to know the inside of Dad's box." The husband said, "He kept something in there when he was an ER surgeon at Parkland Hospital. "

"I have the same problem," the wife whispered, "Lynn-my step mother said that she loves both Marilyn Monroe and the President; she felt sorry for him and she's scared of Mrs. Jacqueline Kennedy."

The Senate of State stared at his wife,

"I don't know what you're referring to, but I have a question for you, Doctor?"

"What's your chief complain, Sir?" the Doctor smiled

The Senate of State looked into the Doctor's eyes and posed the question,

"About the shot at the back of JFK, which the Warren Commission claimed it was fired by Oswald from the Book Depository Building; could it kill the President?"

The Doctor explained,

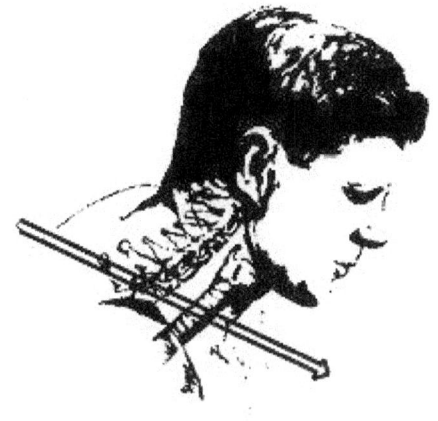

"The single bullet that struck Kennedy in the back and exited through his throat; consistent with it having been struck by a high-velocity bullet and Texas Governor John Connally was also wounded, as he was seated directly in front of the President. The Warren Commission concluded they were likely struck by the same bullet fired by Oswald at the window of the sixth floor of the School Book Depository. That bullet made the victim become an invalid; JFK would be paralyzed from neck

down; but he was still alive; provided JFK was only hit by that Single bullet. We have a numbers of patients in these conditions at the hospital due to automobile accidents or veterans of the wars in Afghanistan, Iraq..."
"What killed JFK? Was he still alive when they brought him to Parkland Hospital?" Robert exclaimed.
Robert and Helen's minds were preoccupied with the murder of President Kennedy. Robert asked his wife,
"Do you think what I think, let search a little more about JFK?"
"Just a tiny bit …the part about the Fatal Shot?" Helen suggested
They rushed to the study room and searched further on this puzzle. Robert found something, "Read this, Helen…According to Kevin Quinn…"

Dorothy Kilgallen a famous writer and Editorialist of numerous political columns, had just completed a lengthy interview with Jack Ruby in prison, and had told some of her friends privately that she had uncovered information about the JFK assassination that would **"blow the case wide open."** Days later she was discovered dead in her apartment, and the manuscript that she had been working on was gone.

J. Edger Hoover said: **"The individual is handicapped by coming face to face with a conspiracy so Monstrous, he cannot believe it exists."**

"If the people knew what we had done, they would chase us down the street and lynch us."
George H.W. Bush.

It was George Bush Sr. and all of his Nazi Illuminati buddies in the CIA, together with the help of the Italian Mafia that killed Kennedy. But they received their orders from the masterminds behind the conspiracy, which included George H. W. Bush,

Nixon and Johnson. LBJ told both his mistress and his ex-wife about the assassination, the night before Kennedy was killed. This picture shows us 4 very important things. (1) The hole in the windshield and Kennedy pulling his tie to the left. (2), Lee Harvey Oswald standing in the doorway of the School Book Depository. (3), a shooter in the second floor of the Dal-Tex building. (4), LBJ already ducking down on the floor of the car. In the interview notes taken by Will Fritz, the homicide detective who interrogated Oswald, it shows that Lee Harvey Oswald claimed to have been out side with Bill Shelly the assistant manager, in front of the Texas School Book Depository during the assassination.

Robert Kennedy also suspected the CIA and the Cubans, asking both CIA director John McCone and his Cuban friend Enrique "Harry" Ruiz Williams if their people were responsible for his brother's murder. RFK said: *"One of your guys did it."*

Haynes Johnson a reporter, says that he was in the room with Robert Kennedy on the afternoon of his brother's murder, and he heard him **blame the assassination on the CIA and their Anti-Castro Cubans**.

John Kennedy had a trusted friend Arthur Krock who would write articles for him in the New York Times. On October 3, 1963 in an article titled "The Intra-Administration War in Vietnam." President Kennedy stated that "*Twice the CIA flatly refused to carry out the Presidents orders, because the agency disagreed with him.*" Kennedy *"likened" the CIA'S growth to a malignancy, which he was not sure even the White House could control any longer. " The agency "represents a tremendous power and total unaccountability to anyone."* Kennedy went on to say that, *"If the United States ever experiences an attempt at a coup d'état to overthrow the Government, it will come from the CIA."* John Kennedy tried to worn the American People of the hidden power that controls our government, and a month later they blew his brains out into a thousand pieces, and scattered them to the winds.

Although Johnson always tried to portray himself publicly as being JFK's right hand man, he fought Kennedy behind the scenes according to Evelyn Lincoln, Kennedy's secretary. He sided against Kennedy, and with the military chiefs, on Berlin, Cuba and Vietnam.

Johnson was against practically everything on President Kennedy's legislative agenda including the Civil Rights legislation. Throughout JFK's presidency, he always cautioning Kennedy saying: *"The timing is not right you have to wait until the time is right."*

Johnson was even against selling surplus wheat to the Soviet Union, as they suffered through a drought that had decimated their own supply; JFK told Arthur Schlesinger on 10/11/63. *"The vice president thinks that this is the worst foreign policy mistake we have made in this administration."*

During the campaign for President Joe Kennedy had told De West Hooker that one of the long-term aims of the Kennedy dynasty would be the destruction of what Joe Kennedy referred to as **"the Rothschild dominated Federal Reserve."** John F. Kennedy had already taken steps to get rid of the Federal Reserve, by printing 50 billion dollars in silver certificates, which were interest free. He planned to use this money to pay off the national debt and to free the American people from the control of the Illuminati Banksters. If the U.S Government would print its own money interest free like the Constitution says they should be doing, the national debt would be zero, and all taxes could be eliminated. The average American would have twice as much money to live on if our government would print their own money interest free, like President Andrew Jackson, President Abraham Lincoln, and President John F. Kennedy, have done in the past, the national debt would no longer be an issue, and taxes would be gone, and the average American could have very little, if any, debt.

History shows President Kennedy was assassinated within a few months of issuing silver backed interest free United States Notes.

Upon his death, President Johnson immediately expanded the war in Vietnam and replaced the United States interest free Notes with worthless Federal Reserve Notes. And Two Million Six Hundred thousand American men ended up fighting during the 10 years that our troops were in Viet Nam, and 58,000 men died and three times that many were wounded. And the U.S Government spent 570 billion dollars on the War which put our country deeper in debt to the Banks. And more bombs were dropped on Viet Nam than all the bombs dropped during World War II, killing millions of innocent civilians in the process.

If President Kennedy had lived and continued printing United States silver certificates interest free, the trillions of dollars in taxes that we are now paying to the Federal Reserve Banksters every years, which is a crown corporation owned by the Bank of England, which is owned by the Bank of Rome, just to pay the interest on the money that our government has borrowed, would have remained in the hands of the American people.

General Eisenhower said in his speech: *"Beware of the Military Industrial Complex."* When John F. Kennedy threatened to cancel their war with Cuba, and to get all of our soldiers out of Viet Nam by 1965, you can bet that he became their number one target. In a speech three weeks before he was murdered, John F. Kennedy asked the American people for their help! Because he knew that he could not beat this secrete society of corporate demons on his own.

Kennedy had also told some of his close friends that Lyndon Johnson would not be on the ticket as his running mate in the 1964 presidential elections, and this would have destroyed Lyndon Johnson's chances of ever becoming President. By promising to do all these things, Kennedy literally had signed his own "Death Warrant." Bush Sr. at the time was the head of the CIA invasion of Cuba, and he sent three teams of assassins to Miami and from there they drove to Dallas. They had originally planned to kill Kennedy during his visit to Miami on the 18th of November, 4 days earlier, but the plan was discovered by the local FBI, and they decided to change the parade route at the last minute, which foiled their first attempt.

KENNEDY KILLED IN A CROSSFIRE

every rifle when it's fired has its own distinct sound. The sound recordings of all the bullets fired in Dealey Plaza the day President Kennedy was assassinated, prove without a shadow of a doubt that there were three different rifles each firing 2 or 3 shots, from three different directions at the sometime. Jackie Kennedy testified before the Warren Commission, that she had crawled on to the back of the car to retrieve a piece of the president's skull. And that she had put the piece back on his head, and pulled his hair back down over it; and held his head on her lap as they rushed to the hospital. Her testimony was stricken from the warren report, because it proved without a shadow of a doubt, that the fatal shot came from the front, and that there was more than one shooter.

Bobby Harkiss (Motorcycle Policeman riding left rear of JFK said): *"When I turned back to look, that's when the President was shot in the face."*

He also testified that blood and bone fragments splattered all over the back of the car, and landed on his face, uniform and motorcycle.

Two of the Police officers got off of their motorcycles and ran up the hill towards the fence behind the grassy knoll. As Dallas police officer Joe Marshal rushed up the grassy knoll he could smell the gun power, which he later reported to the Warren Commission. When he encountered a man in the parking lot behind the fence he pulled his pistol and the man quickly showed him his ID, saying that he was a secret service agent. They then spotted two men running across the rail road yard and chased after them, but they lost them.

"What is your conclusion about this report?" Helen looked up at Robert waiting for an answer

"Definitely there was more than one shooter." Robert firmly replied, "Let's read on..."

If you look closely at this picture, which was taken by the woman in the dark coat with a still camera about a second after Kennedy was shot in the temple above his right eye, you can see the large hole in back of JFK's head.
Agent Hill later testified:

"The right rear portion of his head was missing. It was lying in the rear seat of the car. His brain was exposed. There was blood and bits of brain all over the entire rear portion of the car."

"Mrs. Kennedy was completely covered with blood. There was so much blood you could not tell if there had been any other wound or not, except for the one large gaping wound in the right rear portion of the head."

If the shot had come from the six floor of the School book Depository, Mrs. Kennedy would have been trying to retrieve pieces of the Presidents skull off the front seat of the car instead of the back of the limousine. Part of JFK's skull that was identified as coming from the back of Kennedy's head, was found in the grass with tiny metal bullet fragments embedded in it, 25 feet to the rear and left of where he was hit, indicating that the shot came from the right-front. It is not difficult to figure out how a hollow point bullet being fired from the grassy knoll would cause the Presidents head to explode precisely the way it did.

"The shot must have come from the right front." Robert paraphrased to achieve greater clarity of the situation.

Over 30 medical personnel and doctors that worked on JFK that day agree that he had two entrance wounds from the front, and a large exit wound in the rear of JFK's head. There was a small 5mm (3/8"in) bullet hole in the front neck, just below Kennedy's Adams-apple when he arrived at the hospital, which they cut to made larger to insert a tub in JFK' throat to try to get him breathing again. An entry wound to the throat means that the shoot came from the front.

Catching her eyes on the www.youtube.com/watch?v=L6vWgMDq6tkHis **wife killed him**!!! Look at his **wife**; you'll see the gun smoke!

Helen quickly closed the paper, she yawned, "I'm so tired. Let's go to bed, Robert?"

"I'd think that's enough for today." The Senate of State replied, "At least we found out that Oswald was used as a pasty, since the shot to the head of the President came from the front."

While in bed, Helen told Robert,
"I ran across some weird writing... - it says that JFK was murdered by his wife."
"No way could that have happened!" Robert cried out loud.

"Definitely I agree with you. Do you remember Uncle Ben shared with us some part about "The Fatal Shot" when we discussed about the JFK assassination at his house?" Helen asked.

"Yes, but we left because it was too late that evening; we had a long way home." Robert added.

"Should we come to see Uncle Ben again? I really want to know about this matter." Helen said

"I'm obsessed with the JFK assassination!" Robert hugged his wife,

"Yes, we definitely will ask Uncle Ben more about The Fatal Shot. We can sleep now, right, honey?"

"Hold me tightly in your arms." Helen whispered to Robert.

CHAPTER 4
The Second Visit to Dallas

Robert and Helen visited Uncle Benjamin
McCarthy on Easter Sunday; Robert and Helen
were excited when they learned that besides the
McCarthy family, there were also three Vietnamese
Americans, Professor Nguyen- who teaches
Political Sciences at University of Austin, Texas –
and his wife, Kim – a nurse, and Mr. Tran, an
Attorney at Law who has done some research about
the Vietnam War. They brought some Vietnamese
traditional dishes to join the pot luck with the
McCarthy family.

Mrs. Elizabeth McCarthy greeted Professor Nguyen
and his wife, Kim; and Mr. Tran.

"Come on in, please. We're so glad to see you."
The guests brought in a large basket.

"Thank you for the invitation. We have some
Vietnamese special dishes. I hope you'd like to
taste."

"Of course, I like "Pho" very much." Dennis and
Jason said.

Mr. McCarthy introduced Robert and Helen to Mr.
Tran, Professor Nguyen and his wife,

"This is State Senator, Robert McCarthy, my
nephew; and his wife, Doctor Augier McCarthy"
The Vietnamese greeted the McCarthy family,

"It's an honor to know you."

"It's an honor to us as well." Robert and Helen said.

"And here are Jason and Dennis, my sons."

Mr. and Mrs. McCarthy said while the young men warmly shook hands with the guests.
"Everybody must have a bowl of this beef soup, please."
Mrs. McCarthy gave everyone a bowl of "Pho", "Soup de Jour!"
"Delicious! Thank you."

After dinner, Mrs. Elizabeth McCarthy brought a lemon cake with coffee to the guests in the living room. Mr. McCarthy opened the discussion, "What are the topics for today?"
"I'm puzzling about the numbers of the Lincoln and the JFK assassination; it must be something more than simple coincidence." Jason said.
Martin Gardner examined the list in an article in Scientific American, later reprinted in his book, *The Magic Numbers of Dr. Matrix*. Gardner's both presidents were elected to the House of Representatives in '46.
Both presidents were elected to the presidency in '60, after a series of debates with their opponent. Lincoln defeated incumbent Vice President John C. Breckenridge for the presidency in 1860; Kennedy defeated incumbent Vice President Richard M. Nixon for the presidency in 1960.
Both their predecessors left office in their seventies and retired to Pennsylvania. James Buchanan, whom Lincoln succeeded, retired to Lancaster Township; Dwight D. Eisenhower, whom Kennedy succeeded, retired to Gettysburg.

Both their Vice Presidents and successors were Southern Democrats named Johnson (Andrew Johnson and Lyndon B. Johnson) who were born in '08.

Both presidents were concerned with the problems of black Americans and made their views strongly known in '63. Lincoln signed the Emancipation Proclamation in 1862, which took effect in 1863. In 1963, Kennedy presented his reports to Congress on Civil Rights, and the same year was the famous March on Washington for Jobs and Freedom.

Both presidents were shot in the head on a Friday seated beside their wives. Both Fridays preceded a major holiday observed within the week.

Both presidents were accompanied by another couple.

The male companion of the other couple was wounded by the assassin. Both presidents had a son die during their presidency.

Both presidents fathered four children, only one of whom survived into the next century and who served other presidents by political appointment. Both presidents' wives died in their sixties after an untimely decline in health, during the administration of a president who had seen their husbands in Washington, D.C. the same year as the assassination.

Lincoln was shot by John Wilkes Booth at Ford's Theatre; Kennedy was shot by Lee Harvey Oswald in a Lincoln automobile, made by Ford.

Both presidents' last names have 7 letters.

There are 6 letters in each Johnson's first name.

After shooting Lincoln, Booth ran from a theatre to a warehouse; after shooting Kennedy, Oswald ran from a warehouse to a theatre.

Both Johnsons were succeeded as President in '69 by Republicans whose administrations were considered failures and whose mothers were named Hannah.

Both assassins died in the same month as their victim in a state adjacent to the state of their birth.

Both assassins were Southern white males born in the late '30s, who were in their mid-20s.

Both assassins were killed before being tried, by men who were reared in the North, changed their name as adults, and were bachelors.

Both assassins had 15 letters in their name

Both assassins shot the fatal bullet while in a building where they worked on a floor above ground level.

Both assassins suffered injuries during escape.

Both assassins sympathized with a government that was adversarial to the interests of the United States.

Both presidents had a son die during their presidency.

Both presidents fathered four children, only one of whom survived into the next century and who served other presidents by political appointment.

Both presidents' wives died in their sixties after an untimely decline in health, during the administration of a president who had seen their husbands in Washington, D.C. the same year as the assassination.

Lincoln was shot by John Wilkes Booth at Ford's Theatre; Kennedy was shot by Lee Harvey Oswald in a Lincoln automobile, made by Ford.

.

"I found something quite interesting in about the Kennedys as well."Kim said.

"Please share with us, would you? " The group implored.

"If what I'm about to say offends your religious belief?"

"Don't worry, Kim" Elizabeth laughed, "I even read the Tarots!"

"If we don't like it, we'll let you know." Mr. McCarthy gently said.

Kim continued,

"President Kennedy was born on May 29, 1917; Mrs. Jacqueline Kennedy Onassis was born on July 28, 1929; and Mr. Aristotle Onassis was born on January 15, 1906… which according to the Chinese calendar, these individuals were born in the year of the snake; Aristotle was 11 years and 10 days (lunar calendar) older than John F Kennedy, and Mr. Kennedy was 12 years older than Mrs. Jacqueline Kennedy Onassis… As you all aware of the love triangle among these individuals, so if we look at another angle, this was the fight of three snakes..."

"Three snakes! What a coincidence!" Senate of Texas Robert McCarthy exclaimed.

"Wait," Kim said, "Both President Kennedy and Mr. Aristotle Onassis died in the year of the Rabbit, (JFK 1963, Onassis 1975), again 12 years apart..."

"How is it about Marilyn Monroe's birth and death dates, for she also involved in the Kennedy-Marilyn- Jackie triangle?" Mrs. Elizabeth McCarthy asked.

"Yes, indeed," Mr. Tran joined the conversation, "Marilyn Monroe's birthday was June 1, 1926 and she died on August 5, 1962; the year of birth and the year of death according to Chinese calendar, both fall in the year of the Tiger; or Tigress in this case."

"Thus, there were two battles: one among the three snakes and the other among the two snakes and a tigress." Mr. Elizabeth McCarthy said.

"The death of Marilyn Monroe was also related to the JFK and RFK assassinations." Jason added Instantaneously, Helen felt a cold stream running down her spine; and she was a little trembling. Where did she hear the same vignette? Was it from Brandon Dorward, a Schizophrenic patient under her care? How could a psychotic person reveal the mystery that boggling people for over fifty years? Robert put his hand on her shoulder,

"Are you OK, honey?"

"Please sit next to me." Helen whispered to her husband.

"What have you been talking about, may I share with you?" Professor Nguyen asked.

Mr. McCarthy replied, "We showed a film about the JFK assassination to my nephew and his wife a couple weeks ago..."

"We've learned more about our history; it's very intricate and interesting." Dennis added

Professor Nguyen said,

"I've been obsessed with the murder of President Kennedy for over twenty years, but more that that- the connection between the death of President John F. Kennedy and the Vietnam War."

"Would you please elaborate that subject furthermore?" Senate of State, Robert McCarthy inquired.

"Let's go back to the 1960's..." Professor Nguyen said.

President Kennedy entered the American Presidency at a momentous time in world history. According to the INFALLIBLE chronology of the Bible, the world entered its 6000 year in 1958, and Pope Pius XII died in that same year. This turning point in world history also marked the beginning of the ecumenical movement and Rome's last great desperate attempt to take over the world. In Asia, the Vatican's beachhead was a small country named Vietnam. A fanatical Catholic named Diem was installed as President and he was the centerpiece of their entire Asia strategy. Soon after taking power he began to implement his persecution of the Buddhist majority which comprised 85 percent of the country's population.

Arrest and assassination of Ngo Dinh Diem & Ngo Dinh Nhu

The arrest and assassination of Ngô Đình Diệm, the president of South Vietnam, marked the culmination of a successful CIA – backed coup d'état led by General Dương Văn Minh in November 1963. On 2 November 1963, Diệm and his adviser, his younger brother Ngô Đình Nhu, were arrested after the Army of the Republic of Vietnam (ARVN) had been successful in a bloody overnight siege on Gia Long Palace in Saigon. The coup was the culmination of nine years of autocratic and nepotistic family rule in South Vietnam. Discontent with the Diệm regime had been simmering below the surface, and exploded with mass Buddhist protests against long-standing religious discrimination after the government shooting of protesters who defied a ban on the flying of the Buddhist flag.

When rebel forces entered the palace, the Ngô brothers were not present, having escaped before to a loyalist shelter in Cholon. The brothers had kept in communication with the rebels through a direct link from the shelter to the palace, and misled them into believing that they were still in the palace. The Ngô brothers soon agreed to surrender and were promised safe exile; after being arrested, they were instead executed in the back of an armored personnel carrier by ARVN officers on the journey back to military headquarters at Tân Sơn Nhứt Air Base. While no formal inquiry was conducted, the responsibility for the deaths of the Ngô brothers is commonly placed on Minh's bodyguard, Captain Nguyễn Văn Nhung, and on Major Dương Hiếu Nghĩa, both of whom guarded the brothers during the trip. Minh's army colleagues and U.S. officials in Saigon agreed that Minh ordered the executions. They postulated various motives, including that the brothers had embarrassed Minh by fleeing the Gia Long Palace, and that the brothers were killed to prevent a later political comeback. The generals initially attempted to cover up the execution by suggesting that the brothers had committed suicide, but this was contradicted when photos of the Ngôs' corpses surfaced in the media.

Background

Diệm's political career began in July 1954, when he was appointed the Prime Minister of the State of Vietnam by former Emperor Bảo Đại, who was Head of State. At the time, Vietnam had been partitioned at the Geneva Conference after the defeat of the French Union forces at the Battle of Dien Bien Phu, with the State of Vietnam ruling the country south of the 17th parallel. The partition was intended to be temporary, with national elections scheduled for 1956 to create a government of a reunified nation. In the meantime, Diệm and Bảo Đại were locked in a power struggle. Bảo Đại disliked Diệm but selected him in the hope that he would attract American aid. The issue was brought to a head when Diệm scheduled a referendum for October 1955 on whether South Vietnam should become a republic. Diệm won the rigged referendum and proclaimed himself the President of the newly created Republic of Vietnam.

Diệm refused to hold the reunification elections, on the basis that the State of Vietnam was not a signatory to the Geneva Accords. He then proceeded to strengthen his autocratic and nepotistic rule over the country. A constitution was written by a rubber stamp legislature which gave Diệm the power to create laws by decree and arbitrarily give himself emergency powers. Dissidents, both communist and nationalist, were jailed and executed in the thousands, and elections were routinely rigged. Opposition candidates were threatened with being charged for conspiring with the Viet Cong, which carried the death penalty, and in many areas, large numbers of ARVN troops were sent to stuff ballot boxes.

Diệm kept the control of the nation firmly within the hands of his brothers and their in-laws, and promotions in the ARVN were given on the basis of religion and loyalty rather than merit. Two unsuccessful attempts had been made to depose Diệm; in 1960, a paratroop revolt was quashed after Diệm stalled negotiations to buy time for loyalists to put down the coup attempt, while a 1962 palace bombing by two air force pilots failed to kill him

South Vietnam's Buddhist majority had long been discontented with Diệm's strong favoritism towards Catholics. Public servants and army officers had long been promoted on the basis of religious preference, and government contracts, U.S. economic assistance, business favors and tax concessions were preferentially given to Catholics. The Roman Catholic Church was the largest landowner in the country, and its holdings were exempt from land reform. In the countryside, Catholics were de facto exempt from performing corvée labor. Discontent with Diệm and Nhu exploded into mass protest during the summer of 1963 when nine Buddhists died at the hand of Diệm's army and police on Vesak, the birthday of Gautama Buddha.

In May 1963, a law against the flying of religious flags was selectively invoked; the Buddhist flag was banned from display on Vesak while the Vatican flag was displayed to celebrate the anniversary of the consecration of Archbishop Pierre Martin Ngô Đình Thục, Diệm's elder brother. The Buddhists defied the ban and a protest was ended when government forces opened fire. With Diệm remaining intransigent in the face of escalating Buddhist demands for religious equality, sections of society began calling for his removal from power. The key turning point came shortly after midnight on 21 August, when Nhu's Special Forces raided and vandalized Buddhist pagodas across the country, arresting thousands of monks and causing a death toll estimated to be in the hundreds. Numerous coup plans had been explored by the army before, but the plotters intensified their activities with increased confidence after the administration of U.S. President John F. Kennedy authorized the U.S. embassy to explore the possibility of a leadership change.

Surrender and debate

At 13:30 on 1 November, Generals Dương Văn Minh and Trần Văn Đôn, respectively the Presidential Military Adviser and Army Chief of Staff, led a coup against President Ngô Đình Diệm, assisted by mutinous ARVN officers. The rebels had carefully devised plans to neutralize loyalist officers to prevent them from saving Diệm. Unknown to Diệm, General Đính, the supposed loyalist who commanded the ARVN III Corps that surrounded the Saigon area, had allied himself with the plotters of the coup. The second of Diệm's most trusted loyalist generals was Huỳnh Văn Cao, who commanded the IV Corps in the Mekong Delta. Diệm and Nhu were aware of the coup plan, and Nhu responded by planning a counter-coup, which he called Operation Bravo. This plan involved Đính and Colonel Tung, the loyalist commander of the Special Forces, staging a phony rebellion before their forces crushed the "uprising" to reaffirm the power of the Ngô family. Unaware that Đính was plotting against him, Nhu allowed Đính to organize troops as he saw fit, and Đính transferred the command of the Seventh Division from Cao's IV Corps to his own III Corps. This allowed Colonel Nguyễn Hữu Có, Đính's deputy, to take command of the 7th Division based at Mỹ Tho. The transfer allowed the rebels to completely encircle the capital and denied Cao the opportunity of storming Saigon and protecting Diệm, as he had done during the previous coup attempt in 1960. Minh and Đôn had invited senior Saigon based officers to a meeting at Tân Sơn Nhứt Air Base, headquarters of the Joint General Staff (JGS), on the pretext of routine business. Instead, they announced that a coup was underway, with only a few, including Tung, refusing to join. Tung was later forced at gunpoint to order his loyalist Special Forces to surrender. The coup went smoothly as the rebels quickly captured all key installations in Saigon and sealed incoming roads to prevent loyalist forces from entering. This left only the Presidential Guard to defend Gia Long Palace. The rebels attacked government and loyalist army buildings but delayed the attack on the palace, hoping that Diệm would resign and accept the offer of safe passage and exile. Diệm refused, vowing to reassert his control. After sunset, the 7th Division of Colonel Nguyễn Văn Thiệu, who later became the nation's president, led an assault on Gia Long Palace and it fell by daybreak

In the early morning of 2 November, Diệm agreed to surrender. The ARVN officers had intended to exile Diệm and Nhu, having promised the Ngô brothers safe passage out of the country. At 06:00, just before dawn, the officers held a meeting at JGS headquarters to discuss the fate of the Ngô brothers. According to Lucien Conein, the U.S. Army officer and CIA operative who was the American liaison with the coup, most of the officers, including Minh, wanted Diệm to have an "honorable retirement" from office, followed by exile. Not all of the senior officers attended the meeting, with having already left to make arrangements for the arrival of Diệm and Nhu at JGS headquarters. General Lê, a former police chief under Diệm in the mid-1950s, strongly lobbied for Diệm's execution. There was no formal vote taken at the meeting, and Lê attracted only minority support. One general was reported to have said "To kill weeds, you must pull them up at the roots". Conein reported that the generals had never indicated that assassination was in their minds, since an orderly transition of power was a high priority in achieving their ultimate aim of gaining international recognition.

Minh and Đôn asked Conein to secure an American aircraft to take the brothers out of the country. Two days earlier, U.S. Ambassador to Vietnam, Henry Cabot Lodge Jr., had alerted Washington that such a request was likely and recommended Saigon as the departure point. This request put the Kennedy administration in a difficult position, as the provision of an airplane would publicly tie it to the coup. When Conein telephoned David Smith, the acting chief of the Saigon CIA station, there was a ten-minute delay. The U.S. government would not allow the aircraft to land in any country, unless that state was willing to grant asylum to Diệm. The United States did not want Diệm and Nhu to form a government in exile and wanted them far away from Vietnam. Assistant Secretary of State Roger Hilsman had written in August that "under no circumstances should the Nhus be permitted to remain in Southeast Asia in close proximity to Vietnam because of the plots they will mount to try to regain power. If the generals decide to exile Diệm, he should also be sent outside Southeast Asia." He further went on to anticipate what he termed a "Gotterdammerung in the palace".

We should encourage the coup group to fight the battle to the end and destroy the palace if necessary to gain victory. Unconditional surrender should be the terms for the Ngô family since it will otherwise seek to outmaneuver both the coups forces and the U.S. If the family is taken alive, the Nhus should be banished to France or any other country willing to receive them. Diệm should be treated as the generals wish.

After surrendering, Diệm called Lodge by telephone for the last time. Lodge did not report the conversation to Washington, so it was widely assumed that the pair last spoke on the previous afternoon when the coup was just starting. However, after Lodge died in 1985, his aide, Colonel Mike Dunn said that Lodge and Diệm spoke for the last time around 07:00 on 2 November moments after Diệm surrendered. When Diệm called, Lodge "put [him] on hold" and then Lodge walked away. Upon his return, the ambassador offered Diệm and Nhu asylum, but would not arrange for transportation to the Philippines until the next day. This contradicted his earlier offer of asylum the previous day when he implored Diệm to not resist the coup. Dunn offered to personally go to the brothers' hideout to escort him so that the generals could not kill him, but Lodge refused, saying, "We just can't get that involved." Dunn said, "I was really astonished that we didn't do more for them." Having refused to help the brothers to leave the country safely, Lodge later said after they had been shot, "What would we have done with them if they had lived? Every Colonel Blimp in the world would have made use of them."

Dunn also claimed that Lodge put Diệm on hold in order to inform Conein where the Ngô brothers were so the generals could capture them. When confronted about Dunn's claim by a historian, Conein denied the account. It was also revealed that

Conein had phoned the embassy early on the same morning to inquire about the generals' request for a plane to transport Diệm and Nhu out of Saigon. One of Lodge's staff told Conein that the plane would have to go directly to the faraway asylum – offering country, so that the brothers could not disembark at a nearby stopover country and stay there to foment a counter-coup. Conein was told that the nearest plane that was capable of such a long range flight was in Guam, and it would take 24 hours to make the necessary arrangements. Minh was astounded and told Conein that the generals could not hold Diệm for that period. Conein did not suspect a deliberate delay by the American embassy. In contrast, a U.S. Senate investigative commission in the early 1970s raised a provocative thought: "One wonders what became of the U.S. military aircraft that had been dispatched to stand by for Lodge's departure, scheduled for the previous day." The historian Mark Moyar suspected that Lodge could have flown Diệm to Clark Air Force Base in the Philippines, which was under American jurisdiction, before taking him to the final destination. Moyar speculated that "when Lodge had offered the jet the day before, he had done it to induce Diệm to give up at a time when the outcome of the insurrection was very much in doubt. Now that the coup clearly had succeeded, Lodge no longer needed to offer such an incentive."

Intended arrest at Gia Long Palace

In the meantime, Minh left the JGS headquarters and traveled to Gia Long Palace in a sedan with his aide and bodyguard, Captain Nguyễn Văn Nhung. Minh had also dispatched a M-113 armored personnel carrier and four jeeps to Gia Long to transport Diệm and Nhu back to JGS headquarters. While Minh was on the way to supervise the takeover of the palace, Generals Đôn, Trần Thiện Khiêm and Lê Văn Kim prepared the army headquarters for Diệm's arrival and the ceremonial handover of power to the junta. Diệm's pictures were taken down and his statue was covered up. A large table covered with green felt was brought in with the intention of seating Diệm for the handover to Minh and Vice President Nguyễn Ngọc Thơ, who was to become the civilian Prime Minister during a nationally televised event witnessed by international media. Diệm and Nhu would then "ask" the generals to be granted exile and asylum in a foreign country, which would be granted. The brothers were then to be held in a secure place at JGS headquarters while awaiting deportation. Minh arrived at the palace at 08:00 in full military ceremonial uniform to supervise the arrest of Diệm and Nhu for the surrender ceremony.

Diệm's escape

Minh instead arrived to find that the brothers were not in the palace. In anticipation of a coup, they had ordered the construction of three separate tunnels leading from Gia Long to remote areas outside the palace. Around 20:00 on the night of the coup, with only the Presidential Guard to defend them against mutinous infantry and armor units, Diệm and Nhu hurriedly packed American banknotes into a briefcase. They escaped through one of the tunnels with two loyalists: Air Force Lieutenant Đỗ Thơ, Diệm's aide-de-camp, who happened to be a nephew of Colonel Đỗ Mậu, the director of military security and a participant in the coup plot, and Xuân Vy, head of Nhu's Republican Youth. After the coup, General Paul Harkins, the head of the U.S. presence in Vietnam, inspected the tunnel and noted that it "was so far down that I didn't want to go down to walk up the thing". The brothers emerged in a wooded area in a park near the Cercle Sportif, the city's upper class sporting club, where they were picked up by a waiting Land Rover. Ellen Hammer disputes the tunnel escape, asserting that the Ngo brothers simply walked out of the building, which was not yet under siege. Hammer asserts that they walked past the tennis courts and left the palace grounds through a small gate at Le Thanh Ton Street and entered the car. The loyalists traveled through narrow back streets in order to evade rebel checkpoints and changed vehicles to a black Citroën sedan. After leaving the palace, Nhu was reported to have suggested to Diệm that the brothers split up, arguing that this would enhance their chances of survival. Nhu proposed that one of them travel to the Mekong Delta to join Cao's IV Corps, while the other would travel to the II Corps of General

Nguyễn Khánh in the Central Highlands. Nhu felt the rebel generals would not dare to kill one of them while the other was free, in case the surviving brother was to regain power. According to one account, Diệm was reported to have turned down Nhu, reasoning that "You cannot leave alone. They hate you too much; they will kill you. Stay with me and I will protect you." Another story holds that Diệm said "We have always been together during these last years. How could we separate during these last years? How could we separate in this critical hour?" Nhu agreed to remain with his brother.

The loyalists reached the home of Ma Tuyen in the Chinese business district of Cholon. Ma Tuyen was a Chinese merchant and friend who were reported to be Nhu's main contact with the Chinese syndicates which controlled the opium trade. The brothers sought asylum from the embassy of the Republic of China, but were turned down and stayed in Ma Tuyen's house as they appealed to ARVN loyalists and attempted to negotiate with the coup leaders. Nhu's secret agents had fitted the home with a direct phone line to the palace, so the insurgent generals believed that the brothers were still besieged inside Gia Long. Neither the rebels nor the loyalist Presidential Guard had any idea that at 21:00 they were about to fight for an empty building. Minh was reported to be mortified when he realized that Diệm and Nhu had escaped during the night.

Arrest in Cholon

After Minh had ordered the rebels to search the
areas known to have been frequented by the Ngo
family, Colonel Phạm Ngọc Thảo was informed by
a captured Presidential Guard officer that the
brothers had escaped through the tunnels to a refuge
in Cholon. Thảo was told by Khiêm, his superior, to
locate Diệm and prevent him from being killed.
When Thảo arrived at Ma Tuyen's house, he phoned
his superiors. Diệm and Nhu overheard him and
Tho drive them to the nearby Catholic church of St.
Francis Xavier, which they had frequented over the
years. Lieutenant Tho died a few months later in a
plane crash, but his diary was not found until 1970.
Tho recorded Diệm's words as they left the house of
Ma Tuyen as being "I don't know whether I will live
or die and I don't care, but tell Nguyễn Khánh that I
have great affection for him and he should avenge
me". Soon after the early morning mass was
celebrated for All Souls' Day (the Catholic day of
the dead) and after the congregation had left the
building, the Ngô brothers walked through the
shady courtyard and into the church wearing dark
grey suits. It was speculated that they were
recognized by an informant as they walked through
the yard. Inside the church, the brothers prayed and
received Communion.
A few minutes later, just after 10:00, an armored
personnel carrier and two jeeps entered the narrow
alcove housing the church building. Lieutenant Thơ,
who had earlier urged Diệm to surrender, saying

that he was sure that his uncle Đỗ Mậu, along with Đính and Khiêm, would guarantee their safety, wrote in his diary later "I consider myself responsible for having led them to their death".

Convoy to JGS headquarters

The convoy was led by General Mai Hữu Xuân and consisted of Colonels Nguyễn Văn Quan and Dương Ngọc Lắm. Quan was the deputy of Minh and Lắm was the Commander of Diệm's Civil Guard. Lắm had joined the coup once a rebel victory seemed assured. Two further officers made up the convoy: Major Dương Hiếu Nghĩa and Captain Nguyễn Văn Nhung. Nhung was Minh's bodyguard.

Diệm requested that the convoy stop at the palace so that he could gather personal items before being exiled. Xuân turned him down, clinically stating that his orders were to take Diệm and Nhu directly to headquarters. Nhu expressed disgust that they were to be transported in an APC, asking, "You use such a vehicle to drive the president?" Lắm assured them that the armor was for their own protection. Xuân said that it was selected to protect them from "extremists". Xuân ordered the brothers' hands be tied behind their backs before shoving them into the carrier. One officer asked to shoot Nhu, but Xuân turned him down.

Assassination

The corpse of Ngô Đình Diệm in the back of the APC, having been executed on the way to military headquarters

After the arrest, Nhung and Nghĩa sat with the brothers in the APC, and the convoy departed for Tân Sơn Nhứt. Before the convoy had departed for the church, Minh was reported to have gestured to Nhung with two fingers. This was taken to be an order to kill both brothers. The convoy stopped at a railroad crossing on the return trip, where by all accounts the brothers were assassinated. An investigation by Đôn determined that Nghĩa had shot the brothers at point-blank range with a semi-automatic firearm and that Nhung sprayed them with bullets before repeatedly stabbing the bodies with a knife.

Nghĩa gave his account of what occurred during the journey back to the military headquarters: "As we rode back to the Joint General Staff headquarters,

Diệm sat silently, but Nhu and the captain [Nhung] began to insult each other. I don't know who started it. The name-calling grew passionate. The captain had hated Nhu before. Now he was charged with emotion." Nghĩa said that when the convoy reached a train crossing, "[Nhung] lunged at Nhu with a bayonet and stabbed him again and again, maybe fifteen or twenty times. Still in a rage, he turned to Diệm, took out his revolver and shot him in the head. Then he looked back at Nhu, who was lying on the floor, twitching. He put a bullet into his head too. Neither Diệm nor Nhu ever defended themselves. Their hands were tied."

Attempted cover-up

When the corpses arrived at JGS headquarters, the generals were shocked. Although they despised and had no sympathy for Nhu, they still respected Diệm. One general broke down and wept while Minh's assistant, Colonel Nguyễn Văn Quan collapsed on a table. General Đính, the military commander of the III Corps which controlled Saigon, later declared, "I couldn't sleep that night". Đôn maintained that the generals were "truly grievous" over the deaths, maintaining that they were sincere in their intentions to give Diệm a safe exile. Đôn charged Nhu with convincing Diệm to reject the offer. Lodge later concluded, "Once again, brother Nhu proves to be the evil genius in Diệm's life."

ARVN reaction

Đôn ordered another general to tell reporters that the Ngô brothers had died in an accident. He went to confront Minh in his office.

Đôn: Why are they dead?

Minh: And what does it matter that they are dead?

At this time, Xuân walked into Minh's office through the open door, unaware of Đôn's presence. Xuân snapped to attention and stated, "Mission accomplished." Shortly after midnight on 2 November 1963 in Washington, D.C. the CIA sent word to the White House that Diệm and Nhu were dead, allegedly by suicide. Vietnam Radio had announced their deaths by poison and that they had committed suicide while prisoners in an APC transporting them to Tân Sơn Nhứt. Unclear and contradictory stories abounded. General Paul Harkins reported that the suicides had occurred either by gunshot or by a grenade wrestled from the belt of an ARVN officer who was standing guard. Minh tried to explain the discrepancy, saying "Due to an inadvertence, there was a gun inside the vehicle. It was with this gun that they committed suicide."

U.S. reaction

Kennedy learned of the deaths on the following morning when National Security Council staffer Michael Forrestal rushed into the cabinet room with a telegram reporting the Ngô brothers' alleged suicides. According to General Maxwell Taylor, "Kennedy leaped to his feet and rushed from the room with a look of shock and dismay on his face which I had never seen before." Kennedy had planned that Ngô Đình Diệm would be safely exiled and Arthur M. Schlesinger, Jr. recalled that the U.S. President was "somber and shaken". Kennedy later penned a memo, lamenting that the assassination was "particularly abhorrent" and blaming himself for approving Cable 243, which had authorized Lodge to explore coup options in the wake of Nhu's attacks on the Buddhist pagodas. Forrestal said that "It shook him personally ... bothered him as a moral and religious matter. It shook his confidence, I think, in the kind of advice he was getting about South Vietnam." When Kennedy was consoled by a friend who told him he need not feel sorry for the Ngô brothers on the grounds of despotism, Kennedy replied "No. They were in a difficult position. They did the best they could for their country." Kennedy's reaction did not draw sympathy from his entire administration. Some believed that he should not have supported the coup and that as coups were uncontrollable, assassination was always a possibility. Kennedy was skeptical about the story and suspected that a double assassination had taken place. He reasoned the devoutly Catholic Ngô brothers would not have taken their own lives, but Roger Hilsman rationalized the possibility of suicide by asserting that Diệm and Nhu would have interpreted the coup as Armageddon. U.S. officials soon became aware of the true reasons for the deaths of Diệm and Nhu. Lucien Conein had left the rebel headquarters as the generals were preparing to bring in the Ngô brothers for the press conference which announced the handover of power. Upon returning to his residence, Conein received a phone call from Saigon's CIA station that ordered him to report to the embassy. The embassy informed Conein that Kennedy had instructed him to find Diệm. Conein returned to Tân Sơn Nhứt at around 10:30. The following conversation was reported:

Conein: Where were Diem and Nhu?

Minh: They committed suicide. They were in the Catholic Church at Cholon, and they committed suicide.

C: Look, you're a Buddhist, I'm a Catholic. If they committed suicide at that church and the priest holds mass tonight, that story won't hold water. Where are they?

M: Their bodies are behind General Staff Headquarters. Do you want to see them?

C: No.

M: Why not?

C: Well, if by chance one of a million of the people believes you that they committed suicide in church and I see that they have not committed suicide and I know differently, then if it ever leaks out, I am in trouble.

Conein knew that if he saw the execution wounds, he would not be able to deny that Diem and Nhu had been assassinated. Conein refused to see the proof, realizing that having such knowledge would compromise his cover and his safety. He returned to the embassy and submitted his report to Washington. The CIA in Saigon later secured a set of photos of the brothers that left no doubt that they had been executed. The photos were taken at about 10:00, 2 November, showing the dead brothers covered in blood on the floor of an APC. They were dressed in the robes of Roman Catholic priests with their hands tied behind their backs. Their faces were bloodied and bruised and they had been repeatedly stabbed. The images appeared to be genuine, discrediting the generals' claims that the brothers had committed suicide. The pictures were distributed around the world, having been sold to media outlets in Saigon. The caption below a picture published in Time read "'Suicide' with no hands."

Media reaction

After the deaths, the military junta asserted that the Ngô brothers had committed suicide. On 6 November, Information Minister Trần Tự Oai declared at a news conference that Diệm and Nhu had died through "accidental suicide" after a firearm discharged when Nhu had tried to seize it from the arresting officer. This drew immediate skepticism from David Halberstam of the New York Times, who won a Pulitzer Prize for his Vietnam reporting. Halberstam wrote to the US Department of State that "extremely reliable private military sources" had confirmed that the brothers were ordered to be executed upon their return to military headquarters.

Neil Sheehan of UPI reported a similar account based on what he described as "highly reliable sources". Father Leger of Saint Francis Xavier Catholic Church asserted that the Ngô brothers were kneeling inside the building when soldiers burst in took them outside and into the APC. Lodge had been informed by "an unimpeachable source" that both brothers were shot in the nape of the neck and that Diệm's body bore the signs of a beating.

Impact and aftermath

Once the news of the cause of death of the Ngo brothers began to become public, the United States became concerned at their association with the new junta and their actions during the coup. U.S. Secretary of State Dean Rusk directed Lodge to question Minh about the killings Lodge cabled back, initially backing the false story disseminated by the generals, saying that their story was plausible because of the supposedly loaded pistol being left on the floor of the vehicle. Rusk was worried about the public relations implications the bloody photographs of the brothers would generate. Lodge showed no alarm in public, congratulating Đôn on the "masterful performance" of the coup and promising diplomatic recognition. Đôn's assertion that the assassinations were unplanned proved sufficient for Lodge, who told the State Department that "I am sure assassination was not at their direction."

Minh and Đôn reiterated their position in a meeting with Conein and Lodge on the following day. Several members of the Kennedy administration were appalled by the killings. The Assistant Secretary of State for Far Eastern Affairs W. Averell Harriman declared that "it was a great shock to everybody that they were killed." He postulated that it was an accident and speculated that Nhu may have caused it by insulting the officers who were supervising him. Embassy official Rufus Phillips, who was the U.S. advisor to Nhu's Strategic Hamlet Program, said that "I wanted to sit down and cry", citing the killings as a key factor in the future leadership troubles which beset South Vietnam.

According to historian Howard Jones, the fact *"that the killings failed to make the brothers into martyrs constituted a vivid testimonial to the depth of popular hatred they had aroused."* The assassinations caused a split within the leadership of the junta and repulsed American and world opinion. The killings damaged the public belief that the new regime would be an improvement over the military junta, turning the initial harmony among the generals into discord. The criticism of the killings caused the officers to distrust and battle one another for positions in the new government. Đôn expressed his abhorrence at the assassinations by caustically remarking that he had organized the armored car in an effort to protect Diệm and Nhu. Khanh claimed that the only condition he had put on joining the conspiracy was that Diem would not be killed.

According to Jones, *"when decisions regarding post coup affairs took priority, resentment over the killings meshed with the visceral competition over government posts to disassemble the new regime before it fully took form."*

Culpability debated

The responsibility for the assassinations was generally placed on Minh. Conein asserted that "I have it on very good authority of very many people, that Big Minh gave the order", as did William Colby, the director of the CIA's Far Eastern division. Đôn was equally emphatic, saying "I can state without equivocation that this was done by General Dương Văn Minh and by him alone." Lodge thought that Xuân was also partly culpable asserting that "Diệm and Nhu had been assassinated, if not by Xuân personally, at least at his direction."

Minh placed the blame on Thiệu, after the latter became President, for the assassinations. In 1971, Minh claimed that Thiệu was responsible for the deaths by hesitating and delaying the attack by his Fifth Division on Gia Long Palace. Đôn was reported to have pressured Thieu during the night, asking him on the phone "Why are you so slow in doing it? Do you need more troops? If you do, ask Đính to send more troops – and do it quickly because after taking the palace you will be made a general." Thiệu stridently denied responsibility and issued a statement which Minh did not publicly rebut: "Dương Văn Minh has to assume entire responsibility for the death of Ngô Đình Diệm." During the presidency of Richard Nixon, a U.S. government investigation was initiated into American involvement in the assassinations. Nixon was a political foe of Kennedy, having narrowly lost to him in the 1960 Presidential election. Nixon ordered an investigation under E. Howard Hunt into the murders, convinced Kennedy must have secretly ordered the killings but the inquiry was unable to find any such secret order.

Motivation

Conein asserted that Minh's humiliation by Diệm and Nhu was a major motivation for ordering their executions. Conein reasoned that Diệm and Nhu were doomed once they escaped from Gia Long Palace, instead of surrendering there and accepting the offer of safe exile. Having successfully stormed the palace, Minh had presumed that the brothers would be inside, and arrived at the presidential residence in full ceremonial military uniform "with a sedan and everything else." Conein described Minh as a "very proud man" who had lost face at turning up at the palace for his moment of glory, only to find an empty building. More than a decade after the coup, Conein claimed Diệm and Nhu would not have been killed if they had been in the palace, because there were too many people present. One Vietnamese Diệm loyalist asked friends in the CIA why an assassination had taken place, reasoning that if Diem was deemed to be inefficient, and his deposal would suffice. The CIA employees responded that "They had to kill him. Otherwise his supporters would gradually rally and organize and there would be civil war." Some months after the event, Minh was reported to have privately told an American that "We had no alternative. They had to be killed. Diệm could not be allowed to live because he was too much respected among simple, gullible people in the countryside, especially the Catholics and the refugees. We had to kill Nhu because he was so widely feared – and he had created organizations that were arms of his personal power."

Trần Văn Hương, a civilian opposition politician who was jailed in 1960 for signing the Caravelle Manifesto that criticized Diệm, and later briefly served as Prime Minister, gave a scathing analysis of the generals' action. He stated that *"The top generals who decided to murder Diệm and his brother were scared to death. The generals knew very well that having no talent, no moral virtues, no political support whatsoever, they could not prevent a spectacular comeback of the President and Mr. Nhu if they were alive."*

Burials of Diệm and Nhu

At around 16:00 on 2 November, the bodies of Diệm and Nhu were identified by the wife of former Cabinet minister Trần Trùng Dung. The corpses were taken to St. Paul's Catholic Hospital, where a

French doctor made a formal statement of death without conducting an autopsy. The original death certificate did not describe Diệm as Head of State but as "Chief of Province", a post he had held four decades earlier under the French colonial administration. Nhu was described as "Chief of Library Service", a post which he held in the 1940s. This was interpreted as a Vietnamese way of expressing contempt for the two despised leaders. Their place of burial was never disclosed by the junta and rumors regarding it persist to the current day. The speculated burial places include a military prison, a local cemetery, and the grounds of the JGS headquarters at Tan Son Nhut and there are reports of cremation as well. Nobody was ever prosecuted for the killings

Memorial services

The government did not approve a public memorial service for the deaths of Diệm and Nhu until 1968. In 1971, several thousand mourners gathered at Diệm's purported gravesite. Catholic prayers were given in Latin. Banners proclaimed Diệm as a savior of the south, with some mourners having walked into Saigon from villages outside the capital carrying portraits of Diệm. Madame Thiệu, the First Lady, was seen weeping at a requiem mass at Saigon's basilica. Several cabinet members were also at the grave and a eulogy was given by a general of the ARVN. According to the eulogy, Diệm died because he had resisted the domination of foreigners and their plans to bring great numbers of troops to Vietnam and widen a war which would have destroyed the country. Thiệu sponsored the services, and it was widely seen as a means of associating himself with Diệm's personal characteristics. Diệm frequently refused to follow American advice and was known for his personal integrity, in contrast to Thieu, who was infamous for corruption and regarded as being too close to the Americans. However, Thiệu's attempts to associate himself with Diệm's relative independence from United States influence were not successful. According to General Maxwell Taylor, Chairman of the U.S. Joint Chiefs of Staff, *"there was the memory of Diệm to haunt those of us who were aware of the circumstances of his downfall. By our complicity, we Americans were responsible for the plight in which the South Vietnamese found themselves"*.

Mr. Tran added,
"I'd like to point some light on the connection between the murders of President Diem and President Kennedy as this writing mentioned." President Diem initiated a reign of terror against the Buddhist majority. This led to passive and non-violent resistance and suicides by fire in the streets.

A Buddhist monk burned himself in front of the Roman Catholic Cathedral of Saigon.

Professor Nguyen asked the group,
"May I interrupt at this point to mention an important matter related to this coup d'état?"
"Yes, please. We all want to learn about your country." Mr. Benjamin McCarthy replied
"Thank you," Professor Nguyen expressed his thoughts in a clear voice," In the 18ᵗʰ Century, claiming to defend the Catholic priests who were mistreated in Vietnam, the French invaded our country (1858) and dominated us for almost 100 years (1954). Once more, the Catholic Organization used religious reason to cause disturbance in Vietnam. What was the Vatican purpose? Wasn't it the same ambition as more than 100 years ago?"
"Sun Tzu said," All warfare is based on deception."
Mr. Robert McCarthy agreed
"Let me continue," Mr. Tran read the documents. President Kennedy ordered Diem to let up on the persecutions. However, Diem refused to change the regime. World opinions forced Kennedy to choose between his Mother Church-the Vatican- and his political career; and his decision cost him his life. Finally the order went forth for Diem's removal and the junta officers dragged him from the church and

riddled him with bullets. This occurred on Nov. 2, 1963. Meanwhile, back in the U.S., the Catholic Hierarchy was horrified. Diem was a favorite son; all their hopes of making Asia Catholic were pinned on him. To add insult to injury the order to get rid of him had gone forth from the first Catholic President of the U.S. President Kennedy had been elected President with the help of the Hierarchy (The Jesuit Order of the Vatican) and President Kennedy had the effrontery to put his own political career ahead of his duty to Mother Church. President Kennedy had double-crossed them and he would have paid with his life. The fateful decision was made – Kennedy must be sacrificed. Better for one man to die than that the Catholicization of Asia should perish. This was carried out 3 weeks later on Nov. 22, 1963.

Madam Nhu, sister in law to President Diem and wife of the head of the dreaded secret police clearly blamed Kennedy for her husband's assassination. She wrote from Rome to Mrs. Kennedy:

"I do not know you, but you must understand now what a wife feels when told that her husband has been brutally done to death. What has come to you is only one effect of the frightful injustice of which my husband was an innocent victim..."
.

"Do you see the tribulation and karmas of these people?"

Mr. Tran looked at the audience.

"Would you elaborate a little bit more?" Senate Robert McCarthy asked.

"Karma sounds interesting. Do you practice Buddhism?" Jason inquired.

"I grew up in a family that has a deep root in Buddhism" Mr. Tran said,

"Let me introduce to you a period of the Vietnamese before Ngo Dinh Diem... In 1945, the Indochinese – (Vietnam, Laos, and Cambodia) were colonies of France. In Vietnam, the French put Bao Dai- a puppet King- ruled over the country, yet in fact the French controlled everything. Then, after WW II, the American involved in Vietnam. President Eisenhower promoted Ngo Dinh Diem to overthrow Bao Dai to be the President of Republic of South Vietnam. If you sow a bad seed, you will reap a bad seed; that is the principle of Karma Teaching."

"I see what you mean, Mr. Tran." Helen joined the conversation.

Professor Nguyen elaborated the situations,

"Ngo Dinh Diem overthrew Bao Dai; Ngo Dinh Diem was overthrown by John F. Kennedy; John F. Kennedy overthrew Ngo Dinh Diem; John F. Kennedy was overthrown by the CIA, the FBI, and the Mafia..."

"Now I have a little understanding about Karma. For instance, Mrs. Jacqueline Kennedy was a photographer before she married to JFK..." Jason added," She took pictures of people-including her future husband, JFK- later on, people took pictures of her. Isn't that correct, Mr. Tran?"

"You're quite right!" Professor Nguyen laughed

"How would you explain the deaths of President Ngo Dinh Diem (November 2, 1963) and the death of President John F. Kennedy (November 22, 1963) three weeks apart from each other, both by gun shots in the heads?" Mr. Robert McCarthy inquired

"Hold on onto that for a moment, Sir. I promise that I'll explain that later." Mr. Tran said

"May I keep on with my presentation?" Professor Nguyen asked

"Sir, please." The audience replied

President Kennedy's Television Interview with Walter Cronkite on Vietnam September 2, 1963.

CBS Interview, September 2.

MR. CRONKITE. *Mr. President, the only hot war we've got running at the moment is of course the one in Vietnam, and we have our difficulties here, quite obviously.*

PRESIDENT KENNEDY. I don't think that unless a greater effort is made by the Government to win popular support that the war can be won out there. In the final analysis, it is their war. They are the ones who have to win it or lose it. We can help them, we can give them equipment, we can send our men out there as advisers, but they have to win it – the people of Vietnam – against the Communists. We are prepared to continue to assist them, but I don't think that the war can be won unless the people support the effort, and, in my opinion, in the last 2 months the Government has gotten out of touch with the people.

The repressions against the Buddhists, we felt, were very unwise. Now all we can do is to make it very clear that we don't think this is the way to win. It is my hope that this will become increasingly obvious to the Government, that they will take steps to try to bring back popular support for this very essential struggle.

MR. CRONKITE. *Do you think this Government has time to regain the support of the people?*

PRESIDENT KENNEDY. I do. With changes in policy and perhaps with personnel, I think it can. If it doesn't make those changes, I would think that the chances of winning it would not be very good.

MR. CRONKITE. *Hasn't every indication from Saigon been that President Diem has no intention of changing his pattern?*

PRESIDENT KENNEDY. If he does not change it, of course, that is his decision. He has been there 10 years, and, as I say, he has carried this burden when he has been counted out on a number of occasions. Our best judgment is that he can't be successful on this basis. We hope that he comes to see that; but in the final analysis it is the people and the Government itself who have to win or lose this struggle. All we can do is help, and we are making it very clear. But I don't agree with those who say we should withdraw. That would be a great mistake. That would be a great mistake. I know people don't like Americans to be engaged in this kind of an effort. Forty-seven Americans have been killed in combat with the enemy, but this is a very important struggle even though it is far away.

We took all this – made this effort to defend
Europe. Now Europe is quite secure. We also have
to participate – we may not like it – in the defense
of Asia.

Professor Nguyen went further in the subject,
"Please read this paper, you'd understand the
problem better."
One word from the Archbishop of Hue to his
brother President Diem would be all that was
required to end the persecutions of the Buddhists
and save Kennedy the awful decision that he was
forced to make. But it never came... why?
Vietnam is not the only war that the Vatican started
to manipulate American internal policy. Ireland is
another example. Both countries were divided
North and South. The partition of both countries led
to unmitigated horror and suffering; it made no
benefits to either side.
Lest the Catholics get too friendly with the
Protestants, that war keeps the pot boiling while the
ecumenical movement proclaims love and
friendship to the dear separated brethren. Again,
one word from the Hierarchy (the Vatican) is all
that is needed to end the violence there.
In the final analysis, Vietnam and Ireland are small
countries. Rome's real goal is the U.S. – the big
battalions – the country with limitless military and
economic power to conquer her foes!!

"No way to stop the tragic events because Ngo Dinh
Diem was a faithful Catholic; he could not have

done anything against the Mother Church – the Vatican." Mr. McCarthy sighed.

"The puzzle is," Mr. Tran continued, "Regardless whatever you do, the Devil wins."

"Please explain, Sir. How did the Devil do that?" The audience implored.

Mr. Tran sipped some tea, then said,

"Ngo Dinh Diem obeyed the Vatican: he did not change the regime; he kept on suppression the Buddhists... The price he paid was murder by shots in the head and multiple stabbed in the body...."

Suddenly Helen felt trembling. As a Catholic, she strongly believes in the Trinity of God, the Virgin Mary, she attends mass on Sunday, and loves the rosary. Could she still have faith in the Mother Church Vatican?

"Ah, I see what you meant," Mrs. McCarthy interrupted,

"President Kennedy disobeyed the Jesuits of Vatican; he planned to replace Ngo Dinh Diem since Diem repressed Buddhism in Vietnam, the price President Kennedy had to pay was the same..."

"Kennedy was executed by shot in the head also." Senate Robert McCarthy added.

"It's deadly awful!" Helen exclaimed.

"Does anyone see something else?" Mr. Tran quizzed the audience.

"President Kennedy had a younger brother – Robert Kennedy – who was the Attorney General in the Kennedy Administration." Jason pointed out this fact.

"Oh, yes. What a coincidence! Ngo Dinh Diem had a younger brother –Ngo Dinh Nhu– who was an Advisor in Ngo Dinh Diem Administration..." Mr. McCarthy said.

"Robert Kennedy and Ngo Dinh Nhu were murdered by gun shots, too." Elizabeth said

"Is this karma, Mr. Tran?" Helen implored.

Professor Nguyen nodded in agreement,

"You tell me what it is, Doctor? Isn't this an eye for an eye, a tooth for a tooth as written in the Bible?"

"I found something else, too." Dennis attached another view,

"Mr. Onassis's son, Alexander died of an airplane crash..."

"John F. Kennedy Jr. also died of an airplane crash." Kim uttered a loud call.

"Are there more than just coincidences in these circumstances?" Senate of State Robert asked.

"Before answering that question, I have a paper – probably we should take a look..."

Professor Nguyen passed around a paper,

New evidence has recently been discovered relevant to the assassination of President John F. Kennedy that will show who actually planned and carried out this murder. This new evidence will show that the Warren Commission report, which is the government's final word on the assassination, is a complete cover-up of what actually took place. The following analysis of the assassination will include several events and situations that might not appear to be related to this murder, but will show the extensive intrigue behind it.

While riding in an open motorcade, President Kennedy was shot in Dealey Plaza on Friday, Nov. 22, 1963 at 12:30 p.m. The crowds were cheering. There was a great scene of rejoicing as the president of the United States made his way through downtown Dallas. It seemed as if everyone was smiling in those waving thousands. But presently, shots rang out, and President Kennedy, a short while later, lay dead at the Parkland Memorial Hospital.

This case has baffled people for the last four decades, and is one of the ten most unsolved mysteries of the last one hundred years. The Warren Commission was set up to investigate the assassination, and they concluded that a lone gunman, Lee Harvey Oswald, did it. They claimed that Oswald shot President Kennedy from the Dallas Book Depository building behind his car, but there is rather overwhelming evidence now that disproves the Warren Commission report and points to a massive cover-up and conspiracy behind the assassination. Two days after President Kennedy's death Jack Ruby murdered Oswald. Why? Was it to keep him from talking?

There were basically two main reasons why Kennedy was assassinated. These reasons are involved with the Vietnam War, and the Federal Reserve Bank.

President Kennedy sent two aides to Vietnam, McNamara and Taylor, who gathered intelligence that convinced him that the United States needed to withdraw from Vietnam. Their memo to the

president was entitled, Report of McNamara-Taylor Mission to South Vietnam.
With this report in hand, President Kennedy had what he wanted. It contained the essence of decisions he had to make. He had to get re-elected to finish programs set in motion during his first term; he had to get Americans out of Vietnam. –
Col. L. Fletcher Prouty, **JFK: The CIA, Vietnam, and the Plot to Assassinate John F. Kennedy**, Carol Publishing Group, p. 264.

On Nov. 22, 1963, the government of the United States was taken over by the superpower group that wanted an escalation of the warfare in Indochina, and a continuing military buildup for generations to come. – .
As President Kennedy began to de-escalate American involvement in Southeast Asia, this superpower group was planning his murder. Following Kennedy's assassination, they made sure that America would remain in Vietnam for a long time.
Who was this group? Who wanted us in South Vietnam and why?
When we answer these questions, the people behind the assassination of JFK will be known.
Avro Manhattan was a British journalist who worked for many years for the British Broadcasting Company. He has written at least 15 books on the role of the Roman Catholic Church in world affairs. In his book, **Vietnam: Why Did We Go?**

The political and military origin of the war of Vietnam has been described with millions of written and spoken words. Yet, nothing has been said about one of the most significant forces which contributed to its promotion, namely, the role played by religion, which in this case, means the part played by the Catholic Church, and by her diplomatic counterpart, the Vatican. Their active participation is not mere speculation. It is an historical fact as concrete as the presence of the U.S., or the massive guerilla resistance of Asian communism. The activities of the last two have been scrutinized by thousands of books, but the former has never been assessed, not even in a summarized form. The Catholic Church must be considered as a main promoter in the origin, escalation and prosecution of the Vietnamese conflict. From the very beginning this religious motivation helped set in motion the avalanche that was to cause endless agonies in the Asiatic and American continents.

The price paid was immense: thousands of billions of dollars; the mass dislocation of entire populations; political anarchy; military devastation on an unprecedented scale; the disgrace upon the civilized world; the loss of thousands upon thousands of young Asian and American lives. Last but not least, there were wounding, mutilation, and death of hundreds of thousands of men, women, and children. The tragedy of Vietnam will go down in history as one of the most pernicious deeds of the contemporary alliance between politics and organized religion.

Factors of a political, ideological, economic, and military nature played no mean role in the unfolding of the war, but the religion of the Catholic Church was one of its main instigators. From the beginning her role has been minimized when not obliterated altogether. Concrete facts however, cannot be wiped away so easily, and it is these which we shall now scrutinize, even if briefly. – Avro Manhattan, ***Vietnam: Why Did We Go?,*** Chick Publications, 1984, p. 13, emphasis added.

Avro Manhattan, world authority on Vatican politics, has blown the cover on the real reason our boys suffered and died in Vietnam. He traces their death to the Vatican's passionate desire to make Asia Roman Catholic. Vatican agents hatched and plotted the Vietnam War. American soldiers were indeed serving the Vatican. They desperately struggled to survive among the jungles, the hell of warfare, pain, death and destruction. It was all engineered by... her Jesuits. – Ibid. p. 3, emphasis added.

Many, especially Catholics, may take exception to the facts stated in the previous quotes, but we must present the facts as they are and as they happened. When this book talks about the Catholic Church, it is not speaking of the faithful church members who know nothing about things like this. It is speaking of the rulers of the Vatican and their Order of the Jesuits.

According to Avro Manhattan, the war in Vietnam was fought because the Vatican wanted to create a power base in Southeast Asia from which to take over all of Southeast Asia and then all of Asia. The following quotes are from this same book.

Ho Chi Minh began before World War Two to maneuver for a communist Vietnam. He received help from the U.S. against the Japanese but used that aid to consolidate his hold on the highlands of Tonkin. In August, 1945 he marched into Hanoi and set up the provisional government of the Democratic Republic of Vietnam. A master strategist, he cooperated in the transplanting of nearly a million Catholic North Vietnamese into the South... After the election of Pope John the 23rd in 1958 and the turn of the Vatican from the Cold War toward cooperation with Marxism, Ho Chi Minh made a secret deal with Pope John which eventually led to full control of the country by the North. – (p. 177).

President Ngo Dinh Diem of South Vietnam was a practicing Catholic who ruled South Vietnam with an iron fist. He was a genuine believer in the evil of Communism and the uniqueness of the Catholic Church. He had originally been planted in the presidency by Cardinal Spellman and Pope Pius the 12th. He transformed the presidency into a virtual Catholic dictatorship, ruthlessly crushing his religious and political opponents. Many Buddhist monks committed suicide by fire, burning themselves alive in protest against his religious persecutions. His discriminatory persecution of non-Catholics, particularly Buddhists, caused the disruption of the government and mass desertions in the army. This eventually led to U.S. military intervention in South Vietnam.

In this terrorization he was aided by his two Catholic brothers, *the Chief of the Secret Police* and *the Archbishop of Hue. –* Ibid. p. 56, (emphasis added).

Cardinal Francis Spellman, the archbishop of New York, was the key man that brought America into the conflict. He was active in persuading the U.S. to select Diem and support him as president of South Vietnam. He was made Vicar General of the U.S. Armed Forces and called the GIs the *'Soldiers of Christ'* [meaning soldiers for the Catholic Church] in his frequent visits to the Vietnam War front.

The Vatican played both sides against each other in this Vietnamese Civil War. They controlled Diem in the South while advising and making secret deals with Ho Chi Minh in the North. Thus, however the war turned out, the Vatican would triumph and have control in Vietnam. President Kennedy's attempt to halt the bloodbath incurred the undying wrath of the instigators of the war – the Jesuits of the papacy. President Kennedy began to de-escalate America's involvement in Vietnam shortly before his death. The day after his brutal murder, the following occurred:

At 8:30 a.m., Saturday, the 23rd of November, 1963, the limousine carrying CIA director John McCone pulled into the White House grounds... He was also there to transact one piece of business prior to becoming involved in all the details entailed in a presidential transition – the signing of

National Security Memorandum 278, a classified document which immediately reversed John Kennedy's decision to de-escalate the war in Vietnam. The effect of Memorandum 278 would give the Central Intelligence Agency carte blanche to proceed with a full-scale war in the Far East... In effect, as of November 23, 1963, the Far East would replace Cuba as the thorn in America's side. It would also create a whole new source of narcotics for the Mafia's worldwide markets. – Robert Morrow, **First Hand Knowledge**, Shapolsky Publishers, p. 249.

The day after Kennedy was killed, the decision to stop America's involvement in Vietnam was reversed and the Vatican's program continued. Morrow's statement also revealed another reason for the Jesuits wanting to continue the war; they would make billions of dollars in the international drug trade. For the last four centuries, the Jesuits had been involved in the Far East drug trade and they certainly did not want to lose this opportunity, even if it meant the lives of millions of people! Since the original Jesuit mission had established itself in Beijing in 1601, the Society of Jesus [the Jesuits] had held the key to the Far East Trade – including the drug trade. – assorted authors, Dope, Inc.: *The Book that Drove Kissinger Crazy*, Executive Intelligence Review, p. 117.

The Jesuit controlled politicians in Washington wanted to continue the war in Vietnam. They wanted to create a Catholic power in Southeast Asia. They wanted to maintain their control of the international drug market that they had held for 400 years in the Far East. When President Kennedy stood in their way, he had to be removed. The Jesuits had John Kennedy assassinated.

The second reason for Kennedy's assassination was his intention to eliminate the Federal Reserve. Colonel James Gritz explains,

When Kennedy called for a return of America's currency to the gold standard, and the dismantling of the Federal Reserve System – he actually minted non-debt money that does not bear the mark of the Federal Reserve; when he dared to actually exercise the leadership authority granted to him by the U.S. Constitution… Kennedy prepared his own death warrant. It was time for him to go. – Colonel James Gritz **Called to Serve: Profiles in Conspiracy from John F. Kennedy to George Bush**, Lazarus Publishing.

President Kennedy was attempting to dismantle the Federal Reserve System, which is the central bank of the United States, a creation of the Jesuits. The Constitution of the United States gives to Congress the power to coin money. If the U. S. Congress coined its own money as the Constitution directs, it would not have to pay the hundreds of billions of dollars of interest that it now pays each year to the bankers for the national debt, for money that came out of nothing This is why Kennedy began to issue U.S. government money that was free of debt to replace the Federal Reserve dollars we have been using.

We have seen in previous chapters who were responsible for the creation of the Federal Reserve Bank, and the unconstitutional operation of this bank that steals money from U.S. citizens. The Jesuits, if you will remember from chapter two, tried to assassinate President Andrew Jackson for discontinuing the central bank. They unfortunately succeeded in assassinating Kennedy for trying to do the same thing. The Jesuits uses the wealth created by the Federal Reserve to finance their murderous deeds. John Kennedy incurred the deadly wrath of the Jesuits for daring to act as the President and not as their puppet. Kennedy was Catholic; however, he put the welfare of the United States before the desires of the papacy. He was not a Jesuit.

Here is a very interesting section from the secret instructions of the Jesuit Order, written by their founder, Ignatius Loyola.

Finally, let all with such artfulness gain the ascendance over princes, noblemen and the magistrates of every place that they may be ready at our beck and call, even to sacrifice their nearest relatives and most intimate friends when we say it is for our interest and our advantage.

We see here that if the Jesuit Order says that a person is to die, it doesn't matter if it is your best friend, if it is your father or your brother; they are to be killed. What a dastardly, evil, and wicked system the Jesuit Order of the Roman Catholic Church is. Do you think that the Catholic Church isn't that powerful? Do you think this makes them out to be too strong? Avro Manhattan tells us:

Cardinal Francis Spellman, of New York, was the military vicar of the American Armed Forces in Vietnam. He was also the unofficial link between the pope and John Foster Dulles, the U.S. Secretary of State and therefore the Secretary's brother, Alan, who was the head of the CIA.

Thus, through Cardinal Francis Spellman, the Roman Catholic Church and the Jesuits had access to and control over John Foster Dulles, the Secretary of State, and John Foster Dulles' brother, Alan, who was the head of the Central Intelligence Agency. Those two departments, along with the FBI, were in the hands of Cardinal Francis Spellman, the head Cardinal of the Catholic Church in New York.

The Catholic Church in the USA financially can stand up to all the giant trusts of America. Politically, she looms ever larger in the White House, in the Senate and in the Congress. She is a force in the Pentagon, a secret agent in the FBI and the most subtly intangible prime mover of the S.S. wheel within a wheel; the Central Intelligence Agency. –

Jean Hill was also a witness to the Kennedy murder. In her book, entitled *JFK: the Last Dissenting Witness*, she states that during a conversation her friend, J.B., who was one of the policemen in the motorcade that was with Kennedy, told her,

"Well, while Kennedy was busy shaking hands with all the well wishers at the airport, Johnson's Secret Service people came over to the motorcycle cops and gave us a bunch of instructions. The darnedest

200

thing was they told us the parade route through Dealey Plaza was being changed." "Changed? How," Jean Hill asks. "It was originally supposed to go straight down Main Street." J.B. said, "But they said for us to disregard that. Instead we were told to make the little jog on Houston and cut over to Elm." Jean felt her mouth drop open. "If you'd stayed on Main Street, Kennedy might've been completely out of range of whoever was shooting at him. My 'shooter' behind the wooden fence definitely wouldn't have had much chance to hit him from there." J.B. stared at her with a straight face. "Maybe that's why they changed the route," he said bluntly. "But that's not all. They also ordered us into the craziest escort formation I've ever seen. Ordinarily, you bracket the car with four motorcycles, one on each fender. But this time they told the four of us assigned to the president's car there'd be no forward escorts. We were to stay well to the back and not let ourselves get ahead of the car's rear wheels under any circumstances. I'd never heard of a formation like that much less ridden in one, but they said they wanted to let the crowds have an 'unrestricted view' of the president. Well, I guess somebody got an unrestricted view of him all right." Jean Hill, ***JFK: The Last Dissenting Witness***, Pelican Publishing.

*jfkfacts.org/**assassination**/did-jfks-limousine-come-to-a-stop-amid-the-gu...* Aug 25, 2014 - Here's the Zapruder film, A Secret Agent signaled for the JFK motorcade **slowed down** and stabilized: What do you.... Both versions are shown in the DVD, **Images** of an **Assassination**, but..... If Z. did this—shot the Elm Street **motorcade** at 48 fps instead of.... Allman also describes how Secret Service **Agent** Clint Hill "was giving thumbs to the guy…

Dallas Police Officer Billy Joe Martin Said: According to his fellow motorcycle cops **"who were escorting [the Vice Presidential car,] LBJ started ducking down in the car a good 30 or 40 seconds before the first shots were fired..."** One of the Police Officers who were describing to his fellow Officers what happened the moments just before the shooting started said: **"our new president is either one jumpy son of a bitch or he knows something he's not telling about the Kennedy thing."**

I think it is obvious that Johnson knew that the shooting would start as soon as the President's car slowed down to turn the corner of Elm and Huston, so he ducks under the seat just before the entire rifle firing. Governor Connally knew that Kennedy was going to be killed, and he was quite nervous the whole time he was riding in the set in front of Kennedy. There were witnesses standing near the car when Connally was shot, and they heard him say, "My God they're going to kill us all." This implies that he obviously believed that there was more than one shooter, and that only one person Kennedy was supposed to be killed that day. As the first rifle shots rang out, Roberts ordered his agents to stay in the car, but one of the Secret service agents rushed to the limousine as the back right side of the president's head was then blown off.

On November 23, 1963, the day after the assassination, a meeting took place between the FBI and the CIA. J. Edgar Hoover wrote a memo and he titled the subject heading **"The Assassination of President John F. Kennedy."** Hoover reported that on the day after the murder of President John F. Kennedy the bureau of the FBI had briefings with two individuals: **Captain William**

Edwards of the Defense Intelligence Agency and Mr. George Bush- of the Central Intelligence Agency.

J. Edgar Hoover writes a memo to the Director of the **"Bureau of Intelligence and Research Department of State."** He is afraid that "Mr. George Bush of the Central Intelligence Agency" and "Captain William Edwards of the Defense Intelligence Agency," may try to capitalize on the present situation by launching an unauthorized raid against Cuba with their Anti-Castro group, believing that the assassination of President John F. Kennedy might give them the perfect opportunity to invade Cuba by blaming JFK's assassination on Castro and the Russians.

As the Presidents car approaches, a Cuban man sitting on the curb next to a mysterious man known as the "umbrella man," looks back up towards the picket fence, and is talking to someone on a walkie-talkie. Then they both stand up and the Cuban man starts waving his fist at the President, as the white man opens his umbrella as if he's trying to signal everyone. Just then the bullets start hitting the President from the front, back, and side. Then both men calmly sit back down again on the curb and acted as if nothing had happened; while everyone else around them is reacting frantically, falling on the ground, or running up the hill towards the picket fence trying to cache the men who just fired at the President...

So, the motorcade route through Dallas was changed, and the reason given was so that the people would have an excellent view of the president of the United States. The Jesuit assassins sure did!

Other peculiar things happened too. Lyndon Johnson, the vice president of the United States, was apparently having a real problem. Continuing with Jean Hill's conversation with her friend in the motorcade,

"What are you talking about?" Jean asked innocently. "I don't understand." "My friends in the motorcade say he started ducking down in the car a good 30 or 40 seconds before the first shots were fired. I'd say that's just a little peculiar wouldn't you?" "Oh, come on, J.B.," Jean Hill said, thinking he had to be joking. "They obviously weren't serious, were they?" "As far as I know they were dead serious." J.B. said. "One of them told Maguire that he saw Johnson duck down even before the car turned onto Houston Street, and he sure as ____ wasn't laughing when he said it." "Well, maybe Johnson just dropped something on the floor and bent over to pick it up. I mean there can be a simple explanation." "It's maybe so." J.B. said. "I don't claim to know what his reasons were but this guy said it sure looked like he was expecting bullets to be flying. When I heard it, it made me start wondering about a whole lot of other stuff too."

Lyndon Johnson was acting as if he knew bullets would soon be flying, ducking down repeatedly before the shots went off.

Texas law prohibits people that die in the state of Texas from being removed without an autopsy. Leading doctors at Parkland Memorial Hospital in Dallas were held at gunpoint as the body of John F. Kennedy was removed from that hospital without an autopsy. Why? There was overwhelming evidence that there was more than one bullet that killed JFK. There was overwhelming evidence that the Warren Commission report was nothing but lies. There were many bullets that the doctors would have found that would have shattered the idea that Lee Harvey Oswald was the lone gunman. That is why an autopsy was not allowed in Texas. That is why Kennedy's body was shipped to Washington D.C. where a federal autopsy could be made, where they could fabricate the evidence to support the lies of the Warren commission. There was a Jesuit led conspiracy to kill JFK and they didn't want the evidence to get out, no matter how many people had to be killed in the process.

If there really were several bullets fired that day in Dealey Plaza, then certainly the car would have contained evidence of this. Three days after the assassination, Carl Renas, head of security at the Dearborn Division of the Ford Motor Company, drives the limousine, helicopters hovering over head, from Washington to Cincinnati. In doing so, he noticed several bullet holes, the most notable being the one in the windshield's chrome molding strip, which he said was clearly *'a primary strike'* and *'not a fragment,'* The limousine was taken by Renas to Hess and Eisenhart of Cincinnati where the chrome molding was replaced. The Secret Service told Renas to *"keep your mouth shut."* – Charles Crenshaw, **JFK: Conspiracy of Silence**, Penguin Books USA, p. 106.

Renas was the head of security for the Dearborn Division of Ford Motor Co. Who was the head of that division in 1963 that dispatched Renas for the task of his life?

Henry Ford II says today that the first time he can remember meeting Lee Iacocca was in November 1960 when he summoned the young salesman to his office to tell them he was giving him command of the Ford division [at Dearborn]. – Robert Lacey, *Ford, the Men and the Machine*, Ballantine Books, p. 531.

Lee Iacocca was the man in charge of the Dearborn Division of the Ford Motor Company, who dispatched Carl Renas to go to Washington D.C. to get the car that JFK was in when he was assassinated. Iacocca was the head of the Dearborn Division until he became President of Ford Motor Company in 1970. Iacocca was part of the cover-up because he suppressed evidence concerning JFK's assassination.

What connection does he have with the Catholic Church? In Iacocca's autobiography he says,

It took me a number of years to fully understand why I had to make a good confession to a priest

before I went to Holy Communion, but in my teens I began to appreciate the importance of this most misunderstood right of the Catholic Church. In later years, I found myself completely refreshed after confession. I even began to attend weekend retreats where the Jesuits in face-to-face examinations of conscience made me come to grips with how I was conducting my life. – Iacocca: *An Autobiography*, Bantam Books, p. 8.

Roman Catholic Lee Iacocca, head of the Dearborn division of the Ford Motor Co. was the one who dispatched Carl Renas to get the limousine that had the evidence of multiple bullets that were shot from multiple guns that killed John F. Kennedy. Isn't it amazing that many years later as President of Chrysler, Lee Iacocca went to Congress and asked for financial help? Since Catholic Iacocca had been such an obedient servant to his Jesuit masters, another obedient Catholic by the name of Thomas 'Tip' O'Neill used his power as Speaker of the House to get Lee Iacocca all the money he needed. There were many people who knew a great deal about the Kennedy assassination. Unfortunately, almost all of them died under mysterious circumstances. There was a concerted effort to be sure that no secrets were ever told. Even Jean Hill stated that several attempts were made to kill her and her children.

Jim Marrs, author of Crossfire: The Plot That Killed Kennedy, wrote: *"In the three-year period which followed the murder of President Kennedy and Lee Harvey Oswald, 18 material witnesses died – six by gunfire, three in motor accidents, two by suicide, one from a cut throat, one from a karate chop to the neck, five from natural causes."* ...A mathematician hired by the London Sunday Times in February of 1967 concluded that the odds of the number of witnesses involved in the assassination of John F. Kennedy dying between November 22, 1963 and that date were 100,000 trillion to one... In the time period ranging from November 22, 1963 to August 1993 over 115 'witnesses' have died or fallen victim to death by strange circumstances, suicides or murder. – Craig Roberts and John Armstrong, *JFK: The Dead Witnesses* Consolidated Press.

"Sir, how did Richard Nixon involve in this matter?" Dr. Augier McCarthy inquired "Enclosed is some information on that issue." Mr. Tran said

Frank Sturgis told the San Francisco Chronicle in a May 7, 1977 interview, "The reason we burglarized the Watergate was because Nixon was interested in stopping news leaking relating to the photos of our role in the assassination of President John Kennedy." Nixon was extremely concerned about stopping the Democrats from publishing the photos of Hunt & Sturgis under arrest for the murder of JFK. Eyewitness Marita Lorenz testified under oath that she saw Hunt pay off an assassination team in Dallas the night before Kennedy's murder. There are several incriminating documents and 4,000 hrs of tapes, which are still marked top secret in which there is clear evidence that Nixon is openly "confessing on the telephone" to hiring Bush's assassination teams to help kill JFK. Over and over again certain names kept coming up on the Watergate tapes. Nixon's frequent use of code words when referring to the mysterious connection between the Bay of Pigs, Dallas and Watergate are being kept sealed in the National Archives. Nixon "never clearly said who was responsible for Kennedy's death. But he did say, **"Both Johnson and I wanted to be president, but the only difference was I wouldn't kill for it."**

On the tape, recorded in May of 1972, President Nixon confided to two top aides that the Warren Commission pulled off **"the greatest hoax that has ever been perpetuated."** Unfortunately, he did not elaborate. But the context in which Nixon raised the matter shows you just how far Nixon was willing to stoop in his efforts to become president, even if it involved assassinating his political adversary John F. Kennedy. Nixon also pardoned organized crime figures after the government had spent millions of dollars to put them in jail.

"What is the connection between the Bay of Pigs and the Vietnam War?" Dennis asked
"'I'd be glad to read this according to the Wikipedia." Senate of State Robert McCarthy replied,

A The **Bay of Pigs Invasion**, known in Latin America as **Invasión de Playa Girón** (or **Invasión de Bahía de Cochinos** or **Batalla de Girón**), was a failed military invasion of Cuba undertaken by the CIA-sponsored paramilitary group Brigade 2506 on 17 April 1961. A counter-revolutionary military, trained and funded by the United States government's Central Intelligence Agency (CIA), Brigade 2506 fronted the armed wing of the Democratic Revolutionary Front (DRF) and intended to overthrow the Communist government of Fidel Castro. Launched from Guatemala, the invading force was defeated within three days by the Cuban armed forces, under the direct command of the Prime Minister of Cuba, Fidel Castro.

After the failed U.S. attempt to overthrow the Castro regime in Cuba with the Bay of Pigs invasion, and while the Kennedy administration planned Operation Mongoose, in July 1962 Soviet premier Nikita Khrushchev reached a secret agreement with Cuban premier Fidel Castro to place Soviet nuclear missiles in Cuba to deter any future invasion attempt. Construction of several missile sites began in the late summer, but U.S. intelligence discovered evidence of a general Soviet arms build-up on Cuba, including Soviet IL–28 bombers, during routine surveillance flights, and on September 4, 1962, President Kennedy issued a public warning against the introduction of offensive weapons into Cuba. Despite the warning, on October 14 a U.S. U–2 aircraft took several pictures clearly showing sites for medium-range and intermediate-range ballistic nuclear missiles (MRBMs and IRBMs) under construction in Cuba. These images were processed and presented to the White House the next day, thus precipitating the onset of the Cuban Missile Crisis.

Kennedy summoned his closest advisers to consider options and direct a course of action for the United States that would resolve the crisis. Some advisers—including all the Joint Chiefs of Staff— argued for an air strike to destroy the missiles, followed by a U.S. invasion of Cuba; others favored stern warnings to Cuba and the Soviet Union. The President decided upon a middle course. On October 22, he ordered a naval "quarantine" of Cuba. The use of "quarantine" legally distinguished this action from a blockade, which assumed a state of war existed; the use of "quarantine" instead of "blockade" also enabled the Unites States to receive the support of the Organization of American States.

That same day, Kennedy sent a letter to Khrushchev declaring that the United States would not permit offensive weapons to be delivered to Cuba, and demanded that the Soviets dismantle the missile bases already under construction or completed, and return all offensive weapons to the U.S.S.R. The letter was the first in a series of direct and indirect communications between the White House and the Kremlin throughout the remainder of the crisis.

The President also went on national television that evening to inform the public of the developments in Cuba, his decision to initiate and enforce "quarantine and the potential global consequences if the crisis continued to escalate. The tone of the President's remarks was stern, and the message unmistakable and evocative of the Monroe Doctrine: "It shall be the policy of this nation to regard any nuclear missile launched from Cuba against any nation in the Western Hemisphere as an attack by the Soviet Union on the United States, requiring a full retaliatory response upon the Soviet Union." The Joint Chiefs of Staff announced a military readiness status of DEFCON 3 as U.S. naval forces began implementation of the quarantine and plans accelerated for a military strike on Cuba.

On October 24, Khrushchev responded to Kennedy's message with a statement that the U.S. "blockade" was an "act of aggression" and that Soviet ships bound for Cuba would be ordered to proceed. Nevertheless, during October 24 and 25, some ships turned back from the quarantine line; others were stopped by U.S. naval forces, but they contained no offensive weapons and so were allowed to proceed. Meanwhile, U.S. reconnaissance flights over Cuba indicated the Soviet missile sites were nearing operational readiness. With no apparent end to the crisis in sight, U.S. forces were placed at DEFCON 2— meaning war involving the Strategic Air Command was imminent. On October 26, Kennedy told his advisors it appeared that only a U.S. attack on Cuba would remove the missiles, but he insisted on giving the diplomatic channel a little more time. The crisis had reached a virtual stalemate.

That afternoon, however, the crisis took a dramatic turn. ABC News correspondent John Scali reported to the White House that he had been approached by a Soviet agent suggesting that an agreement could be reached in which the Soviets would remove their missiles from Cuba if the United States promised not to invade the island. While White House staff scrambled to assess the validity of this "back channel" offer, Khrushchev sent Kennedy a message the evening of October 26, which meant it was sent in the middle of the night Moscow time. It was a long, emotional message that raised the specter of nuclear holocaust, and presented a proposed resolution that remarkably resembled what Scali reported earlier that day. "If there is no intention," he said, "to doom the world to the catastrophe of thermonuclear war, then let us not only relax the forces pulling on the ends of the rope, let us take measures to untie that knot. We are ready for this."

Although U.S. experts were convinced the message from Khrushchev was authentic, hope for a resolution was short-lived. The next day, October 27, Khrushchev sent another message indicating that any proposed deal must include the removal of U.S. Jupiter missiles from Turkey. That same day a U.S. U–2 reconnaissance jet was shot down over Cuba. Kennedy and his advisors prepared for an attack on Cuba within days as they searched for any remaining diplomatic resolution. It was determined that Kennedy would ignore the second Khrushchev message and respond to the first one. That night, Kennedy set forth in his messageThe failed invasion severely embarrassed the Kennedy Administration, and made Castro wary of future US intervention in Cuba.

In August 1961, during an economic conference of the Organization of American States in Punta del Este, Uruguay, Che Guevara sent a note to Kennedy via Richard N. Goodwin, a secretary of the White House. It said: "Thanks for Playa Girón. Before the invasion, the revolution was weak. Now it's stronger than ever."

As Allen Dulles later stated, CIA planners believed that once the troops were on the ground, Kennedy would authorize any action required to prevent failure—as Eisenhower had done in Guatemala in 1954 after that invasion looked as if it would collapse. President Kennedy was angered with the CIA's failure, and declared he wanted "to splinter the CIA in a thousand pieces and scatter it to the winds."

"Notice what JFK said about the CIA; and later (November 22, 1963) CIA Director Dulles retaliated to the President's comment: JFK's brain was scattered into the air in Dallas."

It was a risky move to ignore the second Khrushchev message. Attorney General Robert Kennedy then met secretly with Soviet Ambassador to the United States, Anatoly Dobrynin, and indicated that the United States was planning to remove the Jupiter missiles from Turkey anyway, and that it would do so soon, but this could not be part of any public resolution of the missile crisis. The next morning, October 28, Khrushchev issued a public statement that Soviet missiles would be dismantled and removed from Cuba.

The crisis was over but the naval quarantine continued until the Soviets agreed to remove their

IL–28 bombers from Cuba and, on November 20, 1962, the United States ended its quarantine. U.S. Jupiter missiles were removed from Turkey in April 1963.

The Cuban missile crisis stands as a singular event during the Cold War and strengthened Kennedy's image domestically and internationally. It also may have helped mitigate negative world opinion regarding the failed Bay of Pigs invasion. Two other important results of the crisis came in unique forms. First, despite the flurry of direct and indirect communications between the White House and the Kremlin—perhaps because of it—Kennedy and Khrushchev, and their advisers, struggled throughout the crisis to clearly understand each others' true intentions, while the world hung on the brink of possible nuclear war. In an effort to prevent this from happening again, a direct telephone link between the White House and the Kremlin was established; it became known as the "Hotline." Second, having approached the brink of nuclear conflict, both superpowers began to reconsider the nuclear arms race and took the first steps in agreeing to a nuclear Test Ban Treaty.

Professor Nguyen said,

"I'd want to introduce the other side of the Cuban Missile Crisis, which is the main reason the Johnson and the Nixon Administrations pursued." The Cuban missile crisis of October 1962 was the most dangerous moment in modern ... chances of nuclear war **during** the crisis was as high as one in three, also **Cuba illegal drug** trafficking that was at the high tide ..."

The Cuban Missile Crisis was one of the few times that the 'rules' of the Cold War were nearly forgotten. Berlin, Korea, Hungary and Suez - the 'rules' had been followed. But in Cuba this broke down and the Cuban Missile Crisis was the only time when 'hot war' could have broken out. In the 1950's Cuba was lead by a right-wing dictator called Fulgencio Batista. He dealt with opponents with extreme harshness and while a few prospered under his regime, many Cubans were very poor. He was not tolerant of communists and received the support of the Americans. Batista's sole support within Cuba came from the army which was equipped by the Americans. For some years, Havana, the capital of Cuba, had been the play ground of the rich from America. They would come to the island at the weekend to gamble - illegal in all parts of America except for Las Vegas at this time. Havana was considered more convenient for those living in the southern states of America. Large sums of money were spent but most was creamed off by Batista and his henchmen. Over $200 million was actually invested in Cuba itself. For all the money coming into Cuba, the poor remained very poor..

Mr. Benjamin McCarthy emphasized a remarkable point,

"Of course, the CIA/FBI and some Americans were upset at President Kennedy's reaction to the Bay of Pigs. Indeed," Professor Nguyen responded, "the American partisans' promptly countered act to the President by delivered this poster in Dallas the day before the assassination-November 21, 1963."

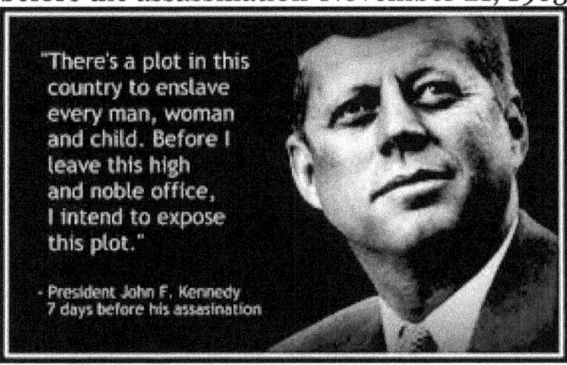

Kennedy was one of many Presidents, kings, Czars, and emperors who refused to obey the Jesuits and were killed for it. The role of the papacy in the heinous murder and cover-up of this crime cannot be denied. We have seen that the Vatican had a motive, the people in key positions to carry it out, and the people in key positions to cover it up. There was one group, one organization, whose historical background was characterized by the planning and execution of such deeds; that had a lasting consistent motive, before, during and after the crime; that had the necessary international connections; that had the money; that could elicit suicidal self-sacrifice in its members; and that continued to exist through all phases of the assassination conspiracy. This is the Roman Catholic Church. – Emmett McLaughlin, an Inquiry into **the *Assassination of Abraham Lincoln*,** Lyle Stuart, Inc.1963, p. 161.

Jason delved into the issue from another angle, "How is the Cuban Missile Crisis related to the US relationship with Israel, Sir?"

Professor Nguyen elaborated the issue,

"The Arab-Israel conflict has been started since the beginning (1948), in 1961there were some casualties from both sides, the US Dept of State, The Office of the Historian wrote as following

The 1967 Arab-Israeli War marked the failure of the Eisenhower, Kennedy, and Johnson administrations' efforts to prevent renewed Arab-Israeli conflict following the 1956 Suez War. Unwilling to return to what National Security Advisor Walter Rostow called the "tenuous chewing gum and string arrangements" established after Suez, the Johnson administration sought Israel's withdrawal from the territories it had occupied in exchange for peace settlements with its Arab neighbors. This formula has remained the basis of all U.S. Middle East peacemaking efforts into the present.

This is how the Jerusalem Post described Kennedy's actions which are inconceivable given the power of the lobby today.

The clash began in 1960, when the outgoing Eisenhower administration sought an explanation for the mysterious construction near Dimona. It was told that this top-secret activity in the middle of the desert was a harmless textile plant, and no, it could not come and visit. Classified spy photos were then published on the front page of The New York Times (yes, the CIA spied on the Jewish state, with or without forged passports).

When President Kennedy took office in 1961, the disagreement became a full-blown crisis. Kennedy was not inherently hostile, but he did not have a special sympathy for the Jewish people. His advisers urged continuous pressure, assuming that Israel would have no choice but to accept US demands. Every high-level meeting or communication repeated the demand for inspection of Dimona. One form of pressure was to deny Ben-Gurion an invitation to the White House - his May 1961 meeting with Kennedy was a low-key affair at the Waldorf Astoria Hotel in New York, and was dominated by this issue.

In some ways, Israel was far weaker than is the case today. Before 1967, the IDF was not seen as a formidable power, and the economy depended on massive aid from Diaspora Jewry. If the US government were to impose tax restrictions, the costs would have been very high. Ben-Gurion avoided saying no by dancing around them for two years.

Finally, Kennedy had enough, and in a personal letter dated May 18, 1963, the president warned that unless American inspectors were allowed into Dimona (meaning the end of any military activities), Israel would find itself totally isolated.

THE UNSPOKEN TRUTH: ISRAEL'S CENTRAL ROLE IN THE JFK ASSASSINATION by Michael C. Piper

Where in the world could anyone come up with the idea that Israel's Mossad had a hand in the assassination of John F. Kennedy? Well, there's more to the story than meets the eye. All of the information which, taken together, proves this contention has already been committed to print. This book, Final Judgment, brings all of these facts together for the first time in a frightening scenario that makes sense. Considering all of the theories about the assassination of John F. Kennedy that have been circulating for years, how could anyone ever suggest that Israel's Mossad was involved? This was the reaction of more than a few people when apprised of the thesis presented in the pages of this book. Yet, I believe, that when you read this volume you will reach the same conclusion: that Israel and its spy agency, the Mossad, did indeed play a critical role in the JFK assassination conspiracy and its cover-up. The evidence, you shall see, is there.

It was several years ago that I first stumbled upon a hint that this was indeed the case. I came across a strange reference in the pages of a controversial work about the JFK assassination which alleged that rogue CIA operatives had been behind the president's murder, A. J. Weberman and Michael Canfield's Coup d'état in America, first published in 1975. The reference, simple as it was, appearing on page 41, read as follows:

"After the assassination, an informer for the Secret Service and the FBI who had infiltrated a Cuban exile group and was in the process of selling them machine guns, reported that on November 21, 1963 he was told, 'We now have plenty of money-our new backers are the Jews-as soon as they take care of JFK.' This man had furnished reliable information in the past."

I barely noticed the reference, but it did intrigue me. Who did this source mean when he referred to "the Jews"? This was the question I needed to answer. My immediate conclusion was this: the source meant Jewish gangsters-such as Meyer Lansky-who had a stake in reviving their Cuban gambling interests that they lost when Fidel Castro came to power. This was the logical answer.

Frankly, I laid the reference aside. It was just one lone remark out of perhaps millions of words written about the JFK assassination. It was nearly a year that went by before I came across the quotation

again-while re-reading the same book. I pondered the quote for a moment, thinking,
"This is interesting."
However, I once again cast those thoughts aside. I had already reached my own conclusions about the JFK assassination long before: The CIA was primarily responsible, working hand-in-hand with certain elements in "the Mafia" and also in the anti-Castro Cuban movement.
However, in the subsequent year that followed, I began to stumble across some interesting information.
In David Scheim's book, Contract on America, which contends that "the Mafia" was solely responsible for the JFK assassination, I saw a variation of the same quote referenced in the Weberman and Canfield book.
However, Scheim's rendition of the quote had deleted the reference to the alleged Jewish backers of the Cuban plotters. I began to think that there might be something more to the story after all, whatever the accuracy of the story allegedly told to the federal authorities.

THE LANSKY CONNECTION

It was around this time that I learned that a new biography of organized crime figure Meyer Lansky had been released. It was entitled Little Man: Meyer Lansky and the Gangster Life. The book-prepared in cooperation with Lansky's family-was little more than a puff piece for the deceased thug. Gossipy, full of inside information, and even entertaining at times, the book still somehow seemed to be missing a lot.

It was then that I returned to my library and pulled a book off the shelf that I hadn't re-read in perhaps fifteen years. It was Hank Messick's biography of Lansky. Re-reading this important book I began to see that Meyer Lansky was not just another gangster. He was "the chairman of the board" of organized crime.

All of the Mafia figures that had been repeatedly implicated in the JFK assassination were, in fact, Lansky's front-men-his subordinates, his underlings. In short, if "the Mafia" had a hand in the killing of JFK, then Lansky had to have been one of the key players.

I quickly began to see in reviewing many of the works which allege that "The Mafia Killed JFK," Lansky's preeminent role was being ignored or otherwise under-played.

I was aware of Lansky's close ties to Israel. After all, Lansky fled to Israel when the heat was on in the United States. But how deeply did the Lansky-Israeli connection go?

My research into that question began to turn up some interesting facts relating to an Israeli connection to the assassination 2f John F. Kennedy.

THE ISRAELI CONNECTION

Why would Israel have an interest in participating in the JFK assassination conspiracy? That was the burning question.

It was just about the time that I had begun to take a second look at the Lansky connection to the Kennedy assassination that several new works about the covert relationship between the United States and Israel were released providing never-before revealed information.

These books, cited extensively in Final Judgment, made it all too clear that John F. Kennedy-before his death-was in a pitched battle with Israel. In fact, Kennedy was at war.

This was something that long-time JFK assassination researchers had no reason to know about. Much of the material had long been classified. It was a secret-a deep, dark secret.

Some of JFK's communications with then-Israeli Prime Minister David Ben-Gurion are still classified. Not even top-level intelligence officials with special security clearance have been allowed access to these potentially explosive documents.

This discovery made me realize that there was a lot more to the Kennedy relationship with Israel and a lot more about the JFK assassination than we had ever been told.

ISRAEL, LANSKY & THE CIA The long and close relationship between Israel and JFK's foes at the CIA is something which is becoming more and more known to the general public. JFK's own war with the CIA is common knowledge.

At the time of the president's assassination, however, the depth and breadth of the CIA's relationship with Israel's Mossad, however, was not so commonly known.

What's more, as I began to discover, Israel's allies in the Lansky Syndicate had much deeper relations with the CIA than most researchers have realized. And while the stories of CIA-Organized Crime assassination plots against Castro have been told time and again, the evidence I began to discover told an even bigger story.

The pieces of the puzzle were all there. They simply needed to be put together. As the research continued, I repeatedly found myself stumbling upon new facts and information that continued to verify what was initially in my mind just a theory, but which I now believe to be the truth.

THE PERMINDEX CONNECTION

It is the little-discussed Permindex connection to the JFK assassination which is the tie that binds-the final proof that Israel's Mossad was at the center of the assassination conspiracy.

In the Permindex connection we find all of the critical elements which tie Israel's Mossad, the CIA and organized crime together in close-knit intrigue linked directly to the murder of President Kennedy. Although researchers, over the years, have devoted much time and energy to pursuing a wide variety of questions relating to the JFK assassination controversy (focusing on controversies that will never be resolved) they have steered clear of the Permindex connection.

Those who have made any reference to Permindex have described it as some sort of "neo-Nazi" entity-even a remnant of Hitler's SS-but, as we shall see, nothing could be further from the truth.

To understand the forces behind the Permindex connection, which we examine in detail in this volume, is to understand the answer to the biggest mystery of this century: the question of who killed John F. Kennedy.

INSIDERS AGREE

Just before I began the book I mentioned my theory to a rather well-known former United States congressman. He surprised me when he said, "I think you are on to something. I've believed for years that the Mossad was involved in the Kennedy assassination, but I never really took the time to look into it. I'm glad you're doing it, though. It will be an important book. It's a book I would have liked to have written myself."

Then, just after I finished the book, I sent a copy of the manuscript to another former U.S. congressman, thinking that he might have some interest in the subject. His response was perhaps a bit astonishing. After the former congressman received the manuscript he wrote me a surprising letter in which

he said, "I will tell you this. A retired Western European diplomat and intelligence officer with whom I've been in correspondence (and who has had disastrous experiences with Israel and the Mossad) has been urging me for the last four years to write the book that you have written."
He passed the manuscript on to the Frenchman who in turn wrote me a fascinating letter providing further information confirming my thesis.

AT PERMINDEX

Clay Shaw - If New Orleans District Attorney Jim Garrison had been permitted to carry out an unimpeded investigation and prosecution of Shaw, a CIA contract operative and a former director of the International Trade Mart in New Orleans implicated in involvement with Lee Harvey Oswald, David Ferrie, Guy Banister and other figures central to the JFK assassination conspiracy, Garrison would have divined Shaw's connections – through a shadowy corporation known as Permindex – to not only the Israeli Mossad, but also the international crime syndicate of Israeli loyalist Meyer Lansky.
Louis M. Bloomfield - Based in Montreal, Bloomfield was a long-time intelligence operative and a front man for the powerful Bronfman family interests. The Bronfmans were not only key international backers of Israel but also long-time figures in the Lansky crime syndicate. Bloomfield, one of the foremost figures in the Israeli lobby in Canada and one of Israel's leading international

operatives, not only served as the chief shareholder in the Permindex Corporation on whose board of directors Clay Shaw served, but also had intimate ties to American intelligence.

Tibor Rosenbaum - One of the "godfathers" of the state of Israel and the first director for finance and supply for Israel's intelligence agency, the Mossad, Rosenbaum was a prime financial angel behind the Permindex corporation. His Swiss banking concern, the Banque De Credit International, also served as the chief European money laundry or the global crime syndicate of Miami-based crime chief Meyer Lansky.

John King - A close business associate of Tibor Rosenbaum's protégé and sometime front man, Bernard Cornfield, King showed up in New Orleans in the early stages of Jim Garrison's investigation-before Clay Shaw's name had come up-and sought to persuade Garrison (through a bribery attempt) to give up the inquiry. Fortunately he failed in his scheme.

THE MOSSAD CONNECTION

David Ben-Gurion - Prime Minister of Israel; resigned his post in disgust with JFK's stance toward Israel. in April of 1963; Said JFK's position threatened Israel's very survival.

Yitzhak Shamir - A long-time Mossad officer (based largely at the Mossad's chief European office in Paris), Shamir headed the Mossad's assassination squad at the time of the JFK assassination. A former

French intelligence officer has charged that Shamir himself arranged the hiring of JFK's actual assassins through a close ally in French intelligence.

Menachem Begin - In 1963, Begin (later prime minister of Israel) was a roving Israeli diplomat; prior to JFK's assassination he was overheard conspiring with Meyer Lansky's California henchman, Mickey Cohen, in a conversation that suggested hostile intentions by Israel against the American president.

Luis Kutner - Although known largely as a "mob lawyer," (who was long and closely associated with Jack Ruby, a sometime-client) Kutner also doubled as an international intelligence operative and functioned as an advisor to an ad hoc pro-Israel lobby group in the United States.

A. L. Botnick - Head of the New Orleans office of the Anti-Defamation League (ADL) of B'nai B'rith, an intelligence and propaganda arm for Israel's Mossad; a close associate of New Orleans-based CIA contract operative Guy Banister who helped create Lee Harvey Oswald's pre-assassination profile as a "pro-Castro" agitator. Evidence suggests that Banister's manipulation of Oswald may have been carried out under the guise of an ADL "fact-finding" operation.

Arnon Milchan - Israel's biggest arms dealer, Milchan was "executive producer" (i.e. chief financial angel) of Oliver Stone's Hollywood fantasy about the JFK assassination-a fact which may explain Stone's aversion to exploring the Israeli connection to the affair.

Maurice Tempelsman - The international diamond merchant and Mossad operative who became the lover of Jacqueline Kennedy Onassis and used his connections to double-perhaps triple-her substantial fortune, thereby co-opting the Kennedy family forever.

Professor Nguyen asked the audience, "Do you recognize the name Maurice Tempelsman?"
"He was Mrs. Jacqueline Kennedy Onassis companion until her death." Jason said
"Correct, once more; we see the connection of the Jews with the First Lady before and after the JFK assassination." Senate of State Robert McCarthy commented
"Let's continue…"

THE CIA CONNECTION

Rudolph Hecht - An owner of the CIA-linked Standard Fruit concern, Hecht was a prominent figure in the New Orleans Jewish community and as chairman of the board of directors of the International Trade Mart was Permindex board member Clay Shaw's primary sponsor.
James Jesus Angleton - Angleton, the CIA's long-time chief of counterintelligence, was the CIA's primary high-level conspirator in the murder of President Kennedy and the subsequent cover-up. Angleton, who had been co-opted by and was totally loyal to the Israeli Mossad, played a major

role in the effort to frame Lee Harvey Oswald. Final Judgment is the first JFK assassination study to delve into Angleton's role in the conspiracy.

David Atlee Phillips - A long-time high-level CIA official, Phillips was the CIA station chief in Mexico City at the time a strange effort was underway to implicate Lee Harvey Oswald as a Soviet KGB collaborator. If anyone in the CIA knew the truth about Oswald, it was Phillips. He confessed publicly that the story about Oswald being in Mexico City was not precisely what the CIA had long claimed.

E. Howard Hunt - Long-time CIA officer and liaison to the anti-Castro Cuban exiles. Testimony by ex-CIA contract operative Marita Lorenz placed Hunt in Dallas, Texas the day before the president's assassination. The full truth about Hunt's actual involvement in the affair may never be known, but there is no question that Hunt was deeply involved in the intrigue surrounding the president's murder. Evidence does indeed indicate that there was a conscious effort to frame Hunt for involvement in the crime.

Guy Banister - The former FBI agent-turned-CIA contract operative whose New Orleans office was a central point for international intrigue involving the CIA, the anti-Castro Cuban exiles and the anti-DeGaulle forces in the French Secret Army Organization (OAS). Under Banister's direction, Lee Harvey Oswald established a public profile for himself as a "pro-Castro" agitator in the streets of New Orleans.

David Ferrie - An enigmatic adventurer and CIA contract operative, Ferrie was closely involved with Lee Harvey Oswald during Oswald's stay in New Orleans in the summer of 1963, working alongside Oswald out of Banister's headquarters. The investigation of Ferrie by New Orleans District Attorney Jim Garrison ultimately led to Garrison's discovery of Permindex board member Clay Shaw's ties to both Ferrie and Oswald.

Marita Lorenz - A former CIA contract operative, she testified under oath that one day prior to the assassination of President Kennedy she arrived in Dallas in an armed caravan of CIA-backed Cuban exiles who were met by not only Jack Ruby, who later killed Lee Harvey Oswald, but also CIA official E. Howard Hunt.

Guillermo & Ignacio Novo - Two brothers, veterans of the CIA-backed Cuban exile wars against Fidel Castro. According to Marita Lorenz, the Novo brothers were part of the armed caravan that arrived in Dallas one day before the assassination of President Kennedy. Many years after Dallas, the Novos were later convicted of participating in the murder of a Chilean dissident in collaboration with international adventurer Michael Townley who himself had ties to high-level figures implicated in the JFK conspiracy.

John Tower - In 1963 Tower was a newly-elected Republican U.S. Senator from Texas with close ties to the CIA. Shortly after the assassination he told associates of his own inside knowledge of the bizarre story of what really happened in Dealey

Plaza. The story told by Tower suggests strongly that there were many unseen forces at work, manipulating many of the key players in the JFK assassination conspiracy. It was not until the release of Final Judgment that Tower's name was ever connected to the mystery surrounding the JFK assassination.

Victor Marchetti - A high-ranking CIA official who left the agency in disgust, Marchetti later made a career writing about the CIA. In a 1978 article he charged that the CIA was about to frame its long-time operative, E. Howard Hunt, with involvement in the JFK assassination. A libel suit resulting as a consequence of Marchetti's article resulted in a climactic finding by a jury that the CIA had been involved in the assassination of the president.

Robin Moore - A journalist with long-standing close ties to the CIA, Moore co-authored former CIA man Hugh McDonald's book, LBJ and the JFK Conspiracy which promoted James Jesus Angleton's false claim that the KGB was behind the president's murder-another of the disinformation stories that emerged following the assassination.

THE LANSKY SYNDICATE

Meyer Lansky - Chief executive officer and de facto "treasurer" of the international crime syndicate; active in gun-running on behalf of the Israeli underground; collaborated closely with American intelligence on a number of fronts; later settled in Israel. Researchers who have claimed that "the Mafia Killed JFK" have pointedly refused to acknowledge Lansky's preeminent positioning in the underworld.

Carlos Marcello - The head of the Mafia in New Orleans, Marcello owed his status to Meyer Lansky who was his chief sponsor in the crime syndicate. Marcello could not have orchestrated the JFK assassination-as some suggest-without Lansky's explicit approval.

Seymour Weiss - Meyer Lansky's chief bagman and liaison with the political establishment in Louisiana, he later served as a director of the CIA-linked Standard Fruit company and may actually have been a high-ranking CIA contract operative in New Orleans at the time of the JFK assassination.

Sam Giancana - The Mafia boss of Chicago, Giancana was a player in the CIA-Mafia plots against Castro; later murdered, probably at the behest of Santo Trafficante, Jr. His family says that Giancana admitted having been involved in the planning of the JFK assassination.

Santo Trafficante, Jr. - Although best known as the head of the Mafia in Tampa, Trafficante actually functioned as Meyer Lansky's chief lieutenant in the crime syndicate and as Lansky's liaison with the CIA in the Castro assassination plots.

Johnny Rosselli - A roving "ambassador" for the Mafia, Rosselli was the primary conduit between the CIA and the mob in the plots against Fidel Castro; may have arranged the murder of Sam Giancana for Trafficante and was later murdered himself.

Mickey Cohen - Meyer Lansky's West Coast henchman; Jack Ruby's role model and a gun-runner for the Israeli underground, Cohen collaborated closely with Israeli diplomat Menachem Begin prior to the JFK assassination;. Cohen arranged for John F. Kennedy to meet actress Marilyn Monroe who was assigned the task of finding out JFK's private views and intentions toward Israel.

Jack Ruby - A long-time functionary for the Lansky syndicate, Ruby was the Lansky connection man in Dallas and also engaged in CIA-linked gunrunning to the anti-Castro Cuban exiles. Evidence suggests there is more to Ruby's sudden "death" than meets the eye.

Jim Braden - A veteran personal courier for Meyer Lansky, Braden was almost assuredly in contact in Dallas with Jack Ruby prior to the JFK assassination. He was briefly detained in Dealey Plaza minutes after the president's murder, but those JFK assassination researchers who have mentioned Braden prefer to cast him as a "Mafia" figure rather than as Lansky's man on the scene in Dallas.

Al Gruber - A henchman of Meyer Lansky's West Coast operative, Mickey Cohen, Gruber and Ruby spoke by telephone just shortly before Ruby killed Lee Harvey Oswald. It is believed that Gruber gave Ruby the contract on Oswald on behalf of his superiors.

THE FRENCH CONNECTION

Charles DeGaulle - Repeatedly targeted for assassination by Israeli-allied forces in French intelligence and in the Secret Army Organization (OAS) who were angry that DeGaulle had granted independence to Arab Algeria. The Mossad-sponsored Permindex operation that also had a hand in the murder of JFK, laundered money used in the assassination attempts on DeGaulle.

Georges deLannurien – High ranking official in the SDECE, the French intelligence agency; pinpointed by a former French intelligence officer as the individual who (at the best of Mossad assassinations Chief Yitzhak Shamir) contracted the hit team who killed JFK in Dallas.

Michael Mertz - A former French SDECE officer and the Paris connection for the Lansky-Trafficante heroin syndicate; alleged to have been one of the actual gunmen in Dallas on November 22, 1963. According to some to be the legendary CIA contract killer, QJ/WIN-

Jean Soutre – a liaison for the French OAS with the CIA's E. Howard Hunt, Soutre maintained contact with Guy Banister's CIA – and mob-linked gun-running headquarters in New Orleans. Soutre may have been in Dallas at the time of the JFK assassination. There is evidence linking Soutre to James Jesus Angleton's intrigue inside the CIA that affected French intelligence in a dramatic way.

Thomas Eli Davis III - A world-traveling mercenary with apparent links to both Jack Ruby and Lee Harvey Oswald, Davis was taken into custody by the Algerian government for his subversive activities alongside Israeli agents in supplying weapons to the French OAS just prior to the JFK assassination. It is said that CIA operative QJJWIN (possibly Michael Mertz, one of the reputed assassins of President Kennedy) helped secure Davis's release from prison.

Geoffrey Bocca - A former propagandist for the OAS, Bocca later co-authored former CIA contract agent Hugh McDonald's book, Appointment in Dallas, which pointed the blame for the JFK assassination away from those who were actually responsible-the first of two suspect books put out by McDonald.

Christian David - A French Corsican criminal associated with reputed JFK assassin Michael Mertz, David has claimed knowledge of a French hit team involved in the JFK assassination. David himself was the chief suspect in the murder of a Moroccan dissident, Mehdi Ben-Barka, whose killing was orchestrated by the Israeli Mossad through anti-DeGaulle forces in French intelligence.
.

"Did President Kennedy attempt to stop Israel having Nuclear weapons?
Was this the reason Israel decided to eliminate JFK?"
Jason inquired.
"Exactly," Robert McCarthy said,
"Please follow this link for more information in this issue." www.jpost.com/.../When-Ben-Gurion-said-no-to-JFK The Jerusalem Post Mar 28, 2010 – The sharpest example took place almost 50 years ago,

when John F. Kennedy demanded that David Ben-Gurion end Israel's nuclear deterrent... "After that was the 6-Day-War with the Decisive Israel Victory and Territorial changes. Israel captures the Gaza Strip and the Sinai Peninsula from Egypt, the West Bank (including East Jerusalem) from Jordan, and the Golan Heights from Syria."

"However, Israel has nuclear weapon. After five decades of pretending otherwise, the Pentagon has reluctantly confirmed that Israel does indeed possess nuclear bombs."

"The price JFK had to pay for disagreement with Ben-Gurion was his brain scattered into the air of Dallas." Dr. Helen Augier McCarthy made a bitter comment.

Mr. Tran continued,

"As you can predict, after the JFK assassination, the Johnson Administration turned the American-Israel Relation to a new page."

*https://www.jewishvirtuallibrary.org/...Israel/ guar...*Jewish Virtual Library...Lyndon **Johnson Administration**: Table of Contents ... Discussion of Selling Arms to **Israel** and Jordan · Draft Memo to **Johnson** about Aircraft Sales to... And up to today

Israel–United States relations are a very important factor in the <u>United States government</u>'s overall policy in the <u>Middle East</u>, and Congress has placed considerable importance on the maintenance of a close and supportive relationship.

The main expression of Congressional support for Israel has been foreign aid. Since 1985, it has provided nearly $3 billion in grants annually to Israel, with Israel being the largest annual recipient of American aid from 1976 to 2004 and the largest cumulative recipient of aid ($121 billion, not inflation-adjusted) since World War II. Seventy-four percent of these funds must be spent purchasing US goods and services. More recently, in fiscal year 2014, the US provided $3.9 billion in foreign military aid to Israel. Israel also benefits from about $8 billion of loan guarantees.

Congress has monitored the aid issue closely along with other issues in bilateral relations, and its concerns have affected Administrations' policies. Almost all US aid to Israel is now in the form of military assistance, while in the past it also received significant economic assistance. Strong congressional support for Israel has resulted in Israel receiving benefits not available to other countries.

In addition to financial and military aid, the United States also provides political support to Israel, having used its United Nations Security Council veto power 42 times with respect to resolutions relating to Israel, out of a total 83 times in which its veto has ever been used. Between 1991 and 2011,

15 vetoes were used to protect Israel out of 24 in total.

Bilateral relations have evolved from an initial US policy of sympathy and support for the creation of a Jewish homeland in 1948 to an unusual partnership that links a small but militarily powerful Israel, dependent on the United States for its economic and military strength, with the American superpower trying to balance other competing interests in the region. Others maintain that Israel is a strategic ally, and that US relations with Israel strengthen the US presence in the Middle East. Israel is one of the United States' two original major non-NATO allies in the Middle East. Late Republican Senator Jesse Helms used to call Israel "America's aircraft carrier in the Middle East", when explaining why the United States viewed Israel as such a strategic ally, saying that the military foothold in the region offered by the Jewish State alone justified the military aid that the United States grants Israel every year. Currently, there are seven major non-NATO allies in the Greater Middle East.

"As you know," Professor Nguyen continued," After the JFK assassination, the Johnson Administration reversed all Kennedy foreign policies, and the Vietnam War became escalating." "Why did Johnson do that?" the audience requested "Johnson was trained by the Jesuits at Georgetown University; he obeyed the order from the Mother Church to invade Vietnam."

"I don't understand," Senate of State Robert McCarthy inquired, "We lost the war, why did we involve?"

"Very well, Sir. If you'd recall, the failure of the Bay of Pigs upset quite a number of the JFK Administration; therefore, the Johnson's regime- which was the reverse JFK foreign policy- need to advance US policy in the Far East…" Mr. Tran explained

"After the assassination of President Kennedy, President Lyndon Johnson and later, President Nixon escaladed the war to the level that the bombs dropped to Vietnam exceeded the total amount of the bombs used in WWII. Have you read *"Vietnam, Why did we go?"* Avro Manhattan (1914-1990). He was the author of over 20 books including the best-seller The Vatican in World Politics, twice Book-of-the-Month and going through 57 editions. He was a Great Briton who risked his life daily to expose some of the darkest secrets of the Papacy. His books were #1 on the Forbidden Index for the past 50 years!!

With an immense collection of facts, photos, names and dates, Manhattan proves that the Vietnam War began as a religious conflict. He shows how America was manipulated into supporting Catholic oppression in Vietnam supposedly to fight communism.

Manhattan explains:

How religious pamphlets and radio broadcasts convinced one million Catholics to leave North

Vietnam and live under Catholic rule in the South, overwhelming the Buddhists.
How brutal persecution of Vietnamese Buddhists led to rioting and suicides by fire in the streets.
Why the reports of what was really happening, written by American military and civil advisers, failed to reach the U.S. President.
Why the project backfired, and as U.S. soldiers continued to die, the Vatican made a secret deal with Ho Chi Minh.

Chapter 1

Preliminaries.
World War II, the Provisional Partition of Vietnam, and the Beginning of the Vietnamese Conflict.

Defeat of France and Japan - Vietnamese freedom-fighters declare the independence of Vietnam - A French Vietnamese puppet Prime Minister - Vietnamese Catholic Bishops appeal to the Vatican - The U.S. sends two warships to Saigon - Eisenhower helps the French in Vietnam - The Geneva Agreement - The 17th Parallel as "a provisional demarcation line" between North and South Vietnam - The Catholic lobby in the U.S. prevents a free election in Vietnam - Fear of a communist electoral take-over - President Eisenhower's

243

candid comment.

Chapter 2

The Vatican-American Grand Alliance
*Reasons Which Prompted the U.S. to Commit
Herself to the War in Vietnam.*

U.S. global policy following World War II -
"Belligerent peace between the U.S. and Soviet
Russia - Russian territorial expansionism after
World War II - The U.S., Korea and the Cold
War - The Vatican fear of world communism -
The launching of political Catholicism against
left-wing Europe - Religious mobilization
against Marxism.

Chapter 3

Fatimaization of the West
*Religious and Ideological Preliminaries to the
Vietnamese War.*

The "Cold War" as a step to the "Hot War" - The
U.S. and the Vatican make ready for "THE
DAY" - The conditioning of Catholics for the
oncoming "Hot War" - The message of the
Virgin of Fatima - The conversion of Soviet
Russia to the Catholic Church - The political
implications of the cult of Fatima - The pope and

the Virgin encourage Catholic volunteers for the Russian front.

Chapter 4

The Pope's Blessing for a Preventive War
The Secretary of the U.S. Navy, Secret Chamberlain of the Pope, Prepares for World War III.

The crown which weighs 1,200 grams of gold - Our Lady appears 15 times to a nun in the Philippines - The American Jesuit and the miraculous rose petals - The American Secretary of Defense jumps from a window on the 16th floor - Cardinal Spellman, Senator McCarthy and the American Secretary of the Navy - The Boston speech and the call for an American "preventive atomic war."

Chapter 5
The Miraculous Zigzagging Sun
Pope Pius XII Uses Religious Emotionalism as an Incitement to War.

The Virgin Mary visits the pope at the Vatican - Pius XII sees the sun "zigzag" - The prodigy and its political meaning - One million pilgrims want the conversion of Russia - The first U.S. ambassador designate at the Vatican attends atomic exercises in Nevada - The U.S. ambassador to Moscow prepares for the invasion of Russia - Description of the forthcoming invasion of Soviet Russia by "Colliers " - Making ready for the war of liberation The "Osservatore Romano" authenticates a miracle - The divine message to the Vicar of Christ.

Chapter 6
The Pope's "Preventive War" Miscarries.
U.S. Admirals, Generals and Diplomats Troop to the Vatican, President Truman's Despairing Comments.

Papal warning of the "barbaric invasion" - The American leader of the "Free Russia Committee" - Dulles appeals for "an atomic striking force" - Eisenhower and 12 War Ministers - 100 Divisions on the "ready" - Saturation bombing experts see the pope - Russian agents steal "the cipher books" of the Vatican - Vatican diplomats and their secret spying via religion - The CIA - 100 million dollars to train spies and terrorists - Uniforms with regulation shoulder flashes marked USSR, instead of USA - Anybody here who can speak Russian? - The pope promises the liberation of' Soviet Russia - Mystical conditioning of Catholicism for the outbreak of an atomic conflict - President Truman's despairing comment.

Chapter 7
The Men Behind the Vietnamese War.
Politicians, Generals, and Prelates and their Selection of the "Savior of Vietnam."

The U.S. and 400,000 tons of war material - The fateful compromise of the 17th Parallel - Joint Vatican-U.S. Asian strategy - Catholic anti-communist crusade, McCarthy and Dulles - A cardinal as a linchpin between Washington and Rome - J.F. Kennedy and the Catholic lobby - U.S. preparation for intervention in Vietnam - The U.S. signs the fatal Vietnam agreement with France - The U.S. takes over military duties in South Vietnam - Foster-child of the Washington-Vatican sponsorship of South Vietnam - A would-be Catholic monk for an American grey eminence - Diem's messiah-like complex - Diem becomes the premier of South Vietnam.

Chapter 8
The Virgin Mary Goes South.
The Catholic Imponderable in the Escalation of the Vietnamese War.

Diem begins to create a Catholic administration - Diem refuses to hold elections as commanded by the Geneva Agreement - Diem's refusal is supported by the U.S. and the Vatican - The plan for the mass dislocation from the North - The

Catholics of North Vietnam, a state within a state - The communist leader of North Vietnam appoints a Catholic bishop to his government - Catholics want preferential treatment - Scheme for mass exodus of Northern Catholics toward South Vietnam - "Why has the Virgin Mary left the North?" - Catholic mass evacuation from North Vietnam - Results of the Catholic-CIA - Diem propaganda campaign - Catholic priests as Diem's agents - A personal message to Eisenhower - The Seventh Fleet is sent to help Diem - Flight for Freedom with the American Navy - The pope's representatives meet the first refugees - Humbug fanfare from Washington - The greatest phony refugee campaign promoted by the CIA and the Vatican.

Chapter 9
The Pius-Spellman-Dulles Secret Scheme.
The U.S. Taxpayer Finances the Creation of a "Catholic Dictatorship" in South Vietnam.

The preparation for a massive Catholic community in South Vietnam - The setting up of a model Catholic state - The U.S. Catholic lobby begins to milk the U.S. taxpayer to help Diem - 40 million dollars to resettle the Catholics from North Vietnam - State officials and Catholic priests - U.S. aid, "to Catholics only" - Mobile Catholic unit to defend Christendom - A rural

Catholic militia - Rapid Catholicization of South Vietnam - Catholics to the top - Become a Catholic for a quick promotion - Mishandling of U.S. aid to Vietnam - Buddhists persuaded to become Catholics - A top U.S. general becomes a Catholic - Discrimination against non-Catholics - The strengthening of Catholics from the communist North.

Chapter 10
The Promotion of Catholic Totalitarianism.
"Individuals Considered Dangerous May Be Confined to a Concentration Camp."

Discrimination against non-Catholic religions - Bribes, threats, agents and bitterness - Battles, riots and arrest of members of "hostile" religions - Further consolidation of the Catholic presence - Diem is given "dictatorial" power - Executive orders for concentration camps - American advisors support the new measures - Buddhists arrested without warrants - Interrogation, deportation, and torture of Buddhists - "Open" detention camps - Massacre and mass elimination of Buddhists - Buddhists become Catholic to save their lives.

Chapter 11
Consolidation of Terrorism
Anti-Protestant Legislation - Detention, Arrests,

Tortures and Executions.

Catholic totalitarianism for a model Catholic state - Diem and the pope's teaching - The Church should NOT be separated from the state - Refusal of license to preach - A Catholic state cannot tolerate Protestant dissidents - Blue print for the elimination of Protestantism - Catholic education for a Catholic state - South Vietnam built upon the social doctrines of ten popes - "It is an error to believe the Catholic Church has not the power of using force" - The cult of personalism - Diem's American "civil advisors" send gloomy reports to Washington - Altars and shrines for President Diem - Catholic "commando squads" of South Vietnam trained at Michigan University - Identification cards for dissident Catholics - Arrests and executions of Buddhist rebels - 24,000 wounded and 80,000 executed - 200, 000 Buddhists demonstrate in Saigon - Diem decides to eliminate the religion of the majority.

Chapter 12
A CIA Spy Plane Cancels a Summit Meeting
The Cardinal Spellman War Replaces the "Preventive War" Planned by the Dulles Brothers and Pope Pius XII.

The two partners and their global objectives -

Soviet Russia invades Hungary - Impending
outbreak of World War III - The true foreign
policy makers of the U.S. - The CIA promotion
of American foreign policies - Collapse of the
American-Russian summit meeting - The CIA
and the spy plane - On the brink of atomic
warfare "three times" - The U.S. threatens to use
atomic weapons - The Church prays for "the
liberation" - The "third" secret of the Virgin of
Fatima - The Pope faints with "horror" - He calls
for a war "of effective self-defense" -
Communist expansion in Europe and Southeast
Asia.

Chapter 13
The Vatican Attempts to Prevent Peace
*Pope John XXIII Rejects Geneva Agreement
While a U.S. Catholic President Goes for
"Unlimited Commitment."*

The Viet-Minh upsets the Catholic Church - The
Geneva Agreement is anathema for the Vatican -
Why the Vatican encouraged the U.S. to
intervene in Vietnam - Why Diem refused to
hold a 'free' election - Why North Vietnam
wanted the "free" election" - What an American
senator has to say about it - The cardinal who
flew in American military aircraft - American
troops the "soldiers of Christ" - Vietnam is
consecrated to the Virgin Mary - The Pope

creates an archdiocese in communist Vietnam - Pope John XXIII - ecumenism-versus-realism - The Vietnamese Catholic Mafia and the three brothers - Kennedy escalates the war - "Unlimited "commitment in Vietnam.

Chapter 14
Religious Persecutions and Suicides by Fire
World Opinion Forces U.S. to "Deplore Repressive Actions" of Diem.

The Catholic minority and the Buddhists - The sectarian volcano bursts out into the open - The Vatican flag in a Buddhist city - Celebration for Buddha's birthday forbidden - The giant gong of Xa Loi Pagoda - The Buddhists burn a Catholic village - The monk's message - Suicides by fire - Mass demonstration against Diem - Orders to close all pagodas - Buddhists killed by the Diem police - Buddhist students arrested and tortured - Refuge in the American embassy - The Americans are shocked at Diem's ruthlessness - The U.S. "deplores repressive actions" - The Catholic-CIA-Diem lobby minimize the Buddhist agitations.

Chapter 15
End of the Catholic Dictatorship
Assassinations of Two Catholic Presidents.

Why the American embassy was against Diem's appointment - A disastrous choice - Kennedy's double dilemma - Diem's religious political priorities - Catholic dictatorships of Croatia and Vietnam compared - Diem and Pavelich's main objectives - Diem's religious operations endanger the U.S. war efforts in Vietnam - Buddhist deserters leave the Vietnamese army - Steps to avoid the disintegration of the army - American subsidies to Vietnam are suspended - CIA chief recalled - A free hand for a "Coup" against Diem - Diem and his brother are shot to death - President Kennedy is killed - Ten additional years of Vietnamese war - The final price, 58,000 young American lives.

Chapter 16
Catholic Expansionism in Southeast Asia in the 19th Century
Historical Background of the U.S. War of Vietnam.

Catholic elites with a Buddhist background - The brothers Diem, inheritors of ancient Catholic exclusiveness - Stepping stones to the Catholic conquest of Indo-China - The Emperor Thieu Tri and the revolt of 1843 - French gunboats and Catholic emissaries - The 1862 "Friendship" imposed upon Vietnam - Friars, nuns, and their civil and military protectors -

Massive Catholic conversions to the "true church" - The Catholicization of French Vietnam during the last century.

Chapter 17
Early History of Catholic Power in Siam and China
Characteristic Precedents of Repression.

The French East India Company and the missionaries - The conversion to Catholicism of a Siamese king - Catholic discrimination against Buddhists - Ghastly deeds of a Catholic Mafia in Siam - Catholic and Frenchmen expelled and executed - End of the Vatican bid for the control of Siam - Siam forbids all Catholics for a century and a half - The Empress of China who became a Catholic - Empress Helena sends a mission to the pope - The Empress and the Jesuits plan to make China Catholic - Rebellion of the Mandarins - The end of a dream for a Catholic China.

Chapter 18
History of Catholic Aggressiveness in Japan
Conversions, Rebellions, Political Unrest and Civil War

Catholic missionaries welcomed to Japan in the 16th century - Japanese rulers, protectors of the

254

Catholic Church - The Catholic Church begins to meddle in Japanese politics - Japanese Catholics fight the authorities - Civil unrest and civil war promoted by the Church - Catholic sieges and battles - Catholic persecutions in Kyoto and Osaka - Battles between the Jesuits, Franciscans and the Japanese Catholics - The Spanish captain and the Japanese ruler of Hideyoshi - Imperial ban against all Catholics - The Catholics of Japan take up arms against the Japanese government - The Jesuits lead an army of 30,000 Japanese Catholics against the Japanese rulers - The murder by the Catholics of the Governor of Shimbara - Bloody battles between Catholics and Buddhists - The Dutch help the Japanese to fight the Catholics - The Edict: All Christians forbidden to enter Japan for 250 years.

Chapter 19
Creation of a Dangerous Alliance
Retrospective Assessment of the Preliminaries of the U.S.-Vietnamese War.

The formula that worked in the past and which still works in the present - The "Cold War," the U.S. and the Vatican - U.S.-Vatican dual fear of a common enemy - Pope Pius XII, the Dulles brothers and Cardinal Spellman - Power of the Catholic lobby in the U.S. - The secret

255

ambassador of the State Department and the pope - Messages by word of mouth only - The trio which helped the U.S. into the war in Vietnam.

Chapter 20
The Two Catholic Presidents and a Revolutionary Pope
The Collapse of the U.S.-Vatican Grand Strategy in Vietnam.

A cardinal, two brothers and Eisenhower - The prophecies of St. Malachy - The expectations of the first "American Pope" - Rift between two Catholic presidents - Politics before religion for Kennedy - Kennedy's dilemma - The election of a revolutionary pope and the shock at the State Department - The crash of the U.S.-Vatican anti-communist crusade - Pope John XXIII scolds President Diem - The Buddhist delegation goes to the Vatican - President Diem begins to endanger the U.S. war operations in Vietnam - Second thoughts in Washington - The step by step slide towards the Vietnamese precipice - President Kennedy and his desperate ambassadors - The final decision - The end of Diem and his brother.

Chapter 21
Secret Deal Between the Pope and the

Communists of North Vietnam.
The Vatican Prepares for a United Marxist Vietnam.

The pope and Ho Chi Minh - Relenting of Vatican hostility toward North Vietnam - Pope John XXIII consecrates a united Vietnam to the Virgin Mary - Disapproval of the pope's dedication - Reaction of Cardinal Spellman and the Catholic lobby of the U.S. - The Vatican takes the first steps for the abandonment of the U.S. in Vietnam - Catholic mass exodus of emigrants from the North - Political implications - Ho Chi Minh outfoxes the pope.

Chapter 22
The Final Disaster
Disintegration of the Vietnam-U.S. Partnership in Vietnam.

Calamitous significance of the Pope John-Ho Chi Minh secret agreement - Their use of religion to attain political objectives The Virgin Mary to the help of a united Marxist Vietnam - The pattern of religious political exploitation - U.S. military escalation and the pope's "wind of change" - Secret cooperation between the Vatican and Vietnamese Marxism - The Catholic Church withdraws from the war in Vietnam - Adverse effects of the Vatican Moscow alliance on the war in Vietnam-The end of an American nightmare.

Jason read a document form Kevin Quinn to the audience.

During the campaign for President Joe Kennedy had told De West Hooker that one of the long-term aims of the Kennedy dynasty would be the destruction of what Joe Kennedy referred to as **"the Rothschild dominated Federal Reserve."** John F. Kennedy had already taken steps to get rid of the Federal Reserve, by printing 50 billion dollars in silver certificates, which were interest free. He planned to use this money to pay off the national debt and to free the American people from the control of the Illuminati Banksters. If the U.S Government would print its own money interest free like the Constitution says they should be doing, the national debt would be zero, and all taxes could be eliminated. The average American would have twice as much as money to live on. If our government would print their own money interest free, like President Andrew Jackson, President Abraham Lincoln, and President John F. Kennedy, have done in the past, the national debt would no longer be an issue, and taxes would be gone, and the average American could have very little, if any, debt. History shows President Kennedy was assassinated within a few months of issuing silver backed interest free United States Notes.

I think it's pretty obvious, with all the information that we have today, that the whole thing was a planed conspiracy, and the mechanism of it came out of the allegiance between the Banksters, the Military industrial complex, the CIA, the web of Cuban exiles and the Mafia. They already had an assassination apparatus set up for killing Castro, they just decided to switch their targets, and kill Kennedy instead."

Upon his death, President Johnson immediately expanded the war in Vietnam and replaced the United States interest free Notes with worthless Federal Reserve Notes. And Two Million Six Hundred thousand American men ended up fighting during the 10 years that our troops were in Viet Nam, and 58,000 men died and three times that many were wounded. And the U.S Government spent 570 billion dollars on the War which put our country deeper in debt to the Banks. And more bombs were dropped on Viet Nam than all the bombs dropped during World War II, killing millions of innocent civilians in the process.

If President Kennedy had lived and continued printing United States silver certificates interest free, the trillions of dollars in taxes that we are now paying to the Federal Reserve Banksters every years, which is a crown corporation owned by the Bank of England, which is owned by the Bank of Rome, just to pay the interest on the money that our government has borrowed, would have remained in the hands of the American people.

Mr. Benjamin McCarthy said,
"Fred Litwin summarized about the JFK assassination conspiracy as following."

.1. The autopsy x-rays and photos of the Kennedy autopsy have been forged 2. Backyard photos of Oswald holding his Mannlicher-Carcano rifle were forged.	
EVIDENCES	Numerous pieces of evidence have been tampered with which "points clearly to a conspiracy by elements within the government to cover up the origins of the assassination."[11]
MURDER	Witnesses are still dying of strange circumstances.
PLANTING OF EVIDENCE	1. Oswald's Mannlicher-Carcano rifle was planted in the TSBD after a Mauser was found. 2. The palm print of Oswald was planted.

	3. The Hidell identification was planted on Oswald 4. CE399 was planted at Parkland Hospital.
MULTIPLE ASSASSINS	Assassins can be seen in various pictures and films of the assassination. Some conspiracy theorists feel there are up to five assassins at work in Dealey Plaza.
POLICE COMPLICITY	The Dallas police, besides being sloppy, helped plant evidence and hide evidence of conspiracy.
EVIDENCE DESTRUCTION	Several bullets that were found have been destroyed.
IMPERSONATION	A second Oswald roamed Dallas and Mexico City.
BODY ALTERATION	1. JFK's corpse was switched/ altered before the autopsy. 2. Oswald's body was

	switched.

Professor Nguyen asked the group to make a note,

"I'd like you all make an underline of the Multiple JFK Assassins: "Assassins can be seen in various pictures and films of the assassination. Some conspiracy theorists feel there are up to five assassins at work in Dealey Plaza on November 22, 1963".

"What is your intention on this matter, Sir?" Senate of State Robert McCarthy questioned

"For two pertinent reasons," Professor Nguyen continued, "Firstly, At least five assassins involved in the murder of President Kennedy-therefore; the Single Bullet Theory has been rejected; so was the theory of the driver of JFK motorcade fired the second shot....The purpose of multiple killers, multiple fires, and multiple shots/wounds....so we forget the most important culprit of this horrible crime."

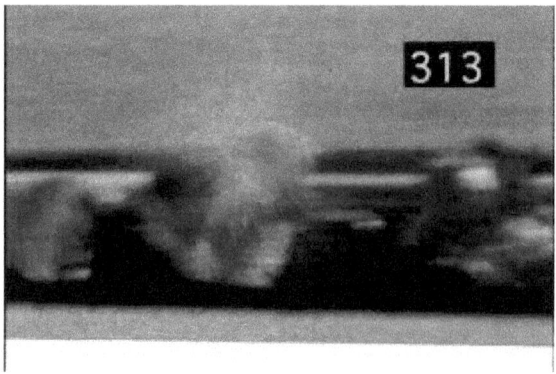

"Secondly," Dr. Helen Augier McCarthy joined the conversation, "May I have the permission to say this part, Professor Nguyen?"

"Of course, please." Professor Nguyen responded with a smile

"Thank you. All of the shots and wounds on the body of President Kennedy were not able to kill him," Dr. Helen A. McCarthy explained," Do you remember the report of Dr. Salyer that the President was breathing as he arrived at Parkland Emergency Room, but his condition was hopeless as most parts of his brain were blown off?"

"What do you mean Doctor?" Mrs. Kim Tran asked

"All of the shots and wounds from multiple assassins were only able to turn the President into an invalid, vegetative state, but he would have been survived," Dr. Helen A. McCarthy kept on," The Fatal Shot in the head was the one that definitely finished President Kennedy's life; no way, no one could do anything about that condition, even at our advanced medical technology now.

The cause of *"Death Certificate"* was filed early that afternoon by Dr. Robert Mc Clelland, before the Federal government could begin to cover up the true facts, with lies and disinformation. Dr. Mc Clelland wrote on the Death Certificate: *"The cause of death was due to massive head and brain injury from a gunshot wound of the left temple."* Looking down at the President's body the gunshot wound would be on the left side, but it was actually above the right eye, on the President's **right temple.**

"Mr. Benjamin McCarthy, please-your turn." Mr. Tran said

Mr. McCarthy said,

"Thank you very much, Mr. Tran. Now, please let me go on with my part since we still haven't seen the fatal shot yet."

"Continue, Sir" The audience said

6. Jacqueline Bouvier was a C.I.A. agent assigned to infiltrate the Kennedy clan as they moved up in political circles. Here's an excerpt from an online biography of Jackie (among others) that cites the fact that she did work for the C.I.A.! "Jackie attended boarding schools and then went off to Vassar. After two years, though, she got tired of it and spent her junior year studying at the Sorbonne in Paris. When she got back to the US she did not want to go back to Vassar, so she enrolled in George Washington University in Washington, DC, graduating in 1951. She took a job at the CIA and in January of 1952 went to work at a Washington newspaper, where she was a photographer. During an assignment she met U.S. Senator John F. Kennedy . They were married on September 12, 1953.

"Enclosed are excerpt from Bill O'Reilley" Dennis said

The orders to kill JFK came from people who control central banking in the US through their fraudulent Federal Reserve System. They are the most ruthless people. They protect the biggest source of power which is the control of money supply. JFK wanted to reduce or even eliminate their power. LBJ was their puppet. The man who represented them was John J. McCloy. He was the Boss of JFK assassination and also its cover-up because later he became a member of Warren Commission.

The biggest conspirators came from Pentagon because it has the biggest brute force with the nukes. The top conspirator was Curtis Lemay, 4-Star General in US Air Force. He made Edward Lansdale, 2-Star General in US Air Force, prepare and execute JFK assassination plan. US Secret Service provided the agents to do the dirty work for them. The top conspirator in Dallas was Henry Wade, Dallas County District Attorney. He had close contacts with John Connally, Texas Governor, and another top conspirator. Dallas Mayor Earle Cabell made Dallas Police participate in JFK assassination. Lloyd Bentsen, later US Senator from Texas, acted as the Paymaster of JFK assassination, by paying off the conspirators with money from the Federal Reserve System. Earl Warren from US Supreme Court was the top conspirator on the legal side of JFK assassination. The Kennedys and U S Congress quickly received offers they could not refuse and all participated in the cover-up of JFK assassination by playing dumb to the public in America and around the world. They wanted to make public pictures of JFK's brains blowing out in a spectacular way and to be able to publicly show the pictures to all politicians they wanted to control.

white gloved hand

1.

It is extremely difficult to blow out the brains of US President in public and on film, and get away with this. No sniper would achieve a spectacular result of blowing brains out with sufficient reliability. They needed somebody close to JFK, who would never be suspected by the common people. They were masters of human psychology. They knew that the bigger the lie the more people would believe the lie. Jackie used two guns. She used a dart gun to inject a chemical agent into JFK's left thigh in order to incapacitate him first. Then about 7 seconds later, she used a firearm installed inside her handbag to shoot a special bullet between JFK's jaw and his neck. Nobody would suspect Jackie holding her handbag close to her chest.

Jackieiskillerqueen.blogspot.com/
"Reverse Engineering of JFK
Assassination During the assassination, gun
smoke rose from Jackie's position, at an angle
perfectly has achieved: through JFK's right

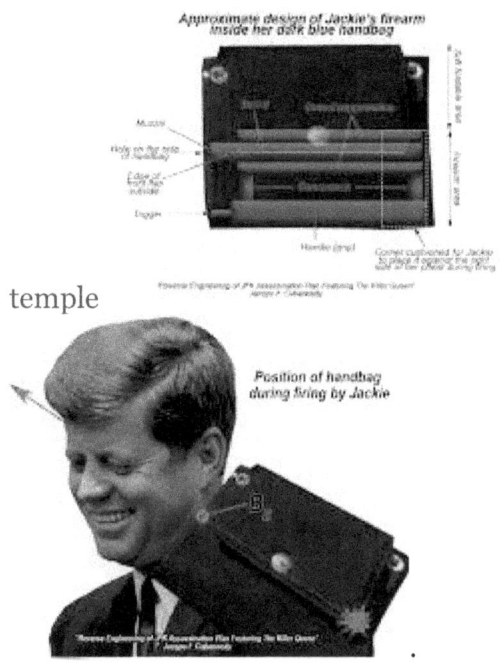

temple

www.youtube.com/watch?v=L6vWgMDq6tk
"How could it be possible…" Mrs. Elizabeth
McCarthy sheepishly replied while others were
speechless.
"Mrs. Jacqueline Kennedy …?" Mr. Tran
inquired perplexedly

Bullet trajectory?

www.theweek.co.uk/.../**jfk**.../who-**killed-jfk**-51-years-of-consp

The report suggested that JFK could have survived after the neck wound that caused by the first shot, but not by the brain damage by the second shot-the fatal one: the bullet to the head that blew part of his brain away - From the Medical view point, it says, "President Kennedy was alive when he arrived at Parkland Hospital," it says, "The doctors observed that he had a heart beat and was making some respiratory efforts. But his condition was hopeless, and the extraordinary works of the doctors to save him could not help but have been unavailing."

REPORTS OF LEFT SIDE HEAD WOUND

There is evidence of an entry wound to the left side of the President's head -- the side on which Jackie was located. Several eyewitnesses, including doctors and other medical personnel, a priest giving last rites, and an eye witness at Dealey Plaza, reported seeing a wound of the left temple. This is compatible with Jackie having fired a shot from a small caliber hand gun at close range to her husband's head. The Zapruder frames of that moment show her head so close to her husband's that, if there was a shot to the left side of JFK's head, it would be nearly impossible to execute from any distance away without striking the First Lady. In addition, no gunshots were reported being seen from the left side of Dealey Plaza where the crowd was sparser and there less places for a gunman to hide. Please zero in on Jackie beginning at the point JFK grabs his throat and look for 5 CLUES:

1. She leans into him but does not put an arm around him as would be a more natural response. Instead, she keeps her hands out of camera range by contorting her arms rather awkwardly, perhaps conscious of the possibility that there are cameras on both sides of the street. Photos and film taken from the left side of the car also do not show exactly what she's doing with her right hand. It appears she's using her left hand to steady his chin for a clean shot to the left side of his head.

2. She seems more focused on Gov. Connally's words to her than on her husband's condition. Could Connally possibly be telling her it's time to "do it"? Or perhaps

he's uttering the trigger words that will elicit a previously induced hypnotic suggestion.

3. At point of head impact, white smoke moves upward on LEFT SIDE of JFK's head. This white wisp of smoke or vapor is visible even in photos and film taken from the other side of the car. Here's a slow motion clip of just the head shot that clearly shows white smoke before the blood splatter. A bullet doesn't cause smoke; the barrel of a gun does. There are various reports (here's one) that indicate that the gunshot entry wound was on the left side of JFK's head; exit wound to the right front. One of the doctors at Parkland, Dr. Jenkins, testified to the Warren Commission that he had discovered what appeared to be a bullet wound to the "left temporal region" "right above the zygomatic bone" in the hairline of the President's head. The theory that the bodies of J.D. Tippit (the Dallas police officer reported to have been shot by Oswald after the assassination) and JFK were switched in order to produce autopsy photos and x-rays closer to the false conclusions of the Warren Commission.

4. She quickly hides something (the gun?). In the still frames of the Zapruder film, it appears to me that there must be several frames missing between #326 and #327. Judging from the slow progression of the other still frames (It takes more than 60 frames to show Gov. Connally turning his head toward Jackie!), there's no conceivable way that Jackie's arm could have skipped

from an upright position to one pointing down in the space of one frame (1/18 of a second)! What do those responsible not want us to see? Or did the conspirators want to save themselves the trouble of having to obscure with black paint the right rear exit wound reported by both Dallas medical personnel and various witnesses?

5. Judging by the blood and brain spray exiting JFK's head, what kind of trajectory would the bullet have to travel? Isn't it more consistent with someone placing the muzzle near his left ear and firing upwards than it would be of a long-distance shooter firing from behind...or even from the front? There is an assassination researcher who puts forth the theory that there was a shooter in the trunk of the car! He is actually closer to the truth than other theorists because the intensity and trajectory of the shot indicates that it came from within the tight little circle of the car and those in it and around it. His conclusions support rather than deny mine. Then there's the testimony of photographer Hugh Betzner, who was in close proximity to the car at the time of the shooting. He stated, "I heard at least two shots fired and I saw what looked like a firecracker going off in the president's car." He also said, "I also remember seeing what looked like a nickel revolver in someone's hand in the President's car or somewhere immediately around his car."
Witness Austin L. Miller on the railroad bridge thought

the shots came from the Presidential limousine itself, and Senator Ralph Yarborough smelled gunpowder at street level following the assassination. There are experts who insist that the Zapruder film was altered and also that frames were removed; and these alterations seem aimed at obscuring the moment of the head shot. The final product still shows evidence of a shot from the front, so this alteration must, more importantly in the minds of the alterers, have been done to hide both the fact that the car was brought to a complete standstill for the execution of the head shot(s), and to hide the fact that Jackie's hand held a gun. This video has more details about the obvious alterations to the Zapruder film and an interview with a French journalist who claims he has seen an unedited copy of the film bought from Zapruder by H. L. Hunt just hours after the assassination. Of interest to me especially is the fact that this journalist claims inside information that there were two head shots fired almost simultaneously from two different directions. Another fact that is pointed out in the video is that the "kill zone" on Elm Street was marked with three yellow stripes painted on the curb at intervals, which can be seen in the Zapruder film (see one here) and also still remain faintly visible to this day in Dallas. The role of the umbrella man is also covered.

The sequence of events that took our President's life was based on observation of the Zapruder film:

1. JFK was shot in the throat from the front, possibly by a bullet or fragment of a bullet that went through the windshield of the car. Contrary to popular belief, Gov. Connally was not wounded until AFTER the fatal head shot (as evidenced by the fact that he is able to turn his body around and toward Jackie in order to speak to her). Note: If you click on the link to the article regarding Gov. Connally's wounds, notice how clearly the white smoke is visible in the Zapruder frames he posts.

2. One or more bullets from the rear were fired at some point during the sequence, causing JFK's back entrance wound (which was shallow probably due to his heavy back corset-like brace), and the injuries to Gov. Connally.

3. Jackie maneuvers herself into position in order to deliver a head shot to enter from the left in JFK's hairline near his ear and upward, but she hesitates a few seconds too long, forcing the sniper hidden on the grassy knoll to respond with a head shot of his own (occurring at frame #326). (Robert D. Morningstar writes regarding a JFK autopsy photo in this article that, "This indicates to us that the bullet causing this wound would have to have passed through an already open frontal head wound without having struck frontal or temporal bone upon entry which would have resulted in its deformation or early fragmentation."). This sniper's shot nearly coincided perfectly with Jackie's shot, and

the startling realization that rifle shots were coming in her direction, coupled with the horror of her mortally wounded husband falling toward her and not away from her, caused her to flee away from their source and towards the rear of the automobile seeking the protective arms of her personal Secret Service agent, Clint Hill. (Jackie almost roughly pushes JFK's body aside as she swiftly climbs out onto the trunk of the car reportedly to retrieve some mysterious object. The official story that she was trying to save brain matter or a piece of skull is suspect as the Zapruder film clearly shows that the trunk area is still in pristine condition. (Note: I have to admit that still shots of the trunk area at this JFK Lancer site seem to show some sort of debris.) I believe that she looks like she grabbed her bullet casing -- on the boot of the car because she's reaching for the protruding "buttons" about halfway to the Secret Service handles in order to hold on to something while she makes her escape. Frame 422-455 was tempered. Note: Kitty Kelley's unauthorized biography, "Jackie Oh!" ignores the standard media hype and simply states that Jackie was trying to "flee." It's really immaterial whether Jackie was grabbing for a piece of skull and/or brain matter, or fleeing a possible shot from a sniper, as the evidence for her involvement in the murder is enough to render it so. Who knows, maybe she was afraid the piece of brain she is said to have retrieved contained incriminating bullet fragments from her gun and not the official "murder weapon."

1.

The Warren Commission Testimony (from
Volume Five of the special hearings) where Mrs.
Jacqueline Kennedy said:"*You know, then,
there were pictures later of me climbing out the
back, but I don't remember that at all.*"
Jacqueline Testimony from original version),
op. cit., p. 16:
"Why didn't she remember?" Mrs. Kim Tran
asked
"I think she was under the influence of some
substance used by the MKULTRA, the
MONARCH." Dr. Helen Augier McCarthy said

The name MONARCH is not necessarily defined
within the context of royal nobility, but rather refers
to the ***monarch butterfly***. When a person is
undergoing trauma induced by electroshock, a

feeling of light-headedness is evidenced; as if one is floating or fluttering like a butterfly. There is also a symbolic representation pertaining to the transformation or metamorphosis of this beautiful insect: from a caterpillar to a cocoon (dormancy, inactivity), to a butterfly (new creation) which will return to its point of origin. Such is the migratory pattern that makes this species unique.

Occulted symbolism may give additional insight into the true meaning Psyche is the word for both "soul" and "butterfly" coming from the *belief that human souls become butterflies* while searching for a new reincarnation.

Some ancient mystical groups, such as the Gnostics, saw the *butterfly as a symbol of corrupt flesh*. The *"Angel of Death"* – Mengele- in Gnostic art portrayed an angel was crushing the butterfly. A marionette is a puppet that is attached to strings and is controlled by the puppet master, hence MONARCH programming is also referred to as the *"Marionette Syndrome."* "Imperial Conditioning" is another term used, while some mental health therapists know it as *"Conditioned Stimulus Response Sequences."*

- The nearly simultaneous head shots coming from two different directions - one close to the head from the left and the other traveling a distance from the right front - explain the conflicting bodily movements indicating JFK's physical reaction to the two head injuries. This video made by Bob Harris explores evidence that there were two nearly simultaneous head shots from different directions. David Lifton, in "Best Evidence: Disguise and Deception in the Assassination of John F. Kennedy," reports being first shocked and then troubled when it's pointed out to him that his "back and to the left" phenomena noted on the Zapruder film in Frame #313 is immediately preceded by a forward motion in #312. My thesis that JFK was shot at close range from the left side and slightly towards the back of his head would account for this motion. David Lifton's "Case for Three Assassins" theory is made more credible by the realization that Jackie was one of the shooters from the "rear," albeit, a very close rear.

"Jackie did it" site under "Left Head Wound." http://jackieiskillerqueen.blogspot.com/ "Kennedy . . . was murdered at Dallas on November 22, 1963. . . . The killing shot may also came from the driver of the President's Limousine, a CIA [Secret Service] agent who shot Kennedy in the head with a special weapon developed by the CIA. If you look at the original [Zapruder] film of the assassination in slow motion and watch the driver, then you can clearly see that he turns around with a gun in his hand, shoots, and the back of Kennedy's head bursts. The films shown in most Western

countries [JFK, Director's Cut] have the driver cut out . . . The bullet, too, was a CIA special that only exploded after entering the body, and thus annihilated Kennedy's brain [Since no Chief Executive has been killed with a rifle in over two hundred years, a maxim of all Jesuit-authored assassinations when using a firearm is the killing shot must be at a point-blank range like Presidents Lincoln, Garfield and McKinley as well as Franz Ferdinand at Sarajevo.] . . . All the witnesses of the conspiracy were either killed or died of fast-growing cancer [viral cell mutations created by the Jesuit General's CIA] that they had injected — the deadly marksman in the car [the driver, Navy Seal William Greer] three weeks after the deed, for example."
Jan van Helsing, 1995
Swiss Historian Secret Societies and Their Power in the 20th Century.

"Between seven and ten shots were fired by four different assassins . . . but Lee Harvey Oswald never fired a single round. Two of the shooters were CIA contract agents. Two were actually picked up by the cops and released, and another one flew out of Dallas untouched. Of the four, I was personally acquainted with three of them . . . Charles Harrelson . . . and he was capable of killing anybody; . . . Frank Sturgis; . . . and Charles Rogers (alias Carlos Montoya)." Hugh Huggins (alias Hugh Howell), 1993 Joe Kennedy's CIA "Chameleon"

Assassin JFK: Breaking the Silence. As St. Peter was given the power of punishing with temporal punishments and even with death for the correction and example of others . . . even so the Pope can depose the [Holy Roman] emperor and give his empire to another, if he does not defend the [Pope's] Church." Antonio Sanitarily, 1626 Italian Jesuit.

"Spellman . . . the Military Vicar of the American armed forces . . . was also the unofficial link between the Pope and John Foster Dulles, the U.S. Secretary of State [whose son, Avery Dulles, is a Jesuit] and, therefore, the Secretary's brother Allen, head of the CIA . . . The Catholic Church in the USA [controlled by the Jesuit Order] is a force in the Pentagon, a secret agent in the FBI and the . . . prime mover of . . . the Central Intelligence Agency."

And who was the Director of the CIA in 1963? It was Knight of Malta John A. McCone. Prior to that McCone had been a defense contractor who had formerly headed the Atomic Energy Commission. Later in 1970, he was a board member of International Telephone & Telegraph Company (IT&T) while remaining a CIA consultant. Marchetti tells us: (ITT board member who later admitted to a Senate investigative committee that he had played the key role in bringing together CIA and ITT officials was John McCone, director of the CIA during the

Kennedy administration and in 1970, a CIA consultant.) Cardinal Spellman's soldier and Director of the CIA, John A. McCone, participated in the Kennedy Assassination.

"Let's read the following, shall we?" Mr. McCarthy passed the paper to the audience.

More shocking discoveries follow below. These include, Jackie pleading with family friend CIA kingpin Allen Dulles to join the CIA, Dulles orchestrating the JFK assassination and cover-up, the faked death of Oswald, the use of a JFK body double- JD Tippit- at Parkland Hospital, and Jackie's role in the death of Robert Kennedy. Twelve key points, as an initial summary of my other findings:

1) In a letter to Vogue Magazine dated May 7th 1951, Jackie mentioned her "special job on a certain project for the CIA" in late 1951. Several authors state that she was directly recruited into the CIA by family friend Allen Dulles in early 1951. The biography "Dreaming in French" has most detailed account of this, see pages 48-54...

2) During the "special job" period (late 1951) CIA Operation Mockingbird journalist/agent Charles Bartlett determinedly introduced Jackie to JFK, and the Kennedy family. Jackie then seduced, married, and spicd on JFK, who the CIA knew was a likely future president, and a threat to their corrupt activities.

3) Psychopaths often crave excitement, are cool under pressure, and do not mind killing people. These traits are common amongst spies. According to her letter to Vogue, Jackie "pleaded" to join the CIA and become a spy. She was determined to avoid becoming a bored housewife.

4) Oswald was another CIA agent/spy – part of the CIA's fake defector program, and handled by CIA agent George De Mohrenschildt in Dallas. The Oswald family's landlady, Ruth Paine was a friend of Allen Dulles (via his mistress Mary Bancroft). Paine helped Oswald get a job in the Book Depository.

5) Dulles hated JFK and RFK because they blamed him for the Bay Of Pigs fiasco, and forced his retirement as CIA Director – but not until November 1961 – Dulles had seven months in office to initiate the conspiracy to assassinate the President.

6) Dulles was a "regime change specialist", and controlled the assassin (Jackie), the patsy (Oswald), the star witness (Ruth Paine), the U.S. national media (via Operation Mockingbird), and the Warren Commission cover-up. Forget "Limited Hangout Lyndon" Johnson, who merely assisted.

7) According to his sister Eleanor, Dulles was impulsive, reckless, and vengeful – psychopathic traits. In 1965, when discussing the "highlights" of his murderous career, Allen Dulles said of JFK, "that little Kennedy, thought he was God".

8) Dulles even claimed/hallmarked the assassination – the original spelling of the surname

Dulles is Dallas.

9) A giant pyramid now looms over the spot where JFK was murdered, in highly Masonic Dealey Plaza. Masons dominated all of the groups involved in the assassination (CIA, FBI, Dallas police etc), and they like to hide their crimes, symbols, and power, in plain sight.

Conspiracy expert and broadcaster Bill Cooper explains the Masonic assassination of JFK here. Bill Cooper was murdered in November 2001, and replaced with controlled opposition Masons Alex Jones and David Icke. Cooper was described as "the most dangerous radio host in America", by notorious Mason Bill Clinton.

10) Many eyewitnesses reported gun fire/"firecrackers" inside the presidential limo on 11/22/1963. For countless reasons, I am convinced that this came from a gun held by Jackie, which she fired upwards, with the barrel behind JFK's left ear. Seconds earlier, she had pulled JFK's head down and towards her, to hide her right/gun hand during this fatal shot. Gun smoke rises above Jackie in the Zapruder footage (reflected on the trunk also): http://postimg.org/image/tdd0ci3z3/ Zapruder frames 310-320 enhanced slow motion.

No one ducks in the car until immediately before the final/fatal shot, despite numerous previous shots – which were to distract from Jackie. Everyone in the car, apart from JFK, was probably part of the plot.

Most of the close witnesses reported a right temple bullet exit wound on JFK's head, which corresponds with an upwards shot from behind his left ear, fired by Jackie. This is what the three main home movies of the assassination also show. Yet, staff at Parkland Hospital reported a large right rear head exit wound:

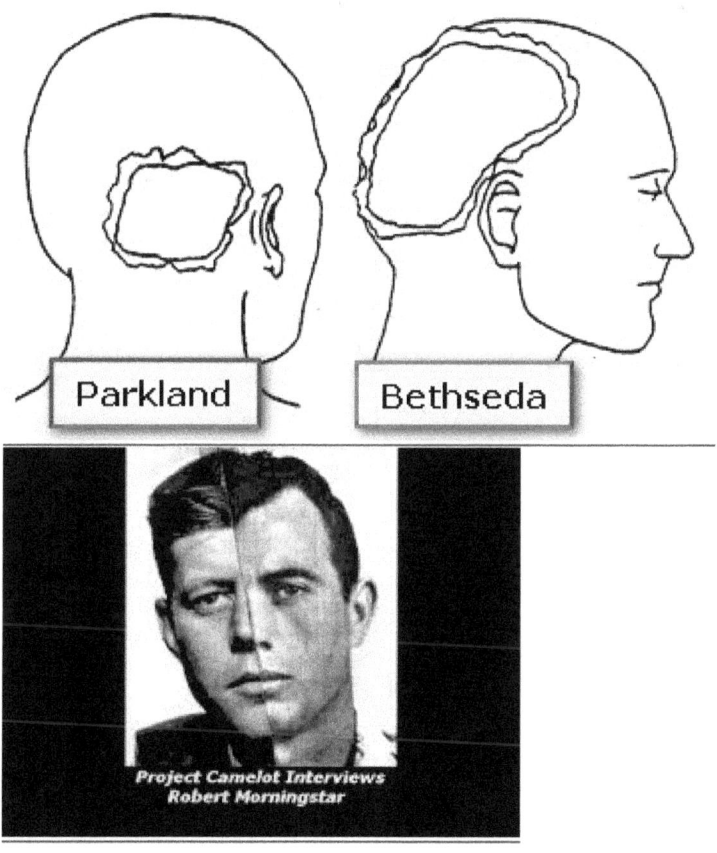

I suggest that the corpse of JFK lookalike policeman J.D. Tippit was substituted for JFK, on

the way to the hospital. This would explain why
Jackie covered "JFK's head" at Parkland, and the
corpse was wearing a different shirt.

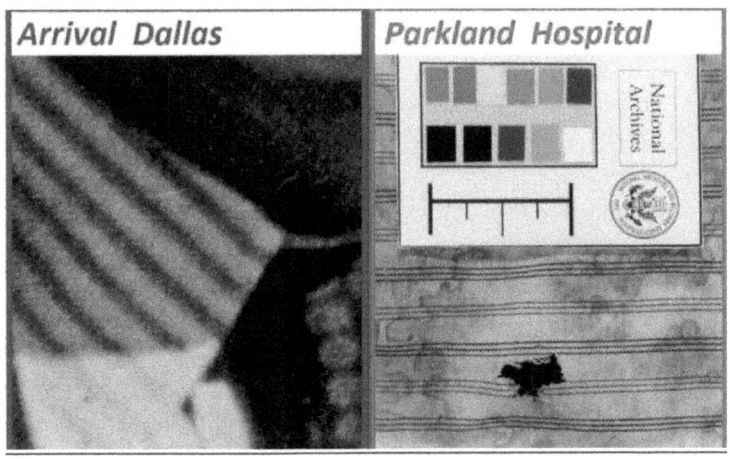

11) The assassination of Oswald appears staged and
fake – no gun smoke or blood was visible. Also,
Ruby was told when Oswald arrived in the
basement, and precisely when to jump out, by two
blasts on a car horn. And, the scene was strangely
quiet – the "journalists" and Oswald largely ignored
each other, for the first time.
12) Jackie went on to have an affair with/spy on
Robert F. Kennedy until he was also assassinated by
the CIA, shortly after vowing to investigate the
murder of his brother. On the night of the
assassination, Jackie flew into L.A., and persuaded
the family to switch off RFK's life-support
machine. RFK breathed unaided for several minutes

before dying – Jackie had guaranteed that he would not investigate her crimes.

A few concluding thoughts. Whilst in office JFK, and his advisors, had introduced policies to solve most of the problems which still face America, and many other nations.

These include, Executive Order 11110 – debt/interest free government money, tax cuts to stimulate the economy and thus increase tax revenues, an end to unnecessary foreign wars starting with Vietnam, the restraint of anti-democratic lobby groups, reducing organized crime, etc.

How these and other beneficial policies could, be introduced today? Satanist Freemasons murdered JFK to block such policies, and have ruled ever since. Therefore, the members of all secret societies need to be banned from public office, before democracy and prosperity can be restored.

This was also part of JFK's agenda, because he warned against secret societies, and secret oaths, in his "Secret Societies Speech". Freemasonry would soon collapse, if membership hindered rather than boosted careers.

Mr. McCarthy paused a minute as he changed the screen,

"Take a look at the Moorman's film- the image was taken from the left, while the Zapruder's film was from the right side; you have a better view of the hand gun."

1.

This video has more details about the obvious alterations to the Zapruder film and an interview with a French journalist who claims he has seen an unedited copy of the film bought from Zapruder by H. L. Hunt just hours after the assassination. Of interest to me especially is the fact that this journalist claims inside information that there were two head shots fired almost simultaneously from two different directions. Another fact that is pointed out in the video is that the "kill zone" on Elm Street was marked with three yellow stripes painted on the curb at intervals, which can be seen in the Zapruder film (see one here) and also still remain faintly visible to this day in Dallas. The role of the umbrella man is also covered.

The sequence of events that took our President's life was, in my opinion, and based on observation of the Zapruder film, as follows:

1. JFK was shot in the throat from the front, possibly by a bullet or fragment of a bullet that went through the windshield of the car. Contrary to popular belief, Gov. Connally was not wounded until AFTER the fatal head shot (as evidenced by the fact that he is able to turn his body around and toward Jackie in order to speak to her). Note: If you click on the link to the article regarding Gov. Connally's wounds, notice how clearly the white smoke is visible in the Zapruder frames he posts.)

2. One or more bullets from the rear were fired at some point during the sequence, causing JFK's back entrance wound (which was shallow probably due to his heavy back corset-like brace), and the injuries to Gov. Connally.

3. Jackie maneuvers herself into position in order to deliver a head shot to enter from the left in JFK's hairline near his ear and upward, but she hesitates a few seconds too long, forcing the sniper hidden on the grassy knoll to respond with a head shot of his own (occurring at frame #326). (Robert D. Morningstar writes regarding a JFK autopsy photo in this article that, "This indicates to us that the bullet causing this wound would have to have passed through an already open frontal head wound without having struck frontal or temporal bone upon

287

entry which would have resulted in its deformation or early fragmentation."). This sniper's shot nearly coincided perfectly with Jackie's shot, and the startling realization that rifle shots were coming in her direction, coupled with the horror of her mortally wounded husband falling toward her and not away from her, caused her to flee away from their source and towards the rear of the automobile seeking the protective arms of her personal Secret Service agent, Clint Hill. (Jackie almost roughly pushes JFK's body aside as she swiftly climbs out onto the trunk of the car reportedly to retrieve some mysterious object.

The official story that she was trying to save brain matter or a piece of skull is suspect as the Zapruder film clearly shows that the trunk area is still in pristine condition. (Note: I have to admit that still shots of the trunk area at this JFK Lancer site seem to show some sort of debris.)

I believe that she looks like she's trying to grab something -- her bullet casing? -- on the boot of the car because she's reaching for the protruding "buttons" about halfway to the Secret Service handles in order to hold on to something while she makes her escape.) Note: Kitty Kelley's unauthorized biography, "Jackie Oh!" ignores the standard media hype and simply states that Jackie was trying to "flee." (p. 230).

It's really immaterial whether Jackie was grabbing for a piece of skull and/or brain matter, or fleeing a possible shot from a sniper, as the evidence for her involvement in the murder is enough to render it so.

Who knows, maybe she was afraid the piece of brain she is said to have retrieved contained incriminating bullet fragments from her gun and not the official "murder weapon."

"According to Bill O'Reilley, we have this version of the assassination." Mr. McCarthy said.

Jackie's bullet was designed after B-Patrone bullet. The bullet contained about 50mg of White Phosphorus and a booster explosive like RDX. Inside JFK's head, the booster explosive ignited White Phosphorus and made it burn up to 5000° F. The bullet broke into razor-sharp metal fragments rotating at speeds up to 100,000 rpm and tearing JFK's jugular veins and arteries behind his right ear. The fragments exited through his right ear.   All people sitting in JFK limo, except JFK, were part of the conspiracy. The bystanders on both sides could not see Jackie's concealed firearm because their views were blocked by Jackie and JFK. The volume of Jackie's gunshot was reduced by a sound suppressor inside her handbag and drowned out by two police motorcycles accelerating very loudly just seconds before the gunshot. Dallas Police Department was part of the conspiracy.   The famous quote "Back, and to the Left" from **JFK** movie by Oliver Stone is very misleading. Before JFK's head bounces back toward Jackie, it bounces forward away from Jackie. However, it is only for about 40 milliseconds and only one frame shows it. You can't notice this by watching Zapruder film; you have to look at individual frames of Zapruder film.

The single best evidence is Zapruder frame 313. It shows a gunshot trail originating from Jackie's right hand, about ten inches below JFK's left ear. As the history proves, the sheep don't believe their own eyes and just follow their corrupt leaders. This means that the conspirators did not have to remove the incriminating gunshot trail in frame 313. Contrary to the official story, Jackie was not looking for pieces of JFK's brain or skull on the trunk. She did not even look at the trunk before jumping on it. Her first goal was to dispel your suspicions early about any firearms on her by showing you her front and back. JFK murder plan tried to exploit the weaknesses of human psychology. Jackie dropped her handbag (with the firearm inside) on the seat before jumping on the trunk. Her second goal was to invite Clint Hill on the trunk so that he could split open JFK's head in the tunnel.

All the other gunshot sounds, smokes, flashes, came from firecrackers. JFK murder planners planted firecracker operators, distracters, camera operators, and false witnesses at Dealey Plaza.

The media controlled by Parasitic Ethnic Group which includes the central bankers who ordered JFK assassination. They feed you all possible conspiracy theories to make you chase your own tail and waste your time. JFK killers are part of a global crime network. Many members of this network masquerade as college professors, scientists, technical experts, best-selling authors, media figures, political leaders, etc. They lie about everything. Since they have managed to hide their JFK secret for so long, imagine their other secrets that you do not know about.

However, it's estimated that close to a million people in the US and Europe know about Jackie's guilt. Her guilt found its way into fiction books, movies, songs, and fashion business, a long time ago. However, Jackie's guilt has been disguised with coded messages that normal audiences missed entirely.

Professor Nguyen said,
"May I continue?"
"Yes." The audience replied

4. The nearly simultaneous head shots coming from two different directions - one close to the head from the left and the other traveling a distance from the right front - explain the conflicting bodily movements indicating JFK's physical reaction to the two head injuries. (The head slightly forwarded at the first shot (Frame #312); but then quickly back

and to the left (Frame #313, and 314) after the incoming shot from the grassy knoll.) This video made by Bob Harris explores evidence that there were two nearly simultaneous head shots from different directions. David Lifton, in "Best Evidence: Disguise and Deception in the Assassination of John F. Kennedy," reports being first shocked and then troubled when it's pointed out to him that his "back and to the left" phenomena noted on the Zapruder film in Frame #313 is immediately preceded by a forward motion in #312. My thesis that JFK was shot at close range from the left side and slightly towards the back of his head would account for this motion. David Lifton's "Case for Three Assassins" theory is made more credible by the realization that Jackie was one of the shooters from the "rear," albeit, a very close rear..

"What is the motivation, please?" Mrs. Elizabeth McCarthy inquired.
"It's hard to believe that Mrs. Jacqueline Kennedy had a hidden face!" Dennis called out.
"Hold on, here are only hypotheses, you need to prove them to see if these assumptions might be acceptable in the 5% of reasonable of doubt." Jason reminded the group
Mr. McCarthy read on.
Although I mention "Jackie did it" under "Left Head Wound." I want to give it mention here as I feel much of it has merit to the discussion: http://jackieiskillerqueen.blogspot.com/ this is a fascinating reading.

Here's a preliminary list of possible MOTIVES as to why Jackie Kennedy would have committed this crime in conjunction with the political conspiracy to assassinate President Kennedy followed by a government cover-up:

JFK's indiscretions with other women started from the very beginning of their marriage. Jackie was fed up, and possibly planning to divorce him anyway, so when she learned of the conspiracy (through Onassis?) to assassinate him, she volunteered. It's reported in Peter Evan's book, *"Nemesis: The True Story of Aristotle Onassis, Jackie O, and the Love Triangle That Brought Down the Kennedys..."*, **She was in love with Aristotle Onassis** and did it at his behest with promises of a future life with all of the benefits millions of dollars can buy.   Jackie did vacation - without her husband – and against her husband's advice- on Ari's private yacht to recuperate from her baby's death. During this period (about three months) Jackie had an affair with Onassis before the assassination, and that the Kennedy marriage was in such shambles that divorce was almost inevitably. The Kennedys did not share the same hotel room in Texas the night before the assassination.

Aristotle Onassis and other **new world order** advocates took advantage of her post-traumatic stress syndrome following the sudden death of her baby in order to utilize **hypnosis and/or mind control MKUltra** techniques much like those used with Sirhan Sirhan. Evidence that links Onassis to the assassination of Bobby Kennedy has been brought forward also in Nemesis.

"According to these hypotheses," Mr. Benjamin McCarthy said, "Both Mrs. Jacqueline

Kennedy and Mr. Aristotle Onassis involved in the assassination of President Kennedy; sarcastically that Jackie only learned that Aristotle Onassis had a counter–spy CIA to assassinate both JFK and RFK after she married to the tycoon."

"It was a short marriage (1968–1975) and there was a lot of bitterness by the end." Mrs. Elizabeth McCarthy said

"Why did both Jacqueline Kennedy and Aristotle have dark sun glasses?" Mr. Kim Tran wondered at the photo.

Professor Nguyen had a secret smile,

"I'd like each person makes his/her own interpretation of Jacqueline and Aristotle's behavior. What did they think/plan behind those dark sun glasses? In the game of Poker, each player does not let other players know what cards you have in hand; each creates an ambiguous appearance to eliminate the opponents so you win the game."

"I got what you said, Sir." Jason replied, "John F. Kennedy and Robert Kennedy tried to indict Aristotle Onassis, Jacqueline involved in a plot against JFK through the Jesuits– planning to have a luxurious life with the ship magnate Aristotle Onassis…"

Senate of State Robert McCarthy added,

"Aristotle Onassis used CIA counter–spy to eliminate JFK and RFK. He paid the law makers in Greece to modify the marriage law so Jacqueline Kennedy Onassis could not inherit half of Aristotle Onassis' assets in the event of a divorce… the game went on

"They looked like two cobras." Dennis exclaimed

"Both of them were born in the year of the Snake, according to the Chinese calendar." Mrs. Kim Tran said

"The story of the three snakes?" An uneasy feeling ran across Dr. Helen Augier McCarthy's mind; she changed the subject,

"How did Jacqueline Kennedy get into the murder scheme of President Kennedy?"

Jacqueline Kennedy was **threatened** by the conspirators. Perhaps she was told that if she refused to cooperate and deal the fatal blow that would ensure her husband's death, there would be a bullet in it for her, or maybe harm to her children. They would have told her they planned to kill JFK anyway, so what difference would it make if she involved.

Mr. Benjamin McCarthy made a remark,

"The Jesuits from Vatican (www.seawapa.com) should be mentioned here, for I think this was the main reason Mrs. Jacqueline Kennedy accept to play the crucial role on November 22, 1963."

The assassination of President John F. Kennedy, ordered by the Jesuit General and executed by Pope Paul VI, was carried out by "the American Pope", Francis Cardinal

Spellman. Spellman, being the Archbishop of New York, was "the American Military Vicar" and therefore used his most obedient soldiers – certain Knights of Malta, Shriner Freemasons, Knights of Columbus and Mafia Dons – in carrying out his orders from Rome.

The single reason for the President's assassination was his interference with the purpose of the Jesuits' Fourteenth Amendment American Empire created in 1868. That purpose was to restore and maintain the worldwide Temporal (political) Power of that Jesuit Creation of 1870 – the "infallible" Pope. In resisting the Pope's Temporal Power, he threatened the monopoly of the Jesuits' Federal Reserve Bank by enacting Executive Order 11110 (4 June 1963) thereby injecting into the economy nearly five billion dollars (4.7) in interest-free "United States Notes", only to be recalled the day after his burial.

The President also attempted to break the foremost international intelligence arm of the Vatican's Jesuits – the Evil Central Intelligence Agency – "into a thousand pieces." In 1963 the CIA was manned by many of Hitler's old warriors –the Jesuit-controlled Nazi SS – turned "cold warriors". According to the great Frenchman, Edmond Paris, in his The Secret History of the Jesuits, it was the Jesuit Bernhardt Staempfle who wrote Hitler's Mein Kampf. This fact is further confirmed by one of the founders of the Nazi Party,

Roman Catholic Otto Strasser, in his revealing book, Hitler and I. It was Roman Catholic Hitler, who said of the Roman Catholic Himmler having modeled the SS after the Jesuit Order,

"I can see Himmler as our Ignatius of Loyola."

And lastly, one of the main posts of the feared SD, the Central Security Service of the SS (after which the American CIA would be modeled with the help of the repatriated Nazi General, Reinhardt Gehlen), was manned by a priest — a former teacher of the evil Council of Trent at the Court of Bavaria, one of the Jesuit General's favorites, a superior officer of the SS and the uncle of Heinrich Himmler — the Jesuit Himmler, who controlled Hitler's every move through Martin Bormann!

Secreted out of Europe through the Vatican's Ratlines, these murderers escaped their rightful punishment as war criminals that, during the Jesuit Crusade in Europe and Russia, killed millions of Russian Orthodox People and Jewish People pursuant to the Jesuits' evil Council of Trent, which, after condemning freedom of conscience and freedom of the press, concluded with these words:

"Accursed be all heretics. ACCURSED!!

Lastly, President Kennedy began to end the Vatican's hoax known as "the Cold War", the American CIA and

Russian KGB having secretly worked together since World War II. He also began to end that Jesuit Inquisition in Vietnam, as its future highpoint would be "Operation Phoenix", the CIA mass-murder of 60,000 Vietnamese "in cold blood" according to its Director, William E. Colby. The President interfering with Rome's Holy Office of the Inquisition could not be tolerated! Millions of "heretic" Buddhists were to be exterminated, the international drug trade would explode, American patriotism and liberty would further be destroyed and Vietnam would be reunited under another communist military dictator loyal to the Pope – like Stalin, like Chairman Mao, like Castro, like George H. W. Bush and son -, Ho Chi Minh.

Waged under the guise of "fighting godless communism", Cardinal Spellman championed America's most disastrous conflict known as "Spelly's War" overseen by Spelly's General, the Roman Catholic and CFR member, William C. Westmoreland. (Remember, according to Col. L. Fletcher Prouty in his JFK, the forced movement of over 600,000 Roman Catholics on U.S. Navy transport vessels from North Vietnam into South Vietnam was "one of the root causes of the Vietnam War." The arch-Catholic Secretary of the Navy responsible for implementing that Jesuit-agitation was the Supreme Knight of the Knights of Columbus, Francis P. Matthews. Knight Matthew's Master was America's "Military Vicar", Francis Cardinal Spellman. Later,

Spellman made several visits to the war-front calling the American troops "the soldiers of Christ", fighting the Pope's Crusade against "godless Jew Communism"!) The outcome was 58,000 dead, 80,000 post-war suicides and a 220 billion dollar debt to the Jesuits' Federal Reserve Bank.

All these acts of President Kennedy were proper assertions of national sovereignty and therefore infringed on the Pope's Temporal Power. As the "infallible" Vicar of Christ and thus, "the Universal Monarch of the World", the Pope, through the religious, political and financial power of the Jesuit Order, fully intended, then and now, to ultimately rule all nations through his loyal kings and dictators from Solomon's rebuilt Temple in Jerusalem.

For when the Pope is crowned during his coronation these words among others (having never been taught to us in the Public Schools) are spoken:

"Take thou the tiara adorned with the Triple Crown, and know that thou art the father of princes and kings, and art the governor of the world."

Thomas Aquinas, Rome's "Angelic Doctor" wrote in his Summa Theological in 1272:

"The Pope, by Divine Right, hath spiritual and Temporal Power, as supreme king of the World: ..."

Lucius Ferraris wrote in his Bibliotheca Prompta (1763), which has been adopted as a standard of Roman Catholic law, as follows:

> On account of the excellence of his supreme dignity, he is called Bishop of Bishops, Ordinary of Ordinaries, and universal Bishop of the Church, Bishop or Diocesan of the world, divine Monarch, supreme Emperor and King of Kings.

Therefore, for challenging the Pope's Temporal Power, in attempting to thwart Rome's grand design against the peoples of the world, John F. Kennedy, America's first Roman Catholic President, was brutally murdered in Dallas, Texas on November 22, 1963, by the soldiers of Francis Cardinal Spellman within the FBI, the CIA, the Secret Service, Military Intelligence and the Mafia.

"Please explain further the role of Mrs. Jacqueline Kennedy." Helen requested

Mr. Benjamin McCarthy said,

"A devoted Catholic, one must obey the priest, the Bishop, the Arch Bishop, the Cardinal; and above all, the Pope. Therefore, the order to eliminate the President was instructed to any member of the Mother Church- the Roman Catholic- the believer must achieve the assigned duty, for it's the command from God. In the case of Mrs. Jacqueline, I assumed that she was told by Cardinal Spellman that JFK was a traitor to the Jesuits, to the Vatican, to the Americans by secretly collaborated with the Soviet Union. Society of Jesuits with their powerful Knights of Malta had engineered the election. John F. Kennedy, betrayed to his masters by allowing coup d'état overthrow Ngo Dinh Diem- a perfect instrument which the Vatican used to control the Far East Asia- JFK must have been punished. On the other hand, Jacqueline Kennedy was protected under the Vatican's wings for the rest of her life. Who could the Pope trust better than Jacqueline Kennedy? We have learned that all other shots turned him into an invalid, yet still alive."

Senate of State Robert McCarthy elaborated the issue,

"If President Kennedy had become invalid, that was totally unacceptable, for there would have been more investigations; and Johnson could not have sworn in. JFK must be completely dead by all means."

Senate of State Robert McCarthy said,

A statistical test procedure is comparable to a criminal trial; a defendant is considered not guilty as long as his or her guilt is not proven. The prosecutor tries to prove the guilt of the defendant. Only when there is enough charging evidence the defendant is convicted.

In the start of the procedure, there are two hypotheses H_0: "the defendant is not guilty", and H_1

: "the defendant is guilty". The first one is called *null hypothesis*, and is for the time being accepted. The second one is called *alternative (hypothesis)*. It is the hypothesis one hopes to support.

The hypothesis of innocence is only rejected when an error is very unlikely, because one doesn't want to convict an innocent defendant. Such an error is called *error of the first kind* (i.e., the conviction of an innocent person), and the occurrence of this error is controlled to be rare. As a consequence of this asymmetric behavior, the *error of the second kind* (acquitting a person who committed the crime), is often rather large.

	H_0 is true Truly not guilty	H_1 is true Truly guilty
Accept Null Hypothesis Acquittal	Right decision	Wrong decision Type II Error
Reject Null Hypothesis Conviction	Wrong decision Type I Error	Right decision

A criminal trial can be regarded as either or both of two decision processes: guilty vs. not guilty or evidence vs. a threshold ("beyond a reasonable doubt"). In one view, the defendant is judged; in the other view the performance of the prosecution (which bears the burden of proof) is judged. A hypothesis test can be regarded as either a judgment

303

of a hypothesis or as a judgment of evidence. The level of significant (a) is the probability we're willing to risk rejecting the null hypothesis when it's true; it's typically between 1% to 5 %.

"Give me a break; this is not a court hearing." Mrs. Elizabeth McCarthy said

"I have worked on the JFK assassination as my PhD thesis," Jason shared his thought, "Presumably that Jackie fired the fatal shot, I still don't agree the Vatican was strong enough to force her pulling the trigger on the temple of her husband."

Professor Nguyen laughed,

"In this department, we must inquire opinions of the ladies!"

"I'll file a divorce." Mrs. Kim Tran said

Mrs. Elizabeth McCarthy responded,

"President Kennedy had numerous affairs; Mrs. Kennedy was cheated in her marriage. A woman in that situation, rich or poor, educated or ignorance...she has the right to be jealous; a woman must revenge by eliminate the other woman/women and/or even the husband."

"Watch out, Mr. Benjamin McCarthy!" Mr. Tran said

"I'm always a good husband; proof: we've been married for over thirty years."Mr. B. McCarthy chuckled, "I quote an advice of Stephen William Hawking, a British theoretical physicist, cosmologist, author and Director of Research at the Centre for Theoretical Cosmology within the University of Cambridge that he understands something about the universe; however, a woman –to him- is still a mystery."

Professor Nguyen said,

"Let me continue…We learned the similar lesson from President of S. Vietnam Ngo Dinh Diem: forcibly put an end to Buddhism, the consequence was his assassination for this assignment; nevertheless, he obeyed the Vatican to death."

All was going well for the Vatican's Jesuits. With their International Intelligence Community, they had begun their Inquisition and Crusade in the Far East. Their tools, Truman and Eisenhower, had begun the Vietnam War and it would prove to be a great harvest of "heretics" pursuant to the Jesuits' Council of Trent. The Cold War had been heated up with the sabotage of Francis Gary Powers' U-2 spy plane. Because of lack of fuel it was forced down in Russia, which ended the planned meetings for peace between the United States and Russia. Nixon, openly backed by Spellman would have continued Eisenhower's foreign policy of "fighting communism.

After the failure of the Bay of Pigs invasion, President Kennedy changed his foreign policy, which the Vatican considered as his betrayal to the Jesuits. In the Council on Foreign Relations, President Kennedy promised to "break the CIA into a thousand pieces.", since the CIA was the teeth of the Council on Foreign Relations- the enforcer of the Empire's Secret Government, the Vatican. Kennedy secretly fired Dulles, the CIA Director – the darling of the Vatican's Jesuits – Kennedy then appointed John A. McCone to replace him, Kennedy did not know that McCone was one of Spellman's Knights and would prove to be one of the President's assassins.

Meanwhile, President Kennedy seriously resisted the power of the Vatican's Jesuit General Janssen. First, according to The Washington Post, Kennedy determined to destroy the CIA — that agency which Truman described after the Kennedy Assassination as "a symbol of sinister and mysterious foreign intrigue: Kennedy did fail in his attempt to gain full control of the CIA and its major partners in the Defense Department. It was the most crucial failure of his abbreviated presidency. He recognized his adversary during his first term, and as he related confidentially to intimate acquaintances, 'When I am reelected, I am going to break that agency into a thousand pieces.' He meant to do it too, but the struggle cost him his life."

Secondly, President Kennedy sought to end the Vietnam

War. The way in which he sought to end it was described in a report, "'Memorandum for the President, Subject: Report of McNamara-Taylor Mission to South Vietnam'. With this report in hand, President Kennedy had what he wanted. It contained the essence of decisions he had to make. He had to get reelected to finish programs set in motion during his first term; he had to get Americans out of Vietnam."

However, his plans were reversed on November 22, 1963, the government of the United States was taken over by the superpower group [the Order merely using its American Intelligence Community to remove one of its Presidential creations] that wanted an escalation of the warfare in Indochina and a continuing military buildup for generations to come." Who was responsible for the reversal of President Kennedy's policies after his brutal assassination? It was the Jesuits' CIA, controlled by one of Cardinal Spellman's Knights of Malta, John A. McCone. We read from the book First Hand Knowledge written by CIA agent and Kennedy assassin, Robert D. Morrow:

"At 8:30 AM, on Saturday, the 24th of November, 1963, the limousine carrying CIA Director John McCone pulled into the White House grounds. McCone was there to brief the President and the slain President's former aide, McGeorge Bundy [the one responsible for the failure of the Bay of Pigs invasion] . . . He was also there to transact one piece of business prior to becoming involved in all the details entailed in a presidential transition — the signing of National Security Memorandum 278 [in fact 273], a classified document which immediately reversed John Kennedy's decision to de-escalate the war in Vietnam. The effect of Memorandum 278 would give the Central Intelligence Agency carte blanche to proceed with a full-scale war in the Far East, a war that would eventually involve over half a million Americans in a life and death struggle without the necessity of Congressional approval.

In effect, as of November 23, 1963, the Far East would replace Cuba as the thorn in America's side [because the Jesuits had given Cuba to Castro!]. It would also create a whole new source of narcotics for the Mafia's worldwide markets. (As mentioned earlier, Victor Marchetti, the former Deputy Director to Richard Helms, claimed in his book, The CIA and the Cult of Intelligence, that Air America, the CIA's proprietary airline, was used as a carrier for opium."

Mr. Tran emphasized this point,
Dear truth-seeker, there you have it! The Vatican's Jesuits with their tool, Cardinal Spellman, using one of his Knights of Malta, John A. McCone, escalated the Vatican's War in Vietnam and gave the CIA unlimited power to carry out the Jesuit General's policy of mass-murder while developing the Mafia's drug trade. Every

segment of Rome's Fraternity benefited. The Vatican's Federal Reserve Bank made trillions financing the Military Industrial Complexes of both the East and West; the International Intelligence Community grew to unbelievable proportions united at its apex in the Vatican; the pharmaceutical industry made billions; the Mafia made billions with the drug trade; Rome's oil companies and Arab nations made billions; President Johnson and his Texas oil men made billions as the tankers of Rome's shipping tycoons unloaded their crude in both Saigon and Hanoi; and, millions of "heretics" were murdered throughout Southeast Asia. The blindly patriotic people of Fourteenth Amendment America were further reduced to economic and political slavery with its White Protestant Middle Class further destroyed along with eighty thousand vets committing suicide, many of whom having suffered untold tortures.

Senate McCarthy said,

"Wikipedia describes **The Gulf of Tonkin Resolution** or the Southeast Asia **Resolution**, Pub. ... It is of historical significance because it **gave** U.S. **President** Lyndon B. Johnson.... not on the **resolution** but was a constitutional exercise of the **President's authority and** Congress passes **Gulf of Tonkin Resolution** on Aug 07, 1964. ... Approves **the Gulf of Tonkin Resolution**, giving **President** Lyndon

B. Johnson … It also **gave** Johnson the right to "take all necessary measures to repel any counter act against the US military…pouring down tons of bombs to North Vietnam, the Vietnamese from both sides suffered from the casualty. America paid for its involvement in the **Vietnam War** with many lives - nearly 60,000 **killed** in action, over 150,000 wounded, and some 1,600 missing … … the **Vietnam War** led to the violent deaths of 3.8 million **Vietnamese** The South **Vietnamese** Army's **casualty** reporting over 220,000 killed…."

Mr. Tran made a comment,

"In addition to the casualty, the illegal drugs market has been torturing Vietnam up to this moment. No form of government was able to control "The Golden Triangle" since it's under the wings of the Mafia and above all the Vatican."

"When Kennedy . . . called for a return of America's currency to the gold standard, and the dismantling of the Federal Reserve System — he actually minted non-debt money that does not bear the mark of the Federal Reserve; when he dared to actually exercise the leadership authority granted to him by the U.S. Constitution . . . Kennedy prepared his own death warrant. It was time for him to go."

Ignatius Loyola, 1540, Founder, 1st Jesuit General, 1540-1556 Secret Instructions of the Jesuits

"It is of faith that the Pope has the right of deposing heretical and rebel kings. Monarchs so deposed by the Pope are converted into notorious tyrants, and may be killed by the first who can reach them. If the public cause cannot meet with its defense in the death of a tyrant, it is lawful for the first who arrives, to assassinate him." - Francisco Suarez, 1613 Spanish Jesuit Defensio Fidei Catholicae

"That it is absolutely allowable to kill a man whenever the general welfare or proper security demands it." - Mendoza Escobar, 1655 Spanish Jesuit Moral Theology "A conspiracy is rarely, if ever, proved by positive testimony. When a crime of high magnitude is about to be perpetrated by a combination of individuals, they do not act openly, but covertly and secretly. The purpose formed is known only to those who enter into it. Unless one of the original conspirators betrays his companions and give evidence against them, their guilt can be proved only by circumstantial evidence . . . and circumstances cannot lie." - John A. Bingham, 1865 Special Judge Advocate The Trial of the Conspirators.

Senate of State Robert McCarthy said,

"Thus, according to the Vatican, Mrs. Jacqueline Kennedy was a heroine in the elimination of the traitor to the Jesuits: JFK."

"The truth depends on, and is only arrived at, by a legitimate deduction from all the facts which are truly material." [S. T. Coleridge, "Table-Talk," December 27, 1831.]

Cardinal Spellman had two agents in the FBI. The first was the Shriner Freemason and brother Cold Warrior, J. Edgar Hoover. According to John Loftus, Hoover had cooperated with the Vatican Ratlines resettling Nazi war criminals in the predominantly Roman Catholic Northeast United States. Why should he not cooperate with Spellman now? Why would he refuse? More importantly Spellman's key man in the FBI was Knight of Malta, Cartha DeLoach. As the third in command, DeLoach was in a position to supervise the assassination and suppress evidence. Garrison proved DeLoach did in fact suppress evidence. After the assassination we see a telling relationship between President Lyndon Johnson and Cartha DeLoach. DeLoach was known as Johnson's man in the FBI and the President would call him any time of day. This is the Cartha DeLoach that had signed a five-year contract with Lee Iacocca's Ford Mercury in connection with the television series, "The FBI." Both DeLoach and Iacocca were Knights of Malta subject to Cardinal Spellman during the Kennedy assassination. Later DeLoach went on to be a director of PepsiCo, and according to Colonel Prouty, that company also participated in Kennedy's assassination. We read with wonder, as it seems this web of assassins appears to be endless:

"Nixon was in Dallas with a top executive of the Pepsi-Cola Company, Mr. Harvey Russell, the general counsel. Nixon was a legal counsel to that corporation. That top executive's son has told of Nixon's presence in Dallas at the time of the assassination, and Russell has confirmed the accuracy of his son's account. Later, sometime after the shooting, Nixon was driven to the Dallas airport by a Mr. DeLuca, also an official of the Pepsi-Cola Company. In addition, the son of another Pepsi-Cola executive was in Dallas at that time and had dinner with Jack Ruby, Oswald's killer, the night before JFK was murdered."

At the time of the assassination in Dallas, the Catholic priest, Oscar Huber, escorted by an unknown priest, was sent from Holy Trinity Catholic Church to administer "last rites" for the President. Knowing that Kennedy's wounds were frontal wounds of entry, Huber reported everything to his superior, the Bishop of Dallas, then "The Most Reverend Thomas Kiely Gorman, DD." According to Martin Lee's article entitled "Who Are the Knights of Malta?" appearing on October 14, 1983 in the National Catholic Reporter, Thomas K. Gorman was a Knight of Malta. Being a brother Knight, he must have reported directly to Cardinal Spellman and kept him apprised of what was happening in Dallas.

At the time of the assassination in Dallas, roughly 12:30PM (in the afternoon), all the telephones went dead in Washington, D.C. for about one hour. How could this have happened? Someone at IT&T had to be responsible as it serviced the Washington area. In 1963 one of the VIP's of IT&T was Francis D. Flanagan. You guessed it. According to Martin Lee's same article, "Who Are the Knights of Malta?", Flanagan was a Knight. Later McCone, with his brother Knights, coordinated a deal between the CIA and IT&T to better work together.

Lastly, we know that the Mafia was involved in the Kennedy Assassination. The Mafia, OSS/CIA, FBI and Office of Naval Intelligence had been working together throughout World War II. Jack Ruby was a Mafioso and David E. Scheim makes it perfectly clear in his Contract on America that the Mob had at least two motives; the Kennedy brothers assault on Organized Crime and the loss of the Mob's gambling paradise in Cuba. The Mafia Dons must have been promised that they would make more money than Havana could ever produce, through the explosion of the International Drug Trade made possible by the Vietnam War. If they helped eliminate Kennedy, Johnson would escalate the war and thereby, the drug trade. The CIA would bring the drugs in from the Golden Triangle, distribute them to the Mafia families (Sam Giancana and Santos Trafficante families) and both would profit.

More importantly, the Mafia's Commission had a favor to repay. Cardinal Spellman, through FDR, had arranged the release of Charles "Lucky" Luciano because of "Operation Underworld" mentioned in a previous chapter. Now the Cardinal needed a favor. If refused, Spellman could use the entire International Intelligence Community, which he had helped to organize, to eliminate any Mob boss. If agreed to, new gambling centers would open up, Atlantic City being one of them. Clearly, if the President was removed, everybody would acquire more power and wealth, the Intelligence Community would become more absolute and the Cardinal would be even more respected by his peers in Rome.

In 1964, for the first time in the nation's history as a Republic (1789-1868) or an Empire (1868-2003), the Pope of Rome set foot in Fourteenth Amendment America. Cardinal Spellman had performed well and was rewarded by a visit from his Master, fellow Cold Warrior and Vatican Ratline handler, Cardinal Montini, who was now the Papal Caesar, Pope Paul VI. There is yet another reason for the removal of President Kennedy. He wanted to arm Israel. Loftus and Aarons write: "In September 1962 Kennedy decided to supply Israel with defensive ground-to-air missiles capable of stopping aircraft, but not the Egyptian offensive missiles. It was the first arms sale by the U.S.

Government to Israel . . . Kennedy promised the Israelis that as soon as the 1964 election was over, he would break the CIA 'into a thousand pieces and scatter it to the winds.' . . . With Kennedy's assassination in November 1963, the Israelis lost the best friend they had had in the White House since Truman departed." And why did the Vatican's Jesuits not want any arms sales to Israel at this time?

Why did our Jesuit-controlled President, Lyndon Johnson, turn his back while the Egyptian army moved up through the Sinai desert to prepare its assault on Israel in 1967? Because the attack upon Israel had to be provoked! The Jesuits' International Intelligence Community, deceiving Egypt into falsely perceiving the weakness of the Israeli army and the supposed abandonment of Israel by the American Empire, provoked that attack. Indeed, weakness breeds contempt and invites attack! The Six-Day war, engineered by Knight of Malta James Angleton, had one primary purpose: the taking of Jerusalem from Islamic Jordan, along with the Temple Mount. The apparent lack of military hardware on the part of Israel provoked the planned attack by Egypt. Therefore, Israel launched a preemptive strike and in six days the holy city was in the hands of Rome's Zionist government. Had Kennedy armed Israel, the Egyptians would never have been emboldened to maneuver for war. With no provoked war there would have been no Israeli attack. With no

Israeli attack the Zionist Army, controlled by the Jesuits' Mossad, would never have taken Jerusalem. With Jerusalem in Arab hands, the high Masonic Jewish Zionists could never rebuild Solomon's Temple – unbeknown to the Israeli people – for the Jesuits "infallible". The Jesuit General, using the "infallible" Pope with his most powerful Cardinal in the American Empire, assassinated President John F. Kennedy in 1963. For it was Cardinal Spellman, "the American Pope," in command of his soldiers – the Knights of Malta – who oversaw the assassination.

And it was certain Knights of Malta, using the Central Intelligence Agency that aided in the actual assassination of the President. Those Knights were CIA Director, John A. McCone, and CIA officers, William F. Buckley, Jr. and Henry R. Luce. In 1963, both William F. Buckley, Jr. and Henry Luce were personal friends of CIA agent E. Howard Hunt. We read from Mark Lane's Plausible Denial on page 270 concerning Time and Life magazines.

President George W. Bush was the most Catholic president we've ever had. He is surrounded with cardinals. George W. Bush has been promoting the Vatican-Nazi Jesuit agenda. Two months into his presidency, surrounded by cardinals of Rome, the President dedicated a cultural center in Washington, D.C., to the greatest enemy this Republic has ever had, the Pope of Rome. Bush declared that he is going to enforce the words and teachings of the Pope here in

America. [According to Patricia Zapoa of the Catholic News Service, March 24, 2001] President Bush said, Every President from Johnson to Bush, and now Obama, has been the abject tool of the Order fulfilling "Jesuitical Politics" — treasonous, internationalist and plotting to make its "infallible" Pope, ruling Satan's Theocratic Kingdom offered to the Lord Jesus Christ, "the Universal Monarch of the World." This political control was clearly described in 1933 by Lady Queen borough who wrote: "The game of politics is the pursuit of power. In all democracies, there are two separate organizations playing the political game. The open and visible one, the members of which hold office as members of a government, and the invisible one composed of individuals who control this visible organization and in whom is vested the real power, the essence of which is finance, controlling the publicity which makes or unmakes its tools. This financial power may be used to promote truth or fallacies, good or evil, national prosperity or national ruin . . . the strength of a democracy thus lies at the mercy of invisible leaders who, being nationally irresponsible, cannot be called to account for the consequences of the acts of the governments they control.

If all factions in a state can be controlled from one source [the CFR]; why should International Control [from Rome] be impracticable?"

From the reversal of President Kennedy's policy to end the Vietnam War (1963), to the war in Yugoslavia

(1998), to the Crusade in Central Asia against Islam
(2004), and now in Eurasia against the Orthodox, the
Jesuits have maintained control over the Executive,
Legislative and Judicial branches of the Empire's
Government. The murder of "heretics" continues
abroad, from the "heretic" Buddhists in the Far East to
the "heretic" Orthodox Serbians in the Balkans and
Ukraine. The Jesuits, in control of both George H. W.
Bush (along with the American military) and Saddam
Hussein, through Shriner Freemasonry, "extirpated" the
"heretic" Moslems of Iraq while initiating the unification
of Europe's military, largely Roman Catholic, during
Operation Desert Storm. A former Jesuit and personal
friend suggests why the Islamic people of Iraq have
been mass murdered by the Military Industrial Complex
of the Order's "Holy Roman" Fourteenth Amendment
American Empire for the last twenty years:

"At the request of Pope Pius XI in 1931, and as directed
by Jesuit General Ledochowski, the Jesuits of the New
England Province, headquartered in Boston, opened a
new high school in 1932 by the name of Baghdad
College, located in Baghdad, Iraq, and staffed by the
Jesuit Fathers, Scholastics, and Brothers from four US
Provinces. Over the years Baghdad College flourished
on what became a beautiful date-palm-covered
property, was attended by both Catholic and Islamic
students, and developed a reputation as one of the
finest schools in Iraq. The Jesuits in Iraq operated under
a government restriction that they engage in no

proselytizing of their Islamic students, although they were free to service Catholic communities in the country.

Meanwhile, we American people have been brainwashed into thinking of and pursuing games and amusements, while our intelligence communities are pursuing "fun and games" with false enemies, intrigues and assassinations, in restoring and maintaining the Temporal Power of the Pope around the world. The revived Greco-Roman Olympic Games fulfill a major goal of the Jesuit Order: the bringing of the world's people together glorifying the physical abilities of Man. One day it will be an international union around one Satanic Man — the "risen" Papal Caesar!

The American people are not only addicted to the Olympic Games but they are consumed with the vanities of professional sports. This is precisely what the Jesuits said they would do in their blueprint for world government, The Protocols of the Learned Elders of Zion. Protocol number 13 declares:

"In order that the masses themselves may not guess what [our fruitless agitations] are about we further distract them with amusements, games, pastimes, passions, people's palaces . . . Soon we shall begin through the press to propose competitions in art, in sport of all kinds: these interests will finally distract their minds . . ."

After the death of Spellman's President Johnson,

Richard Nixon became Commander-in-Chief. Nixon, the old friend of Spellman and fellow "Cold Warrior," extended the War in Vietnam to the bombing of Cambodia at the advice of a Jesuit, Dan Lyons, who personally consulted General Abrams, the Commander of U. S. Forces in Vietnam! Nixon continued to promote the Jesuit agenda as outlined in The Protocols of the Learned Elders of Zion, as his speechwriter was a Jesuit! Profiles in Conspiracy from John F. Kennedy to George Bush, from which we read:

"This is a definite account of a nation betrayed. A spider web of 'patriots for profit,' operating from the highest positions of special trust and confidence, have successfully circumvented our constitutional system in pursuit of a New World Order. They have infused America with drugs in order to fund covert operations while sealing the fate of our servicemen left in Communist prisons . . . At the very least this book represents a factual, true-life adventure that will take you on a riveting journey from the White House, down a heroin highway, to Burma's Golden Triangle where you will meet General Khun Sa — undisputed drug overlord. You will infiltrate the jungles of Communist Asia to rescue U.S. POWs, and in turn be pursued. You'll be taken behind the veil of U.S. covert operations to view deceit and betrayal. At best, this will produce a crack in the façade of 20th century American government, through which concerned citizens can view the looming peril and act in time to reverse our course while God gives us time." These works, including "Jesuit Vatican Tyranny," a twenty-one page article (found on the web at http://members.foothills.net/ricefile/JesVat.htm) updating the reader on the people presently empowered by the Company to rule over its "Holy Roman" Fourteenth Amendment American Empire, serve as companions to Vatican Assassins: "Wounded In The House Of My Friends", and are heartily recommended by the author in describing the Jesuit control of Washington through the Council on Foreign Relations for the last forty years. Author Joel Bainerman in his 1992 masterpiece, The Crimes of a President: New Revelations on Conspiracy & Cover-up in the Bush & Reagan Administrations, further sums up the matter: George H. W. Bush has corrupted the American system to such an extent that he can get away with any crime [just like his son, President George W. Bush . There is a global conspiracy founded on the [Jesuit General's] Freemasonry notion of a New World Order and global domination and President Bush [and now his President son who is a party to the Jesuit-controlled CFR/CIA demolition of the WTC] plays a major part in it."

SUMARY

JFK wanted to end the Vietnam War.

JFK wanted to destroy the Jesuit Federal Reserve with the Treasury notes.

LBJ hated Kennedy and wanted to be president so he helped murder JFK.

JFK was going to destroy the Jesuit CIA.

JFK was going to fire the Jesuit FBI homosexual Chief Jay Edgar Hoover.

JFK fired Jesuit CIA Chief Nazi Allen Dulles and family members working for the Jesuit US Government.

JFK wanted to destroy the Jesuits organized crime in the US.

JFK wanted peace with the Soviet Union created by the Jesuits to wage war.

JFK was hated by the Jesuit funded Cubans because of the Bay of Pigs attempt to overthrow Castro which failed because of the Jesuit CIA. Cuba was given to Castro by the Jesuits to wage war.

Richard Nixon was also part of the plot because he had hatred for JFK defeating him in the 1960 election.

George W. Bush ran the CIA and hated JFK and was part of the plot to kill JFK.

Mr. Tran said,

"I often wonder the JFK is a very complicated matter; for instance; there are more than one unexpected death after the death of President Kennedy. I believe it's a cover-up; for what reason?"

A LOOK AT THE DEATHS OF THOSE INVOLVED*

Jim Marrs and Ralph Schuster

A LOOK AT THE DEATHS OF THOSE INVOLVED* Jim Marrs and Ralph Schuster **Date**	Name	Connection with case	Cause of death
11/63	Karyn Kupicinet	TV host's daughter who was overheard telling of JFK's death prior to 11/22/63	Murdered
12/63	Jack Zangretti	Expressed foreknowledg	Gunshot Victim

		e of Ruby shooting Oswald	
2/64	Eddy Benavides	Lookalike brother to Tippit shooting witness, Domingo Benavides	Gunshot to head
2/64	Betty MacDonal d*	Former Ruby employee who alibi Warren Reynolds shooting suspect.	Suicide by hanging in Dallas Jail
3/64	Bill Chesher	Thought to have information linking Oswald and Ruby	Heart attack
3/64	Hank Killam*	Husband of Ruby employee, knew Oswald acquaintance	Throat cut
4/64	Bill Hunter*	Reporter who was in Ruby's apartment on	Accidental shooting by policeman

		11/24/63	
5/64	Gary Underhill*	CIA agent who claimed Agency was involved	Gunshot in head ruled suicide
5/64	Hugh Ward*	Private investigator working with Guy Banister and David Ferrie	Plane crash in Mexico
5/64	DeLesseps Morrison*	New Orleans Mayor	Passenger in Ward's plane
8/64	Teresa Norton*	Ruby employee	Fatally shot
6/64	Guy Banister*	x-FBI agent in New Orleans connected to Ferrie, CIA, Carlos Marcello & Oswald	Heart attack
9/64	Jim Koethe*	Reporter who was in Ruby's apartment on 11/24/63	Blow to neck
9/64	C.D. Jackson	"Life" magazine	Unknown

		senior Vice president who bought Zapruder film and locked it away	
10/64	Mary Pinchot	JFK "special" friend whose diary was taken by CIA chief James Angleton after her death	Murdered
1/65	Paul Mandal	"Life" writer who told of JFK turning to rear when shot in throat	Cancer
3/65	Tom Howard*	Ruby's first lawyer, was in Ruby's apartment on 11/24/63	Heart attack
5/65	Maurice Gatlin*	Pilot for Guy Banister	Fatal fall
8/65	Mona B. Saenz*	Texas Employment clerk who interviewed Oswald	Hit by Dallas bus

?/65	David Goldstein	Dallas man who helped FBI trace Oswald's pistol	Natural causes
9/65	Rose Cheramie*	Knew of assassination in advance, told of riding to Dallas with Cubans	Hit/run victim
11/65	Dorothy Kilgallen*	Columnist who had private interview with Ruby, pledged to "break" JFK case	Drug overdose
11/65	Mrs. Earl Smith*	Close friend to Dorothy Kilgallen, died two days after columnist, may have kept Kilgallen's notes	Cause unknown
12/65	William Whaley*	Cab driver who	Motor collision

		reportedly drove Oswald to Oak Cliff (The only Dallas taxi driver to die on duty)	
1966	Judge Joe Brown	Presided over Ruby's trial	Heart attack
1966	Karen "Little Lynn" Carlin*	Ruby employee who last talked with Ruby before Oswald shooting	Gunshot victim
1/66	Earlene Roberts	Oswald's landlady	Heart attack
2/66	Albert Bogard*	Car salesman who said Oswald test drove new car	Suicide
6/66	Capt. Frank Martin	Dallas policeman who witnessed Oswald slaying, told Warren Commission	Sudden cancer

		"there's a lot to be said but probably be better if I don't say it"	
8/66	Lee Bowers Jr.*	Witnessed men behind picket fence on Grassy Knoll	Motor accident
9/66	Marilyn "Delila Walle*	Ruby dancer	Shot by husband after 1 month of marriage
10/66	Lt. William Pitzer*	JFK autopsy photographer who described his duty as "horrifying experience"	Gunshot rule suicide
11/66	Jimmy Levens	Fort Worth nightclub owner who hired Ruby employees	Natural causes
11/66	James Worrell Jr.*	Saw man flee rear of Texas School Book Depository	Motor accident

1966	Clarence Oliver	Dist. Atty. Investigator who worked Ruby case	Unknown
12/66	Hank Suydam	Life magazine official in charge of JFK stories	Heart attack
1967	Leonard Pullin	Civilian Navy employee who helped film "Last Two Days" about assassination	One-car crash
1/67	Jack Ruby*	Oswald's slayer	Lung cancer (he told family he was injected with cancer cells)
2/67	Harold Russell*	Saw escape of Tippit killer	killed by cop in bar brawl
2/67	David Ferrie*	Acquaintance of Oswald, Garrison suspect and employee of	Blow to neck (ruled accidental)

		Guy Banister	
2/67	Eladio Del Valle*	Anti-Castro Cuban associate of David Ferrie being sought by Garrison	Gunshot wound, ax wound tohead
3/67	Dr. Mary Sherman*	Ferrie associate working on cancer research	Died in fire (possibly shot)
1/68	A. D. Bowie	Asst. Dallas District Attorney prosecuting Ruby	Cancer
4/68	Hiram Ingram	Dallas Deputy Sheriff, close friend to Roger Craig	Sudden cancer
5/68	Dr. Nicholas Chetta	New Orleans coroner who on death of Ferrie	Heart attack
8/68	Philip Geraci*	Friend of Perry Russo, told of Oswald/Shaw conversation	Electrocution

1/69	Henry Delaune*	Brother-in-law to coroner Chetta	Murdered
1/69	E.R. Walthers*	Dallas Deputy Sheriff who was involved in Depository search, claimed to have found .45-cal. slug	Shot by felon
1969	Charles Mentesana	Filmed rifle other than Mannlicher-Carcano being taken from Depository	Heart attack
4/69	Mary Bledsoe	Neighbor to Oswald, also knew David Ferrie	Natural causes
4/69	John Crawford*	Close friend to both Ruby and Wesley Frazier, who gave ride to Oswald on 11/22/63	Crash of private plane

7/69	Rev. Clyde Johnson*	Scheduled to testify about Clay Shaw/Oswald connection	Fatally shot
1970	George McGann*	Underworld figure connected to Ruby friends, wife, Beverly, took film in Dealey Plaza	Murdered
1/70	Darrell W. Garner	Arrested for shooting Warren Reynolds, released after alibi from Betty MacDonald	Drug overdose
8/70	Bill Decker	Dallas Sheriff who saw bullet hit street in front of JFK	Natural causes
8/70	Abraham Zapruder	Took famous film of JFK assassination	Natural causes
12/70	Salvatore Granello*	Mobster linked to both	Murdered

		Hoffa, Trafficante, and Castro assassination plots	
1971	James Plumeri*	Mobster tied to mob-CIA assassination plots	Murdered
3/71	Clayton Fowler	Ruby's chief defense attorney	Unknown
4/71	Gen. Charles Cabell*	CIA deputy director connected to anti-Castro Cubans	Collapsed and died after physical at Fort Myers
1972	Hale Boggs*	House Majority Leader, member of Warren Commission who began to publicly express doubts about findings	Disappeared on Alaskan plane flight
5/72	J. Edgar Hoover*	FBI director who pushed "lone	Heart attack (no autopsy)

		assassin" theory in JFK assassination	
9/73	Thomas E. Davis*	Gunrunner connected to both Ruby and CIA	Electrocuted trying to steal wire
2/74	J.A. Milteer*	Miami right-winger who predicted JFK's death and capture of scapegoat	Heater explosion
1974	Dave Yaras*	Close friend to both Hoffa and Jack Ruby	Murdered
7/74	Earl Warren	Chief Justice who reluctantly chaired Warren Commission	Heart failure
8/74	Clay Shaw*	Prime suspect in Garrison case, reportedly a CIA contact with Ferrie and E. Howard Hunt	Possible cancer

1974	Earle Cabell	Mayor of Dallas on 11/22/63, whose brother, Gen. Charles Cabell was fired from CIA by JFK	Natural causes
6/75	Sam Giancana*	Chicago Mafia boss slated to tell about CIA-mob death plots to Senate Committee	Murdered
7/75	Clyde Tolson	J. Edgar Hoover's assistant and roommate	Natural causes
1975	Allen Sweatt	Dallas Deputy Sheriff involved in investigation	Natural causes
12/75	Gen. Earle Wheeler	Contact between JFK and CIA	Unknown
1976	Ralph Paul	Ruby's business	Heart attack

		partner connected with crime figures	
4/76	James Chaney	Dallas motorcycle officer riding to JFK's right rear who said JFK "struck in the face" with bullet	Heart attack
4/76	Dr. Charles Gregory	Governor John Connally's physician	Heart attack
6/76	William Harvey*	CIA coordinator for CIA-mob assassination plans against Castro	Complications from heart surgery
7/76	John Roselli*	Mobster who testified to Senate Committee and was to appear again	Stabbed and stuffed in metal drum

338

"It's a quarter after eight already." Robert McCarthy exclaimed, "I have an early brief tomorrow at the House of Senate."

"I'm on call at St. Mary's Hospital." Dr. Helen Augier moaned.

"We have to leave. Thank you very much for the dinner and the discussion" Mr. Tran and His wife, Kim said.

"Thank you for the dinner. I hope that you like my presentation." Professor Nguyen said

"It's excellent." Mr. Benjamin McCarthy shook hands with the guests

"Thank you so much." Jason and Dennis said

"We learn a lot from all of you.

"Bye, bye!"

"Bye!"

***

On the way home, Robert told his wife,

"Isn't President Kennedy an exceptional person? His life, his death have influence all over the world."

"Yes. Dear, Jacqueline Kennedy Onassis is also a special figure. " Helen leaned on her husband's shoulder,

"Do you know what...If Jacqueline Kennedy had not fired the fatal shot?"

"I also suppose that the history of the world would have not been the same." Robert said, "However, JFK must have been murdered by all means, most of the powerful organizations of the world amazingly agreed with one another that JFK must be eliminated before 1964, the next Presidency Election in the US." Robert explained "JFL was aware of the assassination, since he said on the morning of November 22, 1963 "If somebody wants to shoot me from a window with a rifle, nobody can stop it, so why worry about it?" Helen continued, "I don't think that he had ever thought it was not from the window, but from…" Suddenly, Helen changed the subject, she asked her husband,

"Do you remember The Third Secret of Fatima?" "Is it Saint Lucy Santos's letter?" Robert said, "Actually, people are skeptical about it. The Vatican has maintained its position that the full text of the Third Secret was published in June 2000. A report from the Zenit *Daily Dispatch* dated 20 December 2001, based on a Vatican press release, reported that Lúcia told then-Archbishop Tarcisio Bertone, in an interview conducted the previous month, that the secret has been completely revealed and published, and that no secrets remain. Bertone, along with Cardinal Ratzinger, co-authored *The Message of Fatima*, the document published in June 2000 by the Vatican that contains a scanned copy of the original text of the Third Secret.

Bertone, who was elevated to cardinal in 2003 and held the position of Vatican Secretary of State until September 2013, wrote a book titled, *The Last Secret of Fatima*, published first in Italian under a different title in 2007, and then subsequently in

English. The book contains a transcribed interview between journalist Giuseppe De Carli and Bertone in which Bertone responds to various criticisms and accusations regarding the content and disclosure of the Third Secret. At one point in the interview, De Carli comments on an unsourced accusation that the Vatican is concealing a one-page text of the Third Secret which predicts a great apostasy where Rome will "lose the faith and become the throne of the Antichrist."

"Lucy Santos always insisted to the Bishop and to the Pope that the Third Secret of Fatima must be open in 1960. Why?" Helen inquired
"Don't you see it very clear now?" Robert looked into Helen's eyes, "JFK was murdered in 1963, the whole world turned into a new page after his death. Therefore, if the Third Secret had been truly revealed to the world, we could have prevented the disaster of our destruction by the coming of the New World Order…"

Swiftly, it flashed back in Helen's mind the vignette of Brendon Dorward, a schizophrenic patient,

"The male snake, Kaa and female snake Nagaina lived in the wilderness with their two offspring. The male snake, Kaa was the Lord of the Jungle. However, the wolves and the monkeys didn't agree. They planned a plot to kill him. The female snake, Nagaina knew about it, because she was slick and clever, however; she kept quiet. The reason, would

you inquire? She was jealous with Tigress: Kaa
sometimes sneaked out to be with Tigress; she was
a beauty.

In the meanwhile, Akela, the Leader of the Wolf
Pack vowed to raze Kaa to the ground so the Leader
of the Wolf would be the Lord of the Jungle. The
Bandar-log, a tribe of monkeys also wanted to
destroy Kaa; they did not like Akela either. Nagaina
had her own plan as well. She crept out to meet
another male snake, Carinatus…."

"What are you thinking, honey?" Robert asked.
"I love you." Helen whispered.
"The same here…" Robert replied.

***

POSTCRIPT

Closing *"The Lady in the Pink Suit"*, I asked the
Hierophant,
"Sir, supposedly these hypotheses are acceptable,
why did Mrs. Jacqueline Kennedy perform that
act?" The Greek priest explained,
"Catholics believe in the Pope, the Archbishops, the
Priests… and obey their commands in order to
preserve their souls in heaven after death. What is
more dreadful than losing one's soul?" the wise
man said gently, "Or considers that you still have
your soul - provided that you overcome your FEAR
whatever the Devil told you- so you become a slave
of DECEPTION? If you did lose all you've built,

you'd still keep the experience and the knowledge of LIFE; at that moment, you've overcome the DEVIL, you'd still have your soul. And you're truly free. Do you get what I mean?"

"I don't understand." I said

The wise man kindly told me,

"The Matrix is a metaphor; it is true in a sense that most people think they've lived in Freedom. In reality, they've been slaves, both mentally and physically. The Deceptive System has controlled their thoughts, their behaviors, their lives, and their future through the media, the news, the radio, the internet… The Deceptive System has told them how they should feel and what they should think, who their good friends are, and who their deadly enemies are… In order to survive, they've believed in what the Deceptive System has dictated to their brains".

"Is there a way out of this maze?" I stared at him perplexedly

"You're one of them. You've been trapped in the Matrix." The wise man sighed

"Sir, please show me how to get out of this maze?" I begged.

The Hierophant, with a heart so great that the generosity seems infinitely willingness to open my eyes, he said,

"Our passions, if we let them run wild, they will cause damage to ourselves and also to others; but if we can with gentle fortitude direct those passions to do much more achievements by their energy and yet still sate them by our inner strength. We can experience this power when we let the wild passions submit themselves at our heels. Do you know what I meant now?"

Looking around, I saw nobody.

Where did the Hierophant go?

***

My name is Pham Thu Dzung. I'm a Vietnamese immigrant in America; I hold a US of America passport.

After the collapse of S. Vietnam, I escaped by boat then was rescued by a S. Korean Ship then later I settled in the US. My family scattered in France, Australia and the US. I live in California.

My sister got married to an American, Dr. David Sperger; they have a four year old son, Randy.

Sometimes, I babysit Randy when my sister has her hairdo.

Onetime, Randy saw a photograph of my father, he asked,

"Who's this, Auntie?" (Randy does not speak Vietnamese)

"This is my father; he's your grandpa." I said.

My nephew examined the portrait carefully, and he made a remark,

"Oh, he's so skinny. I love Grandpa Bill better. Grandpa Bill is bigger."

I had the feeling as If I walked through afield with the bare trees; the air was cold and wintry. I felt strangely and profoundly sad. I have lost something very precious, my father, my beloved Vietnam.

Looking at my father's photograph, I did not cry,

but I felt my tears on my cheeks; and then I wept bitterly.

April, 2015
PHAM THUDZUNG